Contents

Christianity and Change

Steps to Growth and Healing in Christian Counseling

Ralph H. Armstrong, M.D.

Sheed & Ward

Sheed & Ward™ is a service of National Catholic Reporter Publishing
Company, Inc.

Library of Congress Catalog Number: 89-61930

ISBN: 1-55612-308-6

Published by: Sheed & Ward
                 115 E. Armour Blvd. P.O. Box 419492
                 Kansas City, MO 64141- 6492

To order, call: (800) 333-7373

Acknowledgments

Grateful acknowledgment is made to the following
for permission to reprint:

Excerpts from *Writing the Natural Way*, Copyright© 1983 by Gabrielle Lusser Rico (Jeremy P. Tarcher, Inc., Los Angeles), are used with permission of the publisher.

Excerpts from *The Language of Change*, Copyright© 1979 by Paul Watzlawick (New York: Basic Books, Inc.), are used with permission of the publisher.

Excerpts from *The Clinical Approach to the Patient*, Copyright© 1969 by W. Morgan and G. Engel (Philadelphia: W.B. Saunders Co.), are used with permission of the publisher.

Excerpts from *Uncommon Therapy: The Psychiatric Techniques of Milton H. Erickson, M.D.*, Copyright© 1967 by Jay Haley, editor (The Psychological Corporation), are reprinted with permission of the publisher and the editor.

Excerpts from *Depth Psychology and Salvation*, Copyright© 1963 by Wilfred Daim (The Frederick Ungar Publishing Company), are used with permission of the publisher.

Excerpts from *A Teaching Seminar with Milton H. Erickson*, Copyright© 1980 by J. K. Zeig (New York: Brunner/Mazel, Inc.), are reprinted with permission of the publisher and the author.

"Class of Problem/Class of Solution" figure on page 210 is reproduced from *TAPROOTS, Underlying Principles of Milton Erickson's Therapy and Hypnosis*, by William Hudson O'Hanlon, by permission of W.W. Norton & Company, Inc. Copyright© 1987 by William Hudson O'Hanlon.

Excerpts from *Enchantment and Intervention in Family Therapy*, Copyright© 1986 by Stephen R. and Carol H. Lankton (New York: Brunner/Mazel, Inc.), are reprinted with the permission of the authors and the publisher.

Introduction

The world (and the world within us), struggling with its impairments, seeks relief and hopes to feel good. But maturing Christians, hungry for a deeper relationship with God and more acutely aware of deficits, long for change. Others, such as those who grieve or suffer a mental illness, endure change whether they like it or not. And we suffer as we see those we love suffer; we know they must change, and so we pray. Some of us counsel, hope to see those we work with change, and seek the skill to help them change. We each, then, can read this book in three ways: as a casual observer interested in Christianity and change; from the standpoint of the one being counseled; and from the perspective of one who counsels or desires to learn how to.

The casual Christian reader, curious about the inner workings of people and self, can share with this Christian psychiatrist his struggle to understand and help those who have found change most difficult. In these pages one will find how our faith adds ultimate meaning to the efforts of counselors and psychotherapists. The book orients the reader toward a mind set of *change*; people are most grateful when they experience growth and healing through the gospel.

We cannot help studying these pages from the viewpoint of the one being counseled. We are all impaired, both within and in our relationships, and need healthy change. Many of us need healing. Each chapter has ideas, anecdotes, case illustrations, and exercises that can help us rethink our lives and our faith. I experienced as much as I interacted with our Lord to put the book together. Using it as a guide for a study group can further such objectives.

Ultimately, *Christianity and Change* is meant for counselors. Pastors, chaplains, physicians, medical students, psychiatrists, psychologists, and marriage counselors will find it valuable for their work. The book is ideal as a text for a seminary course on pastoral counseling. In attempting a fresh integration of psychiatry into Christianity, it should stimulate thought, resulting in a deepening view of Christianity and a more comprehensive and effective psychotherapy. Last, it serves the important function of bringing to the attention of the Christian community several state-of-the-art psychotherapies as well as several classic works that are now out of print. Let us go on to explore some of the mysteries of change.

Paradoxically, it is often through frustration in a lack of change that change begins. All who have sought my counsel have had one thing in common: they were at an impasse with some aspect of themselves or others. These impasses contained a destructive element, sometimes mild, sometimes severe; but a facet of someone's self was dying or being damaged. This danger forced these souls to cry out for deliverance. As a Christian, I have worked with the conviction that God played the central role in this: "But deliver us from evil" (Matthew 6:13).*

Deliverance implies change but not the sufferer's passivity. Rather, counselor, counselee, and God must collaborate with intense mental activity to achieve a critical change. Jesus' dramatic ability to heal can blind one to the change of heart he often initiated but left others to struggle with to complete. The woman by the well (John 4) and the man blind from birth (John 9) are examples. The four gospels detail the difficulty Jesus encountered in bringing about real change. Although the gospels can be studied in many different ways, it is useful for the counselor to view them as case records. When Jesus challenged people to change, they often resisted but then struggled and finally broke free. My own process notes depict a similar pattern. But, however else one regards the interactional sequences of the four gospels, the perspective of process notes helps one to see Jesus as the original and ultimate pastoral counselor, to identify with him, and to follow him in his dialogues with others and their rigidities.

Rigid patterns of belief, thought, and relating underlie all impasses and are obstacles to growth and adaptation to changing circumstances. In a world where one must leave home, choose a career, find a mate, raise children, let them go, bury parents, and prepare for one's own death, the ability to stay flexible and the ability to learn are critical. Some patterns preclude flexibility. A repetitive sequence of thought or

*All Scripture quotations are from the Revised Standard Version of the Bible, unless otherwise specified.

action, particularly in a person with serious emotional difficulties, may in essence be an attempt to solve, correct, or assuage an even more fundamental problem.

> *A Christian couple in their 30s ceased having sexual relations: that was the impasse. The wife pursued, the husband withdrew: that was the pattern. The pattern embodied the intended solution of each to manifest or latent problems. Both were attempting self-preservation: he viewed her pursuit as one more attempt by a female to control him; she saw his withdrawal as a rejection of her femininity. This repetitive, unproductive pattern worsened the impasse. Moreover, it arose from a definite starting point: a basic fixation in each.*

Fixation often lies at the heart of such patterns; it is the ultimate sticking point, causing developmental arrest and thereby thwarting God's plan. God made the world good; that is, to work right (Genesis 1:31). We know that if things are working right, there is a progression of personal, interpersonal, and spiritual growth. We see such progression in nature: a plant begins as a seed, sprouts, grows to maturity, flowers, and produces fruit. We should see an unfolding in ourselves. A fixation is like a drought in a flower garden. It grossly interferes with healthy growth, leaving in its place a deformation that is an adaptation to the original condition. All fixations derive from the interruption of one of the core drives of the self: communion and individuation. The interruption, which usually results from the irresponsible use of power by past or present parental or other authority figures, leaves negative emotional reactions of varying severity. One or more fixations are the core problems to be solved. Most counselees will bring, in varying degrees, the following sequence to the counseling situation:

Fixation => negative emotional reactions =>
intended solutions => patterns => impasse

Fixation and the resulting negative emotional reaction, which can produce extreme depression in severe cases, create a basic fault in the sufferer, which is the psychological equivalent of a geologic fault.

The sequence of fixation, depression, intended solution, and pattern constitutes an enduring mosaic in counselees and/or their families, subcultures, or cultures. A ripple effect of change occurs when any of the four elements is altered. This book offers effective methods for having an impact on each of these four points. Christianity for centuries and its new ally psychotherapy for 90 years have sought to provide humanity with the changes needed to live more constructive lives.

Psychotherapy has evolved from the attempts of psychiatrists, psychologists, and others to make sense of the riddles of mental illness. Paralleling the development of other sciences, psychotherapy has used observation, experimentation, and the formulation of hypotheses in an attempt to help people find relief from mental and interactional distress. Psychotherapy, though by no means a unified body of knowledge, turns out to be a modern wisdom movement. Besides providing useful details about many conditions, it has facilitated change in people who were at impasse through its work on patterns and intended solutions. Most psychotherapists are limited, however, by their lack of existential focus.

The church has always been aware of humanity's impasses, misguided solutions, and faults. It has approached the human predicament with a way of life revealed by God. With the hope of new life in Jesus Christ, Christians have offered to a world at impasse the comfort of belief, the joy of conversion, the miracle of prayer, the fellowship of the church, the nurture of communion, the sacraments of confession and forgiveness, and the power of the Holy Spirit. Many struggling with destructive thoughts and actions have used these offerings to their benefit.

In modern counseling, belief in Christ provides the all-important existential framework in which change can take place. I have repeatedly seen how those who believe sooner or later find the answers they need to achieve recovery. It is uncanny to sense in counselees, from a wide variety of denominations, the degree of the Lord's presence. In addition, Christianity is unique in its ability to speak to the core desires of the self as well as in offering new solutions. Christian counseling tends to be futile when it addresses people's impasses yet neglects the sequences of fixations to patterns. The gospel can, if carefully applied, have a profound and lasting effect on fixations, intense negative feelings, and intended solutions and hence lead to the resolution of impasses and the regeneration of the soul.

The book builds on the following basic ideas. The great commandments described by Jesus (Matthew 22:37-39) imply a simple, practical structure of the mind. We have not one mind but two: the *conscious,* logical mind we label the conscious and the imaginative, intuitive mind we label the *unconscious.* The latter, with its crucial role in creativity and hence in change, is an important asset for both counselor and counselee. The *heart,* as spoken of in the Scriptures, holds the potential for both health and disease. A healthy heart is one that is centered on God. A person at an impasse is fixated on some negative aspect of relationships with others or the self. Such a fixation interferes with a full relationship with God. Instead of being centered on God, the personality centers on the fixation and suffers distress. Fixations generate negative emotional reactions, which lead to efforts intended to protect the self. These efforts at self-protection may lead to repetitive and fruitless interactional patterns, which become the impasse. It is primarily the imaginative and metaphoric unconscious mind that represents fixations and the subsequent chain of events to the individual, to others, and to God. Thus, a person conveys the source of distress most poignantly in anecdotes, in body language and voice inflections, in the details of interactions with others, and in dreams. The first two chapters discuss these premises, along with related topics. Subsequent chapters appear in the order most likely found in a typical interview.

To appreciate the heart of another and to help the counselee come to grips with the sequence of fixation to impasse, the counselor must know when to speak and how to understand the implications of what is said. Chapters 3 and 4 discuss fundamental interviewing methods: core interviewing responses, using empathy, and asking specific questions. Chapter 5 (building on Chapter 1) illustrates the importance of opening the counselor's unconscious mind to divine action by *praying without ceasing.* Chapters 6 and 9 describe how the counselor's divinely inspired creative process is used to understand the metaphors and dreams of the counselee, which express imaginatively the heart of the problem. To orient the reader to areas of likely fixation and its effects, three axes of human endeavor are explored: one's relationship with self, with God, and with neighbor. Chapters 7, 8, and 10 discuss how to assess a person's self, his spiritual development, and his interactional system. Chapter 11 describes how to assess a counselee's resources, and Chapters 12 through 16 present several types of interventions. Since a brief problem solving approach has limitations, Chapter 17 deals with referral.

Methods for change include analytic, directive, and specifically Christian approaches. James Masterson, M.D.; the Christian psychiatrist W. Earl Biddle, M.D.; and Frederick Perls, M.D., offer several analytic methods. The more systems-oriented and directive approaches of Milton Erickson, M.D., and Paul Watzlawick, Ph.D., are explored. The Christian counselor may use these methods but is unique in focusing on Jesus Christ as the frame for counseling, recovery, and change and on the Gospel as holding specific solutions for fixations.

Each chapter concludes with classroom-tested exercises and recommendations for further readings. These exercises attempt to give the participants an essential acquaintance with the ideas discussed in the chapters. For this reason, a group approach to the exercises will yield the best results. The exercises can be complemented by guest speakers, pertinent video tapes, or other lectures on such topics as depression, phobias, suicide, schizophrenia, death and dying, etc.

The book's most important exercise is outlined in the appendix. The student is asked to apply the lessons of this book by interviewing the family of origin and writing a *multigenerational family systems* paper. The student is encouraged to keep a journal of dreams, personal observations, and reactions to exercises and the reading material, which can be integrated into the family systems paper. If fully entered into, the various exercises can be a remarkable source of personal and spiritual growth and healing. In summary, a person completing a course with this text should be armed with definite ideas about how to proceed with a counselee.

I acknowledge with gratitude the many people whose work and ideas have inspired me. I particularly thank the Reverend S. Dunham Wilson, an Episcopal priest. Father Wilson saved my life with his counsel. He had an intuitive grasp of virtually every skill discussed in this book. He introduced me to W. Earl Biddle, M.D.; and, he introduced me to *praying without ceasing*. Though alluded to frequently in the Scriptures, I am aware of only two modern authors who have described praying without ceasing in print: Theodore Reik, M.D., and Milton Erickson, M.D., neither of whom was a Christian. I appreciate having met and studied with Dr. Erickson. Much of the modern wisdom of psychotherapy belongs to him. Jerry Greenwald, Ph.D., taught me Gestalt therapy; many ideas and methods from that school have been most helpful. I am grateful to the many clergymen I have known over the years and to members of the Cursillo and Marriage Encounter movements, all of whom have schooled me in the ways of the Lord. Of course, I have learned greatly from my patients and students. Thanks to the Reverend John Borgerding, a Benedictine, I was able to teach at St. John's Seminary, and there craft this work. John East provided invaluable editorial assistance. Pat Van Remortel and Karina East did excellent work typing the manuscripts. Ultimately, all thanks go to our Lord Jesus Christ, who, through all my teachers, helpers, and friends, has multiplied my few loaves and fishes.

1

The Structure of Being

Any counseling that hopes to provide beneficial change first requires an adequate interview. Since any number of lines of inquiry could be pursued, the interviewer needs a map of the person and details of relationships in health and distress. A counselor, to succeed, needs a *model for being* to draw the interview to a successful conclusion. In this age of revolution in attempts to care for the mentally ill, many topographies of minds, some of them quite elaborate, have been proposed. For example, Freud divided the mind into ego, superego, and id. Although this and other systems might offer formats for thinking about the mind, they tend to be at least one step removed from experience. The Scriptures, on the other hand, offer a simple, experience-based, and useful view of being, of the mind as it relates to itself and to others. The Biblical view can be combined with recent neurophysiological discoveries about the brain to produce a pragmatic model of being that helps those who seek our aid.

The Scriptures never explicitly describe a structure of being but rather imply aspects in various texts. For example, Jesus' statement of the great commandment in the law (Matthew 22:37, 39) contains within it much of what we need to know about mind and self.

> *You shall love the Lord your God with all your heart, and with all your soul, and with all your mind. You shall love your neighbor as yourself.*

Mark 12:30 adds the word strength to the formula. Four words in these sentences point to the structure of our selves: you, heart, soul, and mind. You points to the central I, or ego, an executive, an observer. The

1

heart, the existential center, embodies what we believe to be ultimately true in our lives. Strength implies the self as it wills. And, of course, we reason with our minds. The soul is the totality of the self as a living and conscious subject. The act of love toward a neighbor provides the inter- actional element necessary to complete one's being. Understanding and using these structures are steps toward effective counseling.

The I, that central part of us that seems to be the seat of awareness, functions to decide: it is the I that is aware and makes choices in life. To paraphrase the great commandment,

You, using the several structures that comprise your personality, must decide to love . . .

Computer science offers an analogy:

I sit at the keyboard. Inserting a program (heart), I ask the computer (mind) a question. What I do with the answer involves will. So I am aware, and I decide.

In counseling, those who seek our help may struggle with disturbances of heart, mind, or relationships, but heart and mind also reason, learn, remem- ber, and respond and are vital resources for the healing process. Coun- selors must ultimately address their efforts to the heart. Hearts break, need healing, and can rejoice. The second chapter deals with the heart. Mind is more of a thinking device than the seat of attitudes and values, a resource more than the object of healing. We shall first explore the mind and how to enlist its potentials. And not one mind but two!

A study of the mind suggests that we think on two tracks with two distinctly different styles. Consider the contrast between reasoning, as in accounting or engineering, and the imaginative, intuitive, inspirational, more spontaneous thought characteristic of art or literature. Also con- sider the different qualities of thought inherent in dreams versus waking cognition. Madness thinks and speaks differently from sanity. Some biblical writers wrote and spoke with metaphor, vision, and trance, while others wrote in a more verbal, intellectual style. Jesus spoke to some in parables and to others more plainly. Even the Church reflects this duality: with its dogma, canons, and hierarchies, the institution is lifeless without a laity that knows our Lord, relates with him, listens to him, and does his will.

The brain itself exists in duplicate. The two cerebral hemispheres each house a different mind, each a thinking device relatively distinct from the other. Elmer Ambrose Sperry won a Nobel prize for his neuropsychological studies of intractable epileptics who had undergone the surgical division of their *corpus callosa*, the large bundle of nerve fibers connecting the left and right hemispheres, in an effort to control their seizures. His results suggest that the left hemisphere thinks with deductive reasoning, using Aristotelian logic, to verbally and mathematically concentrate its efforts toward thinking about things. The right hemisphere uses space, form, and imagery to represent experience to us. As such, it is closer to memory and emotion, and expresses such qualities as intuition, inspiration, and spontaneity. The psychiatrist Milton H. Erickson (1976) arbitrarily labeled the mind of the left hemisphere the *conscious mind* and that of the right hemisphere the *unconscious mind*. In contrast, the writer Gabrielle L. Rico (1983) labeled them the *sign mind* and the *design mind*, respectively.

Pursuing the experimental evidence for the duality of thinking and its basis in the structure of the brain is beyond the scope of this book. The concept is introduced to dramatize the distinctiveness of each form of thought.

> *A physician challenged me as I presented these ideas in a course on modern hypnosis in psychotherapy. He argued that he was not convinced by the experimental evidence for cerebral lateralization. I agreed but pointed out that the concept was useful as a metaphor, particularly in psychotherapy, where the depotentiation of conscious mental functioning and access to and utilization of unconscious thought forms seem to facilitate positive change. I appealed to him to think more as a poet than as a scientist when doing psychotherapy.*

The conscious mind functions much like the manager of a baseball team. The manager exhorts the team in words, drills the team, and lays down the rules around which the team will carry out its game plan. Then, theorizing about the possible strategies, the manager uses statistics to make player choices. Observing the action, the manager quickly recognizes and corrects mistakes. The team's function may be harmed if there is too much control or if the manager indiscreetly expresses doubts about players or their abilities. The manager is hired for the ability to reason and guide and feels relatively little emotion. Of course, this analogy eventually breaks down, for a good manager should also possess the right hemisphere qualities of artistry, intution, and inspiration. Every person's potential for charisma lies in the right hemisphere.

The editor, accountant, or lawyer within us has a companion poet, musician, or artist who can let go, spontaneously developing a feeling for things, and who expresses for us the metaphors that convey who we are. To illustrate, let me describe an experience I had with my unconscious mind.

> *I was attending a Cursillo.* One afternoon, eight of us were given an assignment that surprised us: create a piece of drama. We were give 90 minutes for the task, but our watches were taken away. The surprise, the lack of specific directions, and the absence of accurate timekeeping served their intended purpose: to disrupt us enough to disorient our conscious minds, our usual methodical patterns. If anything was to emerge, it had to come from God and some other aspect of our beings.*

> *After perhaps 20 minutes of chaos, a pattern began to emerge. The group wanted to portray humorously how they had acted before meeting Christ. Themes of alcohol use and abuse and of self-centeredness predominated. I participated, but acting out our sins lacked both meaning and purpose to me and wasn't funny. I prayed that we could make some sense out of this nightmare. The word nightmare struck a chord, and I had*

---

*Cursillo is a renewal movement that originated in the Roman Catholic church. It is built around three day retreats that are experiential in nature.

a sudden insight on how to frame and conclude the comedy. The completed work stunned me.

The play began with one of the men in our group retiring to bed. The lights dim, and he falls asleep. Next to his bed, the action begins, with several of us lampooning our former sins. When day finally breaks, the dreamer relates his dream to the one who awakened him. "That was a 'what-if' dream," his caller exclaims. "What if Christ had never come? Then we would be stuck in our sins. In Deuterenomy, chapter 30, our Lord, showing Moses the promised land, says 'Today I have set before you life and good, death and evil . . . Choose life.' Since Christ has died and is risen for us, we are indeed free to choose Life. Let us celebrate the Lord of Life today."

The punch line "choose life" penetrated to my heart, healing the self-destructive tendencies I was struggling with at the time. I thought about the metaphor for months.

This example illustrates the richness of the unconscious and how it can use the language of metaphor to produce a figure that speaks to and changes the heart. Erickson (1967) and his followers have systematically explored and exploited the distinctions between conscious and unconscious minds, using metaphors, tasks, paradoxes, and trances to achieve change in the mentally and emotionally disturbed. Rico in writing and Edwards (1979) in art also separate the mind into conscious and unconscious, teaching techniques to enhance expression of the latter, thereby fostering creativity.

Creativity, probably a function of the predominant use of the right hemisphere, is critical to solving behavioral problems. First, counselees are already attempting to describe their conflicts creatively. Psychosis, depression, panic, psychosomatic symptoms, and a host of other neuroses can be thought of as creative attempts to call attention to distress. Furthermore, the sufferer of emotional pain tries through metaphor, body language, and dreams to communicate difficulty; the counselor must match this with creative listening, keeping pace with a person's art of expression with the art of listening. There is art in the cooperative efforts of counselor and counselee working together to synthesize and grasp the various messages. The counselor, once understanding the counselee's difficulty, must creatively respond in the directions given; there is an art to intervention. A purpose of this chapter is to enhance the Christian's use of creativity by helping to access the mind's unconscious processes.

A study of almost any gospel passage shows Jesus' immense creativity; consider, for example, Luke 13:1-9:

> *"There were some present at that very time who told him of the Galileans whose blood Pilate had mingled with their sacrifices. And he answered them, 'Do you think that these Galileans were worse sinners than all the other Galileans, because they suffered thus? I tell you, No; but unless you repent you will all likewise perish. Or those eighteen upon whom the tower in Siloam fell and killed them, do you think they were worse offenders than all the others who dwelt in Jerusalem? I tell you, No; but unless you repent you will all likewise perish.'*
>
> *"And he told this parable: 'A man had a fig tree planted in his vineyard; and he came seeking fruit on it and found none. And he said to the vinedresser, 'Lo, these three years I have come seeking fruit on this fig tree, and I find none. Cut it down; why should it use up the ground?' And he answered him, 'Let it alone, sir, this year also, till I dig about it and put on manure. And if it bears fruit next year, well and good; but if not, you can cut it down.'"*

Perhaps those who told Jesus of Pilate's massacre were baiting him, hoping that he would declare himself a revolutionary or discredit himself by downplaying Pilate's action. But Jesus creatively goes to the heart by raising an existential question, that of the popular belief that suffering results from sin. Negating that belief, he points out that their real need is for personal repentance. He uses the story of those killed by the collapse of the tower at Siloam to make the same point. He closes by crafting a parable of an unfruitful fig tree and a gardener's promise to try to revive it. Jesus thus confronts his listeners with the life-and-death importance of repentance and belief. The short sequence contains the marvelous beauty, poignancy, simplicity, and elegance so characteristic of the Lord of the universe. We are also capable of such creativity.

The counselor can broaden creative capacity by learning and practicing a technique first described by Rico. The technique, called "clustering," allows more "right brain" activity, while allowing the more intellectual and logical left hemisphere mind to rest. In clustering, the person writes a central idea in the center of a page and then "brainstorms" by writing down connecting associations as fast as they occur to awareness. Each emerging thought is written down, circled, and connected with a line from the preceding circled idea. After about five minutes or so, when ideas no longer flow, the counselee begins to write as fast as possible, in paragraph form. Remarkably, the welter of associations begins to take on form and direction, resulting in a product with much more "punch" than conscious effort could produce. The unconscious, given free reign, constructs a coherent and meaningful whole in a more personally pleasurable manner. Rico has, in essence, devised a technique for putting on paper a creative process that ordinarily exists only within the mind, enabling us to learn it.

Consider the following example taken from Rico's book. Heidi Kingsbury, one of Rico's students, wrote letters well, but when she tried to write a story or essay, she involuntarily used her conscious mind to censor and hence inhibit the free flow of ideas. As an exercise, she wrote about her mother, using first her ordinary method, a laborious left brain effort.

> *My mother was a caring person, but she was also a person who had many problems, so she didn't pay as much attention to me as I wanted her to. She would stare in front of her a lot worrying about things I was too young to understand, but it made me feel sad and even a little bit rejected. I guess every kid needs to believe she is the center of her mother's universe.*

Then several days later, she used the clustering technique to write:

> *I remember wanting to tell my mother what happened.*
> *"Mama, listen to me, I want to tell you . . ." I remember that*
> *she only sat there, staring straight ahead. I wanted her to turn*
> *her head and look at me, so I would know definitively she was*
> *listening to me alone, not to some other voice inside, a voice*
> *louder than mine, more insistent than mine. I put my hand*
> *under her chin to turn her head to me. I remember the soft,*
> *warm skin, and I remember the pull of her chin away from me,*
> *until she finally turned her head. I remember my joy as I felt*
> *her turn—and I remember panic as her eyes, unfocused,*
> *looked past me. "What is it, child?" she asked, but I could not*
> *remember what it was I wanted to tell her.*

Rico theorizes that such remarkable differences in literary expression reflect the different functions of the two hemispheres. I do not know whether that is true, but if one deliberately treats the mind as communicating in two distinct modes, the logical and the metaphoric, downplaying the former and encouraging the expressions of the latter, then rich and emotionally powerful productions result. From the above example, I can infer that Heidi's mother had been deeply depressed; such a grasp by both counselor and counselee of the meaning of the mother's lack of responsiveness could prove to be crucial in Heidi's counseling.

A key to both the creative process and counseling is the shift from indeterminate form to focus. Meaning emerged as Heidi first clustered, then wrote about her mother. Such a shift also occurred in the transaction of Jesus noted above: faced with a comment or challenge from without, he grasped the essence of the situation and the hearts of those who spoke with him. His creative responses flowed from this focus. Practice with the process of clustering will help the counselor move the seemingly random to a sense of direction. The instant "aha" marks the crystallization of coherence or meaning for what had previously been regarded as chaos. Effective counseling will depend on using such shifts.

The following example from Rico shows the shift from the superficial to the meaningful, from a welter of random associations to a vivid gestalt. A student was asked to interpret the proverb, "A rolling stone gathers no moss." His literal, conscious mind responded with:

> *A rolling stone is always mossless because it does not stay in any one place long enough to allow the accumulation of living growth on its surface.*

The cluster on the next page was the response of his unconscious mind to his search for something of significance. He clustered around the proverb, writing down thoughts as rapidly as they occurred with no regard as to whether they were serious, inane, relevant, or anything else: he just wrote. Although the process resembles brainstorming, the physical act of drawing lines to and circles around words extends and deepens the process.

After doing the clustering, he began to write as rapidly as he could. He let go, just letting his hand move while holding on to the belief that something meaningful would emerge. Perhaps the shift to the meaningful occurred during clustering, perhaps as he wrote. Whichever, this is what he produced:

> *Of rootlessness. There are times when I envy the bristlecone pine. Nestled on the dry, windy, eastern slopes of the Sierra Nevada, the bristlecone is reputed to be the oldest living thing on earth. Before Lincoln spoke at Gettysburg, before Washington crossed the Delaware, before Columbus sailed from Spain, and even before the birth of Christ, the bristlecone seed sprouted, sent out tendrils, and grew roots.*

> *It is roots that I envy. Not the roots of a cultural heritage, but the roots of permanence, of staying. My roots were first planted in Schenectady, New York, a no-nonsense, cold-as-sin-in-the-winter upstate city that boasted an Indian massacre before California had a white settlement. But the roots, shallow planted, didn't take. So they tried the soil in diverse*

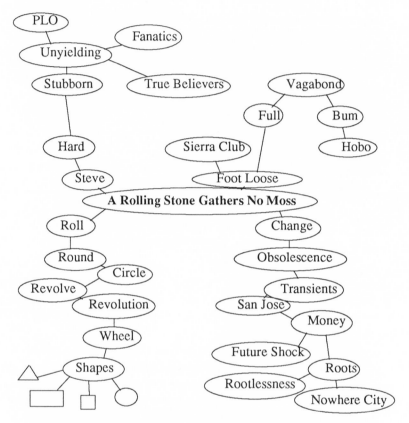

places—Kentucky, Missouri, and Michigan. Finally, itching for new ground to explore, they settled in the peat dust of Central California, only to be transplanted to the concrete adobe hardpan of Los Angeles, the vanishing farmland of San Jose.

There is a loss in this. A loss of security, of identity, of attachment, both physical and emotional. Where I live is Nowhere city. Friendships are fleeting, attachments shallow,

*commitments negligible. Like an Arab following a desert star,
I pull up my tent stakes every five years and move on. The
roots are weak, and anywhere is everywhere.*

In response to an exercise in Rico's book, to cluster around the word
"afraid," I did the following cluster and writing.

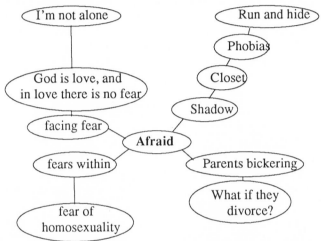

Afraid No More. *Everyone has been afraid. Every child has
feared the shadows of a darkened room, the terror of the bot-
tomless pit just beyond the ajar door to the closet, blackened
within, with forms that move if you just take your eyes off them
for a blink or two. And every child has heard parents bicker
and felt embarrassed or frightened by their anger. One can
march into those fears, assaulting the enemy's beachhead,
blasting him back with force. Or, one can run, hide, dive
under the covers, under the bed, under Mommy's apron, and
grow up phobic, hating oneself in the process.*

*But for me, I managed those fears. The big fight was with the
fears of what was within, fears of my own failings, suddenly
articulated. Banking left in a T-34, suddenly feeling I was*

rolling out, suddenly terrified of my fright—my God, I'm a coward. Or, afraid of an impulse, sudden, too dark to mention, which sent me to psychology textbooks, afraid that maybe I was a homosexual.

I've encountered many more of those inner demons, things within that I feared needlessly, and things I needed to fear but didn't. And in time, God found me and I God, and I didn't need to be afraid anymore. God was in control, redeeming me, loving me, and I was loving God, a part of the body. I was no longer alone, no longer afraid.

In this brief introduction, I have tried to show the impact of the metaphoric, suggesting the existence of a separate mind that communicates through images, symbols, and experience. Metaphor seems to reach our hearts and from there to move us. Furthermore, our hearts, our existential centers, seem to prefer using the language of the unconscious to communicate. And, the heart uses metaphor to have a dialogue with itself. In all our relationships, then, we are constantly communicating on two levels: a digital level to convey factual information, and an analogical level to communicate how we see ourselves, others, and ourselves in relation to others. Our hearts give expression through the unconscious mode. The unconscious is the royal road to the heart. The skilled counselor will learn to use unconscious processes creatively—first to understand the heart of another, then to respond in a manner likely to produce change by reaching the other's heart.

Exercises

1. Take a few moments, relax, perhaps meditate, allowing your mind to quiet. With paper and pencil at hand, think of a word that describes you, choosing the first word that springs into your mind. Write a paragraph about yourself. Now cluster around that word, letting your associations to it spring out as spokes from a hub. When the words no longer come, begin to write, letting your hand write a page or two.

2. Let the name of someone you love come to mind. Write a paragraph about that person. Now, write that name in the center of a sheet of paper, cluster around it, then write a vignette.

3. Consider the proverb, "Still water runs deep." Write out an interpretation of it. Now, writing the proverb in the center of a sheet of paper, cluster and then write a vignette.

4. At the conclusion of the assigned exercises, let the instructor ask the entire class for feedback. Five to ten minutes of such discussion heightens learning and integration.

5. Begin to keep a journal of your observations, insights, and thoughts as the course progresses. Record your dreams as well. This material will be useful for the family systems paper and for exercises pertaining to dreams (Chapter 9).

Suggested Reading

Rico, Gabrielle L. *Writing the Natural Way,* J.P. Tarcher, Inc., Los Angeles, distributed by Houghton Mifflin Co., Boston, 1983.

2

The Heart

If psychiatry has contributed anything to Christianity in this century, it is the idea that to understand a person's motivations more fully requires looking past the surface to a deeper part, to the closely held beliefs, attitudes, and values that constitute the center. Psychiatrists have noted that law, dogma, and conventional wisdom are ineffective in producing desired change in those suffering emotional distress. Rather, encouraging the expression of hidden or unexpressed core ideas seems to produce change, relieve suffering, and yield personality growth. Furthermore, recent advances in understanding the nature of change, how people resist change, and how they can be helped to change have enhanced the possibilities of healing and growth. If we take this idea of a hidden, existential center; look more closely at where and how people need to change; reexamine the Scriptures and our faith; and only begin to tap the creative power of God, we begin to see remarkable transformation in a variety of emotional and relational disturbances.

Although much of the theory and practice of psychiatry and psychology assumes a motivational center, few theorists have attempted to delineate it explicitly or to use it to achieve constructive change. In contrast, the Scriptures repeatedly refer to the heart as the existential center, describing it as the focal point of God's action with people. Let us first consider a psychological viewpoint. Watzlawick (1978) succinctly describes the idea of a distinctive world view in the following quotation:

Psychotherapy is concerned with change. But opinions differ widely about what it is supposed to change, and these divergences have their roots in the widely different views about the nature of man—and thus is a question that is philosophical, even metaphysical, and not just psychopathological . . . Anybody seeking our help suffers . . . from his relation to the world . . . that he suffers from his image of the world, from the unresolved contradiction between the way things appear to him and the way they should be according to his world image. He then can choose one of two alternatives: He can intervene actively in the course of events and adapt the world more or less to his image; or, where the world cannot be changed, he can adapt his image to the unalterable facts. The first alternative may very well be the object of advice and counseling . . . whereas the latter is more specifically the task and the goal of therapeutic change . . . We are thus faced with two Realities: One that is thought to exist objectively . . . and one which is the result of our "opinions" and our thinking, which constitutes our "Image" of the first. Thus if we talk about and suffer from "Reality," we mean a construct whose origin and premises are likely to be known to the good Lord only: a construct of which we have forgotten—if we ever knew it—that we are ourselves its architects and which we now experience "out there" as a supposedly independent "real" reality . . . We must think of a world image, then, as the most comprehensive, most complex synthesis of the myriads of experiences, convictions, and influences, of their interpretations, of the resulting ascription of value and meaning to the objects of perception, which an individual can muster. The world image is, in a very concrete and immediate sense, the outcome of communication . . . It is not "the world," but a mosaic of single images which may be interpreted in one way today and differently tomorrow; a pattern of patterns, an interpretation of interpretations; the result of incessant decisions about what may and what may not be included in these meta-interpretations, which themselves are the consequences of past decisions.

This chapter examines what constitutes the world view and the heart, for the counselor must grasp these concepts firmly to assist in therapeutic change.

The World View

Watzlawick's paragraph suggests that a world view is an image of the world and the way things "should be." Such an image results from a host of choices and interpretations, springing from one's experience. It is also often a child's view of reality built out of the stuff of a child's world, and hence potentially idiosyncratic and limited in scope. Thus, a world view might well be rich in superstition, fantasy, and animism, containing elements of the magical. Hence, the world view might, though intended to be a construct representing reality, be loose and contradictory. Culture helps determine one's world view, but it is the daily occurrences of family life that most profoundly influence the details of one's image of the world. In that regard, the essence of a world view relates to the qualities of and interpretations ascribed to important relationships. But the world view obviously results from a synthesis. Just how does a person go about organizing a world view? If we could know this, and if change and healing have anything to do with a change in one's world view, then changing the organizer of the world view would be crucial. Consider the following world view, a paranoid image made explicit in a psychotherapy:

> *Walter was a 35-year-old white male. Wounded as a Marine in Vietnam, he had since suffered anxiety, depression, difficulties concentrating, insomnia, and nightmares. For seven years following his discharge, he had abused multiple street drugs. He said he hated everyone and was tense, easily startled, jumpy, on guard, and afraid he might lose control of his anger and hurt someone. He intensely resented the government, was bitter toward the Marines and the public, trusted no one, and thought about Vietnam all the time. He felt guilt over the wounding of a friend, and feared the recurrence of a breakdown he had experienced after his friend was hurt. Therapy revealed intense feelings of vulnerability and pervasive guilt.*

Early treatment issues involved establishing rapport, trust, and empathy. The decisive moment came when we dealt with his recurrent nightmare, a terrifying dream he had endured for years and that expressed the essence of his world view. Although the specifics of the dream varied, the basic theme never changed. "I am surrounded by Gooks in black pajamas, armed with pitchforks and hoes. They have killed everybody and are going to get me too." In the therapy session, I told him to close his eyes and picture the Gooks. He instantly began to shake. "Tell them to go ahead and kill you, if they must," I said. That was new to him, but he complied. "They look puzzled," he stated. Next I instructed him to "Tell them that before they do you in, you'd like to share your C-rations with them, sort of as a last meal." His face reflected intense mental activity as he exclaimed, "They've put down their weapons!" I next said, "As you eat together, take out your wallet, and show them a picture of your baby girl." Tears rolled down his cheeks as he pondered, then said, "They're people, just like me. They are showing me pictures of their kids." He terminated therapy shortly thereafter, remarking repeatedly, "It was so simple."

Walter organized his world view around the profound experience of war. Through his psychotherapy, he could reorganize it around gentler aspects of life.

Certainly, then, cultural, family, and personal experiences influence one's world view. But, given these variables, what is it that dictates that one person interpret experience one way, and a second person an entirely different way? Let us look to the scriptural concept of the heart, both for its commentary on a person's center and for clues as to what the central organizer of the world view might be.

The Heart

The Scriptures imply a core motivational center in the repeated use of the word heart. The term appears about a thousand times in English Bibles as a translation from about ten Hebrew and Greek words. Grouping these references into five rough categories gives us a fresh picture of the nature of the human center that will prove useful in facilitating change:

- The heart and core aspects of character
- The heart and thinking, imagining, and learning
- The heart and following, allegiance, loyalty, and commitment
- The heart and straying, idolatry, hardness, and deception
- God as the creator of a new heart.

The heart contains core aspects of character. It thinks deeply and engages in a dialogue with itself. The heart uses the imagination and learns, particularly learning wisdom. The heart aligns with another, participating in following behavior. It may center on God, know and be directed, taught, or molded by God; hence, God brings about change in the heart. Sadly, however, the heart is also the center for evil, hardness, lust, pride, and irreligion; Satan speaks to and influences the heart. Law is inadequate in changing the heart; we need a new heart. God acts to create within us a new heart through a redeeming relationship with Jesus Christ. Let us examine each of the five categories in more detail.

A single word can sometimes describe the *essential core* of a person. For example, "war was in his heart" (Psalms 55:21) points to the core aspect of one person's character. Generosity as a character trait is summoned in Exodus 35:5: "whoever is of a generous heart, let him bring the Lord's offering." Brokenness and contrition find their essences in the heart: "a broken and contrite heart, O God, thou wilt not despise" (Psalms 51:17). Matthew 11:29 describes our Lord's basic humility: "for I am gentle and lowly in heart." All these references locate the fundamentals of character in the heart.

Furthermore, the heart *thinks deeply* and maintains a dialogue with itself. Judges 5:15 says, "Among the clans of Reuben there were great searchings of heart." I Samuel 27:1 says, "And David said in his heart, 'I shall now perish one day by the hand of Saul.'" Psalm 10:13 says, "Why does the wicked renounce God, and say in his heart, 'Thou wilt not call to account'?" Luke 2:19 describes deep thought: "But Mary kept all these things, pondering them in her heart." That the heart utilizes imagination is explicit in Genesis 8:21: "for the imagination of man's heart is evil from his youth." Proverbs 2:1-3,5 describes the essential role of the heart in learning: "My son, if you receive my words and treasure up my commandments with you, making your ear attentive to wisdom and inclining your heart to understanding . . . then you will . . . find the knowledge of God." Thinking, having a dialogue, imagining, and learning with the heart imply those actions on the most profound, most basic levels of personality.

The Reverend S. Dunham Wilson, an Episcopal priest, offers an interesting interpretation of the Noah story (Genesis 8 and 9). The story metaphorically poses a theological question about the nature of mortals and their relationship to evil. Thus, it is a "What if?" story. God, seeing the evil in our hearts, wonders, "What if I found a righteous one. If I wiped out all the evildoers, would the offspring of the righteous have clean hearts?" The conclusion is: "No, it would do no good to start over, for the heart is evil from infancy."

It is important to give operational definitions to such words as evil, bad, good, right, and wrong. Counselors commonly work with people who have deep concerns about being bad, evil, or wrong. I explain that these terms are best used to describe actions or attitudes that are constructive or destructive. So, God tries to tell us our hearts are evil; that, without God, we ultimately think and act in ways destructive to our well being.

The Scriptures relate the heart to the *act of following;* we all follow something. That part of us that casts its lot, aligns itself, commits itself, and is loyal, is referred to as the heart. We center on where our hearts are. "For where your treasure is, there will your heart be also (Matthew 6:21). Consider also Judges: "and their hearts inclined to follow Abimelech, for they said, 'He is our brother.' " A variety of passages call us to follow our Lord, to place him at the center of our hearts. "O Lord, God of Israel, there is no God like thee . . . showing steadfast love to thy servants who walk before thee with all their heart" (I Kings 8:23).

But we *stray away,* and serve other gods. From our hearts we bring forth evil (Matthew 12:34-35, 15:18), deceit (Proverbs 23:7), and pride (Jeremiah 49:16). The heart hardens and refuses to learn or listen (Exodus 4:21, Mark 3:5). Irreligion (Psalms 14:1) and idolatry (Ezekiel 14:3-7) take hold in the heart. The devil speaks to and may seduce the heart (John 13:2, Acts 5:3). We deceive ourselves and others and hide our hearts, but God searches our hearts (Jeremiah 17:10) and is not fooled by externals: "Man looks on the outward appearance, but the Lord looks on the heart" (I Samuel 16:7).

External obedience to the law does not touch the heart: a moral heart cannot be legislated. Wise persons cry to God, "create in me a clean heart" (Psalms 51:10), and God promises "A new heart I will give you, and a new spirit I will put within you; and I will take out of your flesh the heart of stone and give you a heart of flesh" (Ezekiel 36:26). He gives us a heart to know God (Jeremiah 24:7) by sending his Son. Then, by faith, the eyes of the heart are illuminated (Ephesians 1:18), and Christ dwells in the heart (Ephesians 3:17). "And because you are sons, God has sent the Spirit of his Son into our hearts, crying, 'Abba! Father!'" (Galatians 4:6). And as we come to know him, to recognize him, to see him, "our hearts burn" (Luke 24:32). Jesus invariably moved to the heart of the matter with those who came to him. Consider the rich young ruler, the woman by the well (John 4:7-38), and the Pharisees, to name just a few. The main purpose of this book is to help you think in terms of your counselees' hearts, to enable you to speak to them in ways that can lead to beneficial change.

The Relationship of the Heart to the World View

The heart ultimately is that part of us that commits itself to something, that follows someone, and out of which core aspects of character and hence action issue. The heart, then, is the organizer of the world view. Who we follow, who we commit ourselves to, what we fix our attention on, shapes and colors our world view regardless of culture, family, or personal experience. Ultimately, our self-image, our very identity, depends on who or what we have identified with and committed ourselves to.

At the Cursillo at the Mission San Miguel, an original Spanish mission in California, one of my tasks was to deliver a talk on the subject "Who am I?" On my way to give my talk, I walked through the courtyard, a large atrium and garden with an ancient fountain at its center. I noticed a mother goose, followed by several goslings. After the talk, we took colored pencils and sketched some of our impressions concerning the subject of my talk. In an instant of inspiration, my hand sketched the mother goose and her brood. Under the sketch, I wrote 'We are who we follow.' Our Lord had given me an elegantly simple metaphor for a complex subject.

We are all followers, all slaves to something. We are free in the sense that ultimately we can choose to whom we enslave ourselves. The image of sheep in the Scriptures is meant to depict this reality. Following is reflected in the child's following of parents and teachers; we often adopt the customs, traditions, and even the abnormal behaviors of our elders. The child's propensity to follow evolves into the hierarchical structure inherent in all societies. But every trend in the personality has its polar opposite: we often like to think of ourselves as self-sufficient, independent, and followers of none. Thus, as adolescents or adults we may follow the prevailing cultural lifestyles and become materialistic or ascetic in rebellion. Some of us follow seemingly powerful leaders and join a cult or a rigid religious group. In the extreme, some give up all individual decision making; the Jonestown tragedy is an example. It is to be hoped that we eventually come to commit ourselves to a church that is open-ended enough to allow individuality. The ultimate following, however, is an intimate prayer relationship and knowing of God the Father, God the Son, and God the Holy Spirit, achieved in part through a relationship with other believers.

"I am the light of the world; he who follows me will not walk in darkness, but will have the light of life" (John 8:12).

Development of the Heart

The heart of a person develops over time. The process of learning to follow goes through predictable steps during maturation. Chapter 8 describes a scheme of spiritual development. The Christian counselor, in helping a person move to the next step in development, initiates beneficial change, particularly if it is true that *we are who we follow*.

Self-sufficiency => conversion => fear of God, fear of self => breakdown => Thy will be done => knowing Christ => love, the fulfillment of the self

Chapter 7 discusses the progress of the self as working through masks to feelings to the achievement of communion and individuation, and Chapter 10 the development of interpersonal relationships as:

Leaving home => marriage => children => growth through intimacy and work => letting go of children => becoming grandparents => letting go of parents => retirement => old age and dying

These flow charts are of value to the counselor, for they allow diagnosis of a person's or family's progress and suggest the direction for the next step. Change can occur as a person progresses in any of the three cycles.

Impasses and Fixations

Many people lack a smooth development and instead find themselves at impasse with themselves or in relation to others or to God. Such impasses include impasses in marriage, with a child, with a parent, with addiction, with the law, with a mental illness, with poverty, or with a job or the lack of one. Ordinarily, a person reaches several developmental landmarks, such as graduating from high school, leaving home, getting a job or starting a career, getting married, having children, letting go of grown children, becoming grandparents, and negotiating old age (Haley 1973). But others do not leave home, cannot seem to marry or stay married, cannot or will not work, will not let go of children, *etc.* Such people also tend to realize little progress spiritually. People suffering impasses such as these will be driven to seek counsel, if only to find relief for their pain.

Impasses have their own paths of development. One or several fixations may underlie impasses. Fixations give rise to intense negative feelings, leading in turn to the struggle to get free from those feelings. The net result, for the person at impasse, is an unproductive pattern of thought and interaction. Such patterns can involve whole families or even cultures. In an approach from a Christian perspective, the counselor may direct diagnostic, then therapeutic efforts at the counselee's religious framework, fixation points, intense negative feelings, unproductive intended solutions, or patterns. The Christian counselor has the particular capacity to deal with fixation, intended solutions, and the religious framework. The following list details points of arrest and hence of intervention.

Religious Frame: relationship with God

- Refusal to believe negates God as a resource for change (Matthew 13:1-23).

- A believer's judgmental attitude likewise negates God as a resource for change (Matthew 7:1-5).

Fixations: pertain to frustrations of one or both of the two basic drives of the self (the drive for communion and the drive for individuation)

- Fixations to lack of permissions or to unhealthy life scripts or metaphors.

- Fixations around loss. Pathological grief usually points back to an earlier fixation.

- Fixations to traumatic experiences.

- Fixations to overcritical, intrusive, abusive, alcoholic, neglectful, or otherwise poorly functioning parental or other authority figures.

- Fixations to bad parental images.

- Fixations related to ongoing relationships to the family of origin.

- Fixations due to resentment, the refusal to forgive, and/or the wish to get even.

Intense Negative Feelings: guilt, anger, abandonment, engulfment, helplessness, hopelessness, powerlessness, and humiliation are some of the feelings that derive from frustrations of the two basic drives.

Unproductive Intended Solutions: people's intended solutions to suffering can complicate life.

- Repeated use of solutions that do not work.
- The wish to be taken care of—the clinging solution (II Thessalonians 3:6-13).
- Sexual, drug, and alcohol addictions—can become the problem to be solved before other fixations can be approached.
- Masks—defensive styles of living and relating, such as acting out, projection, pride, self-sufficiency, and denial.

Patterns: complexes of thought and/or interaction.

- People at impasse think, behave, or interact in repetitious, predictable fashion. Whole families, organizations, or cultures may interact in circular, dialectical manners that obstruct the communion between and individuation of participants.

Impasses

Daim (1963) related the psychoanalytic concept of fixation to Christian thought. He described several cases in which his patients painfully separated themselves from an over-possessive figure, usually a parent. He denoted the problem as one of fixation: the sufferer fixated on another person. Successful resolution of the fixation through the analysis was termed a partial salvation, analogous and parallel to the complete salvation achievable through our Lord Christ. One who is fixated is termed eccentric, and a parallel is drawn with idolatry; we need to become centered on Jesus Christ. I have seen numerous similar cases where people have become mired in adhesive family systems or with domineering, critical, or overly possessive parents, with resulting symptoms of disease and stultification or personality. I use the concept of fixation constantly in therapy, assuming that most who consult me are stuck somewhere within their hearts, either in the inward person or in an important relationship. Common to fixation at any point is the replacement of the heart's ability to think deeply with obsessional thinking, a repetitive, compulsive, and unproductive form of intellectual activity. Lacking the capacity to think deeply, the sufferer has increased difficulty relating and learning, which further arrests spiritual development. In other words, the fixated person cannot follow freely. The resulting pain drives the person to the counselor and paradoxically often opens the possibility of marked spiritual growth.

The counselor can use the techniques of interviewing and assessment described in subsequent chapters to help bring into focus patterns, intended solutions, feelings, and fixations. Treatment (prayer, a Scriptural passage, a personal experience, a confrontation, a story, or a task) can then be more specific, in language the counselee can understand. The following case shows how a man mastered his fears by resolving fixation.

Andrew, a 56-year-old agoraphobic, suffered frequent panic attacks and feared driving, being alone, heights, closed spaces, and much more. He drank to enable himself to do even small tasks. He blamed his condition on his wife, a chronic alcoholic. After coming to a group for agoraphobics intoxicated, he admitted he had a drinking problem and arranged to admit himself to a program for alcoholics at a nearby hospital. As he prepared to leave, his wife declared she would divorce him if he left. Shaken but determined, he proceeded, but decided to call his father, hoping for support. His father responded with a whining "But who is going to take me to my doctor's appointments?" At the hospital, his counselor asked, "Have you ever thought that your wife and father are selfish?" Andrew was stunned by this remark, for he had always thought of them as taking care of him. Now, dealing with the heart of the matter, he recalled his childhood role of taking care of his parents, preventing their fights, soothing their feelings, and listening to their troubles. On her deathbed, his mother enjoined him to take care of his father. Thereafter, until his fear of driving interfered, he drove him everywhere, even though his father was quite capable of driving himself. Andrew could then realize how, through nagging his wife about her drinking, he was, underneath it all, "taking care" of her to the extent that she was not taking responsibility for herself. He subsequently told his father to drive himself and his wife that if she wanted to drink, it was her liver. In time, she quit drinking, and his phobias diminished markedly.

The Language of the Heart

Before going further, write a brief paragraph about yourself entitled "Who am I?" No one is to see your effort. Next, write "Who am I?" in the center of a clean sheet of paper. Quickly cluster around that theme, continuing until you can find no more associations. Then, write a paragraph as quickly as you can. Now consider what you have written.

Note that the more metaphoric your paragraph is, the more anecdotal, the more you use words such as "like" and "as if," the more affective, feeling-tinged, graphic, and moving portrait you will paint of yourself. The point is that the language of the heart is the language of action, feeling, and experience. In other words, a person's actions are metaphors for self. "You shall know them by their fruits" (Matthew 7:20). The heart and the world view use the language of imagination to represent them; furthermore, the heart listens most to metaphor. Thus, the unconscious mind, the mind of the right hemisphere, speaks for the heart. To quote Watzlawick (1978) again:

> We are now at the point where the two main themes developed so far—hemispheric asymmetry and the concept of the world image—may be brought together. The translation of the perceived reality, this synthesis of our experience of the world into an image, is most probably the function of the right hemisphere . . . To change this seemingly unchangeable reality, one needs to know first *what* has to be changed (which means that one must grasp the world image in question), and secondly, *how* this change can be practically achieved . . . from these two foci, the *what* and the *how*, there follow important conclusions for the language and the technique of

psychotherapy . . . As far as the language is concerned . . . it is the language of the right hemisphere. In it the world image is conceived and expressed, and it is, therefore, the key to our being in, and our suffering in relation to, the world . . . As regards technique, there are three approaches which in the practice of psychotherapy offer themselves in varying degrees and combinations: the use of right-hemisphere language patterns; blocking the left hemisphere; specific behavior prescriptions.

Metaphor translates our unarticulated views of life and what life should be into tangible figures that in turn affect our being. For example, while dining at a medical society meeting, a family practitioner nearing retirement age told several of us he had recently completed a coast-to-coast bicycle trip. After describing his adventure, he suddenly glared at me and asked, "Now what does that mean?" At first I had no answer, but as I thought about it I realized the trip was a metaphor for his life. Furthermore, as the heart speaks in the language of metaphor, so it also listens: it is no accident that the Scriptures were written in anecdotes, stories, parables, dreams, and the stuff of trance. All are in the language of the heart. A basic theme of this book is that if the counselor can hear and understand the language of a person's heart and can respond in kind, change and healing can more rapidly and effectively be brought about.

The language of the heart brings out another aspect of the relationship between heart and world view and between the spiritual and temporal orders. The images our unconscious minds construct to portray for us our inner convictions, our views of reality, and our important relationships metaphorize, analogize, and parallel our spiritual relationships. All external objects and our inner representations of those objects are windows through which we may view God. In other words, the concrete objects of the temporal world, and the immaterial but nonetheless real images of our imaginations, have sacramental as well as temporal significance. "Ever since the creation of the world, His invisible nature, namely, His eternal power and deity, has been clearly perceived in the things that have been made (Romans 1:20).

Our images are the portraits, representations, and inner symbols of the world around us. Each child from birth mentally illustrates important people. The child begins with the mother image and follows soon with the father image. Encountering destructive elements in life, both in parental failures and in personal anger, the child forms evil images alongside the kindly images that nurture. The ensuing struggle within parallels the war between God and evil. As a counselor helps a person mold images into a closer likeness of God the good Father, marked beneficial change follows (Biddle, 1962).

To summarize, I have argued that each of us possesses an unconscious mind that thinks with metaphor in its various forms, using symbols to depict and construct an inner reality out of our experiences with the external world in relation to ourselves. Since families are basic to the development of the self, parental images as well as self-images will contribute to the make-up of this internal reality. Indeed, parental images become part of the self-images. The central organizer of that inner reality, the world image, is the heart, that part of us that thinks deeply and commits itself or aligns to something greater than the self. But because of our own marked failings as well as those of our caretakers, we may develop fixations that inevitably lead to chaotic, contradictory, or destructive forms of thinking and action that lead in turn to impasses and the desperate need for outside help. Effective Christian counseling will consist of first understanding the language of the heart; then grasping the counselee's world view and fixations; and finally offering the person of Christ in the person of the counselor, through example, words, explanations, teachings, and directives. Such an interaction may stimulate the counselee to think deeply, to be open to God's actions, to discard fixations, and hence to be healed.

Exercises

1. Divide into groups of three. Have each person in sequence complete the sentence, "I feel very strongly that . . ." Then, with the help of the other group members, go back in time to an incident or phase of life that produced that strong feeling or opinion. Let each person do that as

many times as time allows. Discuss the role the incident played in the development of your heart.

2. Do the same with the sentence, "It is important to me that I . . . "

3. In groups of three, have each discuss a present or past hero.

4. In groups of three, have each discuss a favorite story. This might be a story read in childhood or recently, a story told by someone else, or a story enacted in a play, motion picture, or television production.

5. Cluster around the words "my heart," then quickly write a paragraph.

Suggested Reading

Daim, Wilfred, *Depth Psychology and Salvation,* Frederick Ungar Publishing Co., New York, 1963.

3

Interviewing

To come to appreciate the heart of another, we must interview in a manner that will allow an unfolding to transpire. People will reveal to us their most closely held opinions only if we can both establish rapport and engage in a dialogue with them in such a way that they come to express thoughts or ideas that they may never have articulated even to themselves. A kind of mutual search is required, led by the counselor, to encourage the counselee to bring forth the necessary ideation. This chapter presents a model of the interview and a survey of interviewing responses and maneuvers to accomplish this objective.

The essence of the method is clustering in reverse. Breaking the process down, the interview resembles a series of inverted cones: each base represents the starting point of data collection, each apex a grasp of some aspect of the counselee's experience. The apexes of several cones become in turn the base of another cone, its apex pointing more toward the heart of the counselee's difficulty. The early phase of investigation of a particular question, the base of the cone, consists of three kinds of interviewer actions: open-ended questions, active listening, and facilitations. The cone narrows as the counselor asks more specific questions in moving toward an understanding of this particular segment of the counselee's experience. Concomitantly, the relationship is established by attending to the counselee's comfort, showing interest, following associations, and working toward an empathic understanding of the counselee's world view. In addition, the counselor simultaneously contributes cognitions to the periphery of the cluster, prays without ceasing (Chapter 5) and listens with the third ear to the anecdotes, metaphors (Chapter 6), symbols, and body language of the counselee, thus gaining

30

more ideas about the heart and the basis of difficulty for the counselee. The counselor may also ask specific questions that help locate the counselee along the spiritual, personal, and family developmental pathways. Counselor and counselee now put all this together, essentially clustering in reverse. To this end, the counselor may offer explanations or interpretations of what appear to be the central or key issues. The counselee invariably responds to these offerings with anecdotes and body language that confirm or deny the accuracy of the counselor's assessment. Once the fundamental difficulty is grasped, treatment can be applied. The neophyte counselor errs most commonly in offering advice before the basic issues are understood. This and subsequent chapters deal in detail with each of the above steps.

Opening the Interview

It is good to begin and end every counseling session with a prayer. Opening and closing prayers model a prayerful approach to life for the counselee and metaphorically frame the counseling relationship and the counselee's problem. Counselors in secular settings may choose not to do so, at least not initially, because the choice of a secular counselor probably indicates the counselee is not opting for the spiritual perspective. I try to meet the counselee's view of the world, later introducing the gospel directly or indirectly after I have come to understand the counselee's stages of spiritual, interpersonal, and personal development, and any impending fixations. Even in secular counseling, I will continue to pray without ceasing (Chapter 5).

The usual courtesies, including a firm handshake, are offered at the start of each session. The counselor opens with a general question, such as:

> *Can you tell me what brings you here, something of your difficulties; how might I be of help?*

This and subsequent open-ended statements and questions allow a spontaneous unfolding of the counselee's fundamental difficulties. The counselor should pay careful attention to the first words of the counselee; referring back to these words can help maintain the thread and direction of the interview. Although the counselor will at least initially want to keep the focus on the thoughts, experiences, and feelings of the present, the counselee should have plenty of free reign for expression. At the beginning and throughout all interviews, the counselor uses responses, queries, and statements to establish communication, empathy and rapport, and to lead to a mutual grasp of the fixations of the heart of the counselee. The counselor is thus like a parachutist who searches for the ring that, when pulled, leads to the opening up of the entire structure. This and subsequent chapters will deal in detail with these techniques.

Early in the interview, perhaps even before the open-ended initial questions are posed, the counselor will want to attend to the comfort of the counselee. Profound emotions envelop a person seeking counseling for the first time. Some find asking for help humiliating, while others may be embarrassed by their symptoms or life situation. Hope or desperation or both may be present, perhaps combined with simple nervousness. Others have been coerced into counseling by irate or worried relatives. People seeing a psychiatrist for the first time may feel despair because they imagine this to be the end of the line: a psychiatrist, after all, is only for crazy people. Often the counselor can, by attending to body language, facial expression, or voice inflection, gain an intuitive understanding of how the counselee feels about coming. Empathic statements by the counselor, such as: "You look unhappy; I would imagine it was a big decision to come here!" may allow the counselee to voice feelings and to feel understood by the counselor. Or, the counselor might indirectly empathize with the counselee by telling an anecdote. For example, a counselor, sensing the counselee fears being crazy, might tell a story of another person with similar fears. The counselee's nonverbal responses, signs of assent and relaxation to the reassurance built into the anecdote, indicate a sense of feeling understood. Empathically recognizing and discussing the counselee's concerns build trust in the counseling situation. Empathy is discussed in detail in the next chapter.

Core Intervention Responses

Having opened the interview, the counselor explores with the counselee in an open-ended manner. As the counselee narrates concerns, the counselor can help the process along with four types of responses (Benson *et al.*, 1985):

- Open-ended questions
- Active listening
- Facilitations
- Reflections

Open-ended questions or statements ask for information in a general manner, not specifying the kind or form of information sought. Open-ended questions are used throughout the interview and in subsequent therapy, even when focusing on specific issues. They allow a counselee to relate stories in a familiar way. Open-ended questions are more likely to elicit unconscious responses, close-ended questions to elicit "yes," "no," or other single-word responses. "Tell me something of how you spend your day?" and "If my video camera could follow you around for a day, what would it see?" are examples of open-ended questions. Open-ended questions or statements should also be used when any new topic arises. For example, "Tell me about your husband."

Active listening is used by the counselor to convey interest in the counselee, receptivity, attentiveness, and the wish that the counselee continue unfolding the story. Active listening is a nonverbal communication that is received by the unconscious mind of the counselee: it employs silence plus nonverbal indications of interest, such as nodding; maintaining an open, receptive body stance; leaning forward; and maintaining eye contact. Silence is usually interpreted positively if the attention of the counselor during a silence is on the counselee. Active listening is probably the single most effective tool in interviewing. Deliberately using the body language of active listening is also good for the counselor. For example, a counselor who has already seen several people that day may have difficulty getting interest up for another. But adopting active listening techniques can actually engender interest. Note, however, that silence may be inappropriate if the counselee is very ill, very frightened or intimidated, or otherwise mute.

Facilitations are communications that encourage the counselee to say more, but are open ended. Examples are "OK," "uh huh," "You were saying?" "Please go on." These simple verbalizations are extremely important in aiding a counselee's revelation. They are useful throughout the interview but especially along with active listening early in the interview, with new topics, and after open-ended questions.

Reflections are responses that echo, repeat, or mirror a portion of what the counselee has just said; such responses facilitate further expression in the counselee's own words. Reflections are another indirect communication that tends to stimulate unconscious, more spontaneous verbalization. A more complex reflection is a summary of several points that the counselee has made earlier, even in past sessions. For example,

So far, you have told me that you've had lots of recent changes and stresses on top of being an anxious person in the past. You have job pressures, and you've been in therapy in the past, but never finished.

The counselor communicates having followed the counselee and implicitly asks for more definition of the difficulty. Reflections are extremely effective in conjunction with active listening and simple facilitations: not only do they encourage the counselee to continue, they show an interest in and memory for the counselee's words.

The interview moves from the general toward the specific, from the description of complaints to the specifics of thought, behavior, and relationships as the interviewer asks more specific questions, becoming somewhat more directive in the process. Morgan and Engel (1969), writing on medical interviewing for physicians and medical students, describe the strategy:

Encouraging the patient to speak freely continues to be the basic requirement for a productive interview, since only the patient can describe what he has been experiencing. On the other hand, he usually does not appreciate all that the interviewer needs to learn from him. In order to accomplish his task of diagnosis, the student must subtly direct the course of the interview. Far from being merely a passive listener, he indicates to the patient by his responses and questions the need for certain organization and content. The patient soon comes to appreciate that events must be dated, sequences established, and symptoms described precisely. At the same time, such direction must not be achieved at the expense of prejudicing the patient's responses or of blocking the free flow of his associations. The amount of direction needed in the interview varies with the patient. Some will wander and discuss unproductive areas in minute detail; others will gloss over important historical points, and still other patients will represent a coherent story where little intervention is needed. It is most important that the student be flexible in his interview technique, learn to adapt to the patient's style of reporting, and still remain in control of the situation. The student should neither passively listen to volumes of irrelevant detail, nor should he conduct the interview in the manner of a courtroom lawyer by firing repeated questions. Obviously, much practice and experience are needed to achieve the proper balance.

The two objectives, to encourage the patient's spontaneous associations and to provide direction, are best achieved by always initiating the inquiry into each new area with open-ended (nondirective) questions and by following with progressively more specific (directive) questions until the subject is fully clarified. This means that the interviewer must have clearly in his mind what detail is necessary to understand the illness yet not prematurely impose his ideas on the patient. For example, he may begin the investigation of a symptom with the request, "Tell me more about it" or "What was it like?" This allows the patient to say whatever he wishes about the symptom and to bring up his own associations, unprejudiced by the interviewer. The student, as he listens to the patient's account, is alert to omissions and ambiguities, and periodically indicates what needs to be clarified; *e.g.,* "That was when?" "What was the feeling?" "Which came first?" As the patient completes his more spontaneous account, the interviewer then follows with whatever specific questions are necessary to complete the picture. In so doing, he always tries to formulate each successive question on the basis of what the patient has just said. In essence, just as is done in sustaining a conversation, the student picks up where the patient leaves off. By following the patient's lead, he avoids the disruption of the patient's train of thought and important associations emerge naturally under such conditions. When a series of direct questions are posed early in the interview, the patient may respond simply by waiting passively for the next question. Only when the interviewer is satisfied that he has obtained all the information that he needs by following the patient's associations, does he again take the initiative to change the subject and introduce a new topic. Each new area is pursued in the same manner. Thus, the interview typically consists of a series of interconnected sequences, each one of which begins with open-ended questions and progresses to increasingly more specific questions until the issues are fully defined.

Throughout the interview, the student remains attentive to the patient's spontaneous associations, even when at first they may seem to be irrelevant. The patient is allowed to digress long enough to establish whether the information is pertinent to the history. If so, he is encouraged to continue. All the while, however, the student must keep in mind what information the patient has not yet clarified, so that he can return later to ask necessary questions at an appropriate time.

As the cones of the interview narrow, specific questions (such as *probes* and *clarifications*) are used to seek more information in areas already mentioned by the counselee. For example:

"When you say you've been depressed, can you tell me more of what you mean by the word 'depressed?' Tell me more about your drinking in recent days."

"Can you give me an example of (feeling, thought, action, relationship) you just mentioned?"

Thus, these questions and statements can retain an open-ended quality, yet focus the field of discussion. Clarifications and probes are used to move from the general to the specific or when the counselor does not understand some part of what the counselee has said. Probes and clarifications help counselor and counselee arrive at the ultimate goal of that segment of the interview: a shared understanding of an aspect of the counselee's experience.

Specific Questions

In the medical model, the interviewer asks specific questions that, hopefully, will lead to a diagnosis. In counseling, too, these core interviewing responses may lead to a diagnosis, albeit a psychiatric diagnosis. Indeed, many who seek counseling in parish settings, a doctor's office, or with a marriage counselor may well fall into such categories as a borderline personality or other personality disturbance, major depression, panic disorder, schizophrenia, or the like. Such diagnoses are valuable because they have strong implications with respect to treatment and prognosis. Chapter 17 deals with psychiatric diagnosis in more detail. But, moving past the linear questioning leading to diagnosis, the Christian counselor wants to have a feeling for the person's point of view and stage of development and, more specifically, a grasp of the person's impasses and fixations. Although much of this grasp comes from listening, observing, praying, and feeling, specific questions narrow the cone or cones.

In general, the counselor provides a sense of purpose, which is soon sensed by the interviewee. Both can then cooperate in pursuing the goal of the interview: to go to the heart of the matter, that heart comprised of the relationships of the self to itself, to others, and to God; their inner representations; and the self's efforts to correct impasses and fixations in those relationships, inner and outer. As a counselee develops an indepth understanding of relationships, steps to solve the problem become clear. In addition, the counselor can begin to communicate new solutions and choices to the counselee. Although this can be done explicitly or implicitly, the implicit (or indirect) method is superior since it uses the language of the unconscious, that structure that communicates most directly to the heart. Several of these methods for facilitating therapeutic change are covered in subsequent chapters.

The counselor uses specific questions to close interview cones. The counselor can use any of six categories of questions in working toward a lively dialogue leading to productive change.

No Specific Questions At All

A few counselees talk so freely that they seem to dominate the interview. The counselor can distinguish the dominating or defensive person from the one who is largely self sufficient with little prompting by noting that the latter readily develops interview cones with little more than active listening on the part of the counselor. For example:

> *Edna, a 50-year-old woman in treatment, initiated a session with a statement that she had had a nightmare the night before. Then she talked about a trip to see her father-in-law, who was dying of cancer. She described interchanges with him, his wife, and the doctor managing the case. She left in a good frame of mind. On returning home, she suddenly felt exhausted and went to bed. Once asleep, she had a nightmare in which her father-in-law reached for her from a hospital bed, unable to breathe with a look of "it's over" on his face. Edna described awakening perspiring, then remarked, "I must be going through suffering with him because I didn't do it with my father," indicating to me an unfinished relationship with her deceased father. Thus, she had gone from the exposition of various details to a heartfelt concern without any help from me. Now understanding her point of fixation, I became active, inviting her to have a dialogue with her father, using the empty chair technique (described in Chapter 14). In past sessions, Edna had expressed considerable resentment about her father's alcoholism, but in this dialogue she thanked him for the good things he had given her. This expression of gratitude allowed her to complete the relationship with him and let him*

go. Thinking that perhaps the nightmare voiced concerns about the inevitability of her own death and wanting to assess her spiritual responsiveness, I told a story of a friend of mine dying from Parkinson's disease. I described to her how I had realized that God does not offer us reasons for suffering so much as he gives us the solution to suffering in the life, death, and resurrection of Jesus Christ. Thus, I asked her heart a question indirectly. But her body language indicated that she was not touched by what I had said.

Specific Questions that Pinpoint Events Initiating Symptoms and the Meaning of those Events to the Person

Those who seek counsel often complain of distressing symptoms, such as anxiety, depression, confusion, unhappiness, or actions destructive to self or to others. At the outset of counseling, they see no connection between the events of their lives and their symptoms. Establishing such connections is important and can sometimes lead to a rapid resolution of symptoms. Consider the following case:

A 34-year-old man had suffered recurrent panic attacks for about two years. These attacks, which would begin suddenly, consisted of a pounding heart, shortness of breath, a terrible feeling of imminent doom, and fear of an impending heart attack. This second fear reinforced the first. We managed to control these attacks with medication, and he saw no connection between them and his external life. One morning, however, after a symptom-free period of several weeks, he returned in a state of panic. Specific questioning established that he had felt fine the evening before but had awakened in the morning with a panic attack. I maintained that something had happened to trigger the attack, but he could think of nothing. I proceeded to ask in detail the events that had occurred before he went to sleep. He mentioned casually that he had approached his wife to make love, but she had turned him down. I exclaimed, "That's it. You must have felt angered or hurt." He looked stunned and said, "I can't believe it! My panic attack just this instant stopped!" He went on to describe that he and his wife had struggled for years over their difference in sexual interest, and that her refusal had indeed angered him. However, in characteristic fashion, he had said nothing.

The key to progress here is the counselor's conviction that symptoms do not just happen but rather stem from the interaction of the sufferer's world view with certain events. The counselor pursues this conviction with questions that bracket that event. The event itself will invariably have produced emotion, and from it the counselee will have experienced some kind of loss. Loss of a sense of nurture, of a sense of sexual identity, of self-esteem, or of an ideal are commonly discovered. These senses of loss undermine the integrity of the self and cause symptoms as long as they remain out of awareness. Retrieval of the event and the emotional recognition of its meaning can lead to dramatic and often immediate relief. This class of specific questions forms the basis for the techniques of crisis intervention. The suggested reading for this chapter expands on this important skill.

Specific Questions that Cover a Wide Range of Relationships to God, Family, and Self

Often, in the initial interview, the counselor will sense that interview cones have closed about as much as they can and will want to inquire about the counselee's past and present relationships. Such inquiry often uncovers information that broadens the counselor's grasp of the counselee. Questions such as those that follow sample the person's functioning over a span of years to the present: "What is your earliest memory?" "The one after that?" Open-ended questions, however, allow the counselee to open up spontaneously. Here are some examples: "Give me a thumbnail sketch of your mother." "Your father." "Their relationship."

"How would you describe yourself as a person?"

"Can you tell me some of what you dream when you sleep?"

"Can you tell me something about your sex life?"

"Do you have any religious beliefs?"

Such samplings help the counselor to mentally "build a person," or, more to the point, help in grasping the counselee's world view and any impasses or fixations. A lengthy exercise at the end of Chapter 7 will allow readers to experiment with these questions.

Specific Questions that Elicit the Details of Concrete Interactions

As the counselor comes to appreciate the counselee's impasses or fixations, pinpointing experiences that metaphorize, typify, or illustrate those stuck points can be helpful. In other words, all of the impasses and fixations listed in Chapter 2 are lived out in concrete, discrete actions or avoidance of action in the person's daily life. Detailed inquiry will invariably reveal that those actions occur and recur in almost stereotyped fashion; simply put, they are patterns. A grasp of such patterns may allow the counselor to initiate change through assigning a task that intervenes in, disrupts, or promotes a minimal change in that pattern. Consider the following case:

> *A very beautiful 20-year-old oriental woman came in complaining of the recent onset of mental confusion and paranoid delusions. I helped her symptoms with medication and then learned that her symptoms resulted from her mother's inability to let her go. Work with both mother and daughter led to a resolution: her mother let her go, and her symptoms disappeared. Two years later she returned with identical symptoms. She was engaged to a successful young attorney of Hispanic origin. He was quite dominating and controlling, a replay of her mother; she had not learned to cope with such behavior on the part of others. Specific questions about their interactions revealed that the essence of the impasse was played out every morning in her apartment, when she was making his lunch. She described how, as she was about to slice an item, he would object, take the knife from her, and say, "Let me show you how to do it right." She exclaimed in despair, "No matter how I cut it, it isn't right!" She reported numerous battles over the*

subject, but he persisted. Feeling caught between a love for him and a desire to marry and a loss of her individuality, she became psychotic. I decided to assign her a task that would make one small change in this stereotyped pattern. I instructed her, on the next occasion of his complaining, to hand the knife to him and say, "Show me how, O great one, to cut the tomato. You are obviously wiser than I, and I will sit at your feet and learn." She returned the following week with a triumphant glow on her face and reported the disappearance of her symptoms; her fiance, upon hearing her words, had exploded in rage and, after quieting down, had said, "I think I've got some things to learn." Their relationship proceeded more smoothly after that, and she was discharged from treatment.

Thus, a particular interaction had come to be a metaphor for this woman's life. Intervening in the details of that metaphor led to a rearrangement of the balance of power between two people. The woman had a new metaphor and hence a new world view, with resolution of symptoms. Interactional systems and the use of tasks in counseling are further discussed in Chapters 10 and 16.

Questions that Ask the Counselee to be Specific

The linguists Bandler and Grinder (1975) studied the grammar of people suffering emotional distress. They argued that as people attempt to put their world views into words, they often do so inadequately. Furthermore, people can literally mislead themselves by the obscurations their own language brings about. Bandler and Grinder discuss three ways a person may poorly represent a world view, through the processes of *deletion, nominalization,* and *generalization.*

In *deletion,* the counselee omits, perhaps inadvertently or defensively, substantial pieces of the world view. The counselor may respond to a deletion in one of three ways: by not recognizing the deletion and hence accepting it, by asking for the missing piece, or by guessing at it. I suggest the counselor note the deletion and at a timely point ask for it. Consider the following case:

A 50-year-old man had possessively dominated his wife for years. He broke down when she fled into an extramarital affair. In discussing his spiritual life, he described attending Mass, but he had neither taken communion nor confessed his sins in years. Noting that the word "sins" failed to refer to anything in particular, I asked, "Which sin?" He blushed and then described his periodic affairs.

In *nominalization*, the counselee linguistically turns an ongoing process into an event or an accomplished fact. Once an event occurs, its outcome is fixed and nothing can be done to change it, while to see something as a process is to be able to alter it. Nominalizations distort the truth of a given situation. The counselor must challenge them. For example, Joe, a 14-year-old boy says of his father:

J.: I hate him!

A.: Could you say you are angry with him for what he did
to you?

A common example of nominalization is the use of "being" language in place of "action" language. Contrast "You are a bad boy" with "I'm mad because you still haven't picked up your toys." Thus, people can be the victims of as well as the initiators of nominalizations:

A conscientious 29-year-old man suffered occasional impulsive drug use. Frightened by these impulses, he sought help. He proved to be prone to plunges in self-esteem and, in turn, vulnerable to acting out. His mother had always been highly critical of him, but her severest blow to him occurred when she derided an essay he wrote for admission to college, saying, "I wouldn't hire you to be the trash man." In doing so, she condemned his being. Far better to have said, "I think it's a lousy essay." He always assumed that his mother hated him. However, her criticisms and condemnations were really a way of clinging to him, of saying to him, "Don't leave me." Recovery of the crucial incident and its reframing led to new strength in resisting temptations.

Related to nominalization is *generalization*. In generalization, a person builds a world view with respect to one category of experience from a single or a few experiences in that category. Clearly, we all generalize. The process of healing and change in counseling involves the ability of the counselee to face, look at, think deeply about, and rethink generalizations, combined with the ability of the counselor to facilitate that process.

Metaphoric Questions

A skilled counselor may ask questions indirectly by telling a story about someone or something else, as, for example, fishing for information about a counselee's mother by talking about the mother goose at the San Miguel mission, describing her as she cared for her brood. Or, talking of another patient's mother or a wife as she mothers, *etc*. Such indirect specific questioning can lead to important, unguarded information from the counselee.

We have so far considered core interviewing responses, specific questions, and how these techniques can help a counselee focus on areas of impasse and fixation. The following abbreviated narrative of an actual case is presented to illustrate some of these points. Gene, a man of 52, was referred by his family doctor for depression.

A.   Can you tell me something of what brings you here?

G.   Six months ago, I traveled to Texas. My sister's son had died. He was an alcoholic. When I returned home, my youngest son announced he was moving out. Then, in early January, I helped my friend take his wife to the hospital.

A.   Uh huh.

G.   On February 2, while shaving, I suddenly felt outside myself, like I wasn't real.

A.   *(Shifts, leans forward to match G's position, nods.)*

G.   After that I started having panic attacks and have become claustrophobic. I don't want to be alone. I'm not myself.

A. Hm.

G. And I'm nervous and depressed.

A. Depressed?

G. Yeah, and I'm crying a lot. And I feel angry!

A. Angry? At whom?

G. (*Pauses, reflects*) I don't know. Maybe myself. How dare I let myself get into this.

A. (*Specific questioning establishes that G. is moderately depressed and in a chronically dissociated state. He has continued to work and has improved slightly with medication from his family doctor, but he is not happy with how he feels. He hates seeing a psychiatrist but is afraid he is losing his mind.*)

Such a sudden and dramatic onset. It suggests you've lost something. (*We have closed one cone, that of psychiatric diagnosis. Now we pursue another, an inquiry into loss as a point of fixation. I have kept in mind his first words, the comment about the death of his nephew.*)

(*G. goes back to his nephew's death, his yellow color, and his agonal vomiting of blood. His voice inflection conveys his shock over the scene, but he also manages to use the word "stupid" during the description.*)

A. I'm thinking of your description of your nephew's death, and of your sudden dissociation in front of the mirror. The latter sounds like a kind of, uh (gropes for the right word) . . .

G. Shock!

A. That's it. Shock!

G. I was in shock once, in a car accident! Just like it!

A. A delayed reaction to the death of your nephew!

G. That's right! (*Thus far, we have succeeded in connecting symptoms to his experience. He is looking better already. At this point a second cone is closed. Now we can deal more directly*) *with his feelings about his nephew. I use the empty chair technique, described more fully in Chapter 14.)*

A. Would you be willing to imagine that your nephew is sitting in that chair there? Tell him how you feel about him, his illness, his death.

G. You failed your mother! You failed me! I'm furious with you!

A. Try saying "I forgive you."

(G. sobs, long pause)

Closure

The interviewer bears the responsibility to keep track of time and guide the interview to a smooth close. At a suitable moment, the counselor may signal with body language (putting down pad and pencil, closing books, leaning forward in the chair toward the door, *etc.*) or with a statement such as, "We must stop shortly." This is a time for summary statements or final questions such as, "Is there anything else I should know before we stop?" A discussion of fee or plans for the next interview can take place here. The interviewee's sensitivity to closing is illustrated by the following incident:

A 21-year-old male, suffering a schizophrenic condition and hospitalized at a state hospital, proved to be a talented hypnotic subject. Toward the end of a session of hypnosis, I realized I was almost out of time and blurted out "time's up." The instant I said it I knew I had said the wrong thing. I recovered and asked the patient to have a closing hypnotic dream, actually a way to ask the patient's unconscious mind for feedback regarding the session. He dreamed, "There was a clock man. He said 'time's up' and threw me into a warehouse. ["Warehouse" is a common nickname for a state hospital.] I wound up in a sink and went down the drain. I was no bigger than a thumb." I never forgot his metaphoric chastening for my improper ending.

As with the opening, the interviewer attends to the comfort of the interviewee. If the interview has been upsetting, this should be discussed. The careful counselor notices the body language of the counselee, inquiring about any manifestations of distress, irritation, or bewilderment. Only with a final, empathic understanding can the interview properly close. If after the interview the counselor feels uneasy, the process should be reviewed and, perhaps, the counselee should be called.

Exercises

1. Obtain a videotape of a pastoral counseling or psychotherapeutic interview. After viewing the tape, critique the interviewer's conduct of interview, focusing on the opening, the use of core interviewing responses, closure of interview cones, the use of specific questions, and closure.

2. Locate people or couples who have received counseling and who are willing to share their experience with the class. This counseling may have been for marital problems, bereavement, depression, alcoholism, personality disorder, fears and phobias, *etc.* Let a student interview the person or couple around the question: "What was it like to have had marital problems?" "Depression?" *etc.* in front of the class. Have the class critique the opening, use of core interviewing responses, *etc.*

3. Assign students the task of summarizing a pastoral counseling case they have had experience with. In my experience, second year seminarians have one or two interesting cases; third and fourth year students have several more. These vignettes will be useful for future role-playing exercises.

4. Divide into groups of three or four and practice interviewing, utilizing these vignettes or others provided by the instructor.

Suggested Reading

Switzer, David K., "Crisis Intervention and Problem Solving," in *Clinical Handbook of Pastoral Counseling*, Paulist Press, New York and Mahwah, New Jersey, 1985.

4

Empathy

The core interviewing responses of open-ended questions, active listening, and facilitations are empathic in that through active interest they encourage the counselee to open up. Indeed, only through empathizing with the counselee can the counselor hope to learn of and reach the counselee's heart, because love and empathy are intimately associated, and ultimately only love can truly win another person. Love has been defined in many ways, but operationally love is to perceive the needs of another and then to take action to meet those needs. Empathy is essential to love, for only through empathy can one come to appreciate the heartfelt position and hence fundamental emotional, psychological, and spiritual needs of another person.

Dictionaries define empathy as an imaginative projection of one's own consciousness into another's being, mentally entering into the feeling or spirit of a person or thing, appreciative perception or understanding, and, interestingly enough, motor mimicry.

Often, the body language of interviewer and interviewee reflects the development of rapport during an interview. In interviews with high rapport, the interviewee regularly adopts the posture and motor movements of the interviewer, in mirror fashion crossing legs, gesturing, putting hands to face, etc. Erickson (1976) regularly and deliberately but subtly mimicked his interviewee's body language, mannerisms, speech pattern, and even breathing rate to accelerate the development of rapport. After matching the interviewee for a time, he would shift his own demeanor to a more relaxed, confident, or open position, thereby communicating such subconscious messages as, "Relax!" or "Be open!"

In practice, empathy is the plumbing of another person's thinking, feeling, and experience with the simultaneous setting aside of considerations of morality, with respect to what is being expressed. It involves a willingness and the patience to hear the other person out, to gain an effective grasp of the essence of another person's story. It embraces a belief that the other person has a story worth listening to, a story that one can come to appreciate only with patient effort and by avoiding the pitfall of jumping to conclusions about the basic motivations and intentions of the other. The parish priest in the following example illustrates a lack of empathy and the damage that can cause.

> *For most of her life, a 13-year-old girl had experienced extreme verbal abuse from her mother. Disturbed by vivid fantasies of slaying her mother in her sleep, she confessed to her parish priest that she was angry with her mother. "I got a 30 minute lecture," she stated.*

Empathy requires recalling one's own feelings, imaginations, experiences, and failings in evaluating those of another. Empathy is not an intellectual exercise but an effort of imagination and emotion, faculties associated with the unconscious mind. *I can imagine how you must feel!* Empathy requires the counselor to hold a fundamental respect for the other, a belief that there is a child of God somewhere inside, with a story worth listening to and considering.

> *The 13-year-old child mentioned above went on to marry a verbally and sometimes physically abusive man, with whom she stayed for about 15 years. Her profound masochism, stemming from guilt surrounding her homicidal wishes, coupled with her desire to "help" her sadistic mate, kept her in the marriage. In her thirties, sick of mistreatment, she left her husband. However, later she fell into a similar relationship, in which she got pregnant. Desperate to escape, she had an abortion, an action very much against her principles. Knowing the whole story, one could see that the abortion, in itself a*

morally reprehensible act, was the last link in a chain of events extending back to childhood. For the counselor, the act of loving this woman began with the empathic understanding of her experience. Knowing her need, the counselor could begin to take action to meet her need, to help the child in her grow past the masochistic fixation on the mother.

Empathy as Attitude

Empathy needs first to be considered as an attitude within the counselor. An empathic posture or its polar opposite, a judgmental posture, is always highly visible to the unconscious mind of the counselee in the body language, voice inflections, and implications of the speech of the counselor. We are all fine tuned to the nonverbal manifestations of judgment. The body language of empathy is similar to that of active listening, described in Chapter 3, often possessing the "motor mimicry" described above. Voice inflections in empathy reflect friendliness, respect, and interest, while judgment rings with inflections of criticism, condescension, superiority, or disgust. For example, I once listened to a psychiatrist interview a 50-year-old woman, a hapless alcoholic. The interview closed with the psychiatrist saying, "We've helped a lot of people like you." The phrase "people like you" carried with it an inflection of condescension and implied an inferior status for the interviewee. The Christian should remember that status with God can change quickly: Judas was an apostle, while the thief crucified next to Jesus went with him to paradise.

Empathy as Technique

The second aspect of empathy is its use as technique: the actual verbalizations that facilitate the careful touching of another's feelings. The student initially using these techniques might feel them awkward and contrived. However, their practice can induce a more empathic posture over time. The latter half of this chapter deals with these techniques. Empathy as an interview technique is especially useful when the interviewee is sick, in pain, in shock, suffering a loss, or otherwise suffering. Erickson (1976) illustrates techniques of empathy in dealing with an injury of his 3-year-old son, Robert. In this example, Erickson empathized sequentially with several aspects of his son's feelings, leading to a beneficial outcome of a traumatic situation.

> *Robert fell down the stairs, split his lip, and knocked an upper tooth back into the maxilla. He was bleeding profusely and screaming loudly with pain and fright. A single glance confirmed the emergency. No effort was made to pick him up. Instead, as he paused to breathe for fresh screaming, he was told quickly, simply, sympathetically, and emphatically, "That hurts awful, Robert. That hurts terrible." Right then, without any doubt, my son knew that I knew that I was agreeing completely with him. Therefore, he could listen respectfully to me, because I had demonstrated that I understood the situation fully. Then I told Robert, "And it will keep right on hurting." In this simple statement, I named his own fear, confirmed his own judgment of the situation, demonstrated my intelligent grasp of the entire matter and my entire agreement with him. The next step was to declare, "And you really wish it would stop hurting." Again, we were in full agreement and he was ratified and even encouraged in this wish. And it was his wish, deriving entirely from within him and constituting his own urgent need. With the situation so defined, I could offer a suggestion with some certainty of its acceptance. This suggestion was, "Maybe it will stop hurting in a little while, in just a minute or two." This was a suggestion in full accord with his own needs and wishes and, because it was qualified by a "maybe it will," it was not in contradiction to his own understandings of the situation. Thus, he could accept the idea and initiate his response to it. The next procedure was a recognition of the meaning of the injury to Robert himself—pain, loss of blood, body damage, a loss of the wholeness of his normal, narcissistic self-esteem, of his sense of physical goodness so vital in human living. He knew that he hurt, that he was a damaged person; he could see his blood upon the pavement, taste it in his mouth and see it on his hands. And yet, like all other human beings, he too could desire narcissistic distinction*

*in his misfortune, along with the desire for narcissistic com-
fort. (Nobody wants a picayune headache, but since a
headache must be endured, let it be so colossal that only the
sufferer could endure it. Human pride is so curiously good
and comforting!) Therefore, Robert's attention was doubly
directed to two vital issues of comprehensible importance to
him by the simple statements, "That's an awful lot of blood on
the pavement. Is it good, red, strong blood? Look carefully,
Mother, and see. I think it is, but I want you to be sure."
Thus, there was an open and unafraid recognition in another
way of values important to Robert. He needed to know that his
misfortune was catastrophic in the eyes of others as well as his
own, and he needed tangible proof thereof that he himself
could appreciate. Therefore, by declaring it to be "an awful
lot of blood," he could again recognize the intelligent and
competent appraisal of this situation in accord with his own
actually unformulated, but nevertheless real, needs. However,
we qualified that favorable opinion by stating that it would be
better if we were to examine the blood by looking at it against
the white background of the bathroom sink. By this time he
had ceased crying and his pain and fright were no longer
dominant factors . . . Instead, he was interested and absorbed
in the important problem of the quality of his blood. His
mother picked him up and carried him to the bathroom, where
water was poured over his face to see if the blood "mixed
properly with water" and gave it a "proper pink color." Next
came the question of suturing the lip. Since this could easily
evoke a negative response, it was broached in a negative
fashion to him, thereby precluding an initial negation by him,
and at the same time raising a new and important issue. This
was done by stating regretfully that, while he would have to
have stitches taken in his lip, it was most doubtful if he could
have as many stitches as he could count. In fact, it looked as if
he could not even have ten stitches and he could count to twen-
ty. Regret was expressed that he could not have seventeen
stitches, like Betty Alice, or twelve like Allan; but comfort was*

offered in the statement that he would have more stitches than Bert, Lance or Carol. Only seven were required, to his disappointment, but the surgeon pointed out that the suture material was of a newer and better kind than any his siblings had ever had, and that the scar would be an unusual "W" shape, like the initial of his daddy's college. Thus the smaller number of stitches was well compensated for by greater advantages.

Erickson first identified and named Robert's pain. He did not try to talk him out of it or tell him he should not feel that way. Next, he empathized with Robert's fear for the future. Then he empathized with his wish, his hope. He followed with a suggestion, but Robert's doubts were named, and hence empathized with, in the word "maybe." He next empathized with Robert's pride and simultaneously with his need for his mother. Even his negativity was considered. Lastly, his sense of sibling competition was included.

Countertransference

To stay with another person's experience, to refrain from disagreeing with it, judging it, or trying to change it, requires a temporary sacrifice of our own closely held opinions about how things should be, and how others should think or behave. During a counseling session, various emotional reactions may arise within the counselor to tempt him to interrupt, criticize, condemn, withdraw, or prematurely offer advice. These emotional reactions, perhaps strong and confusing, may spring from consciously held opinions, negative self-images of which the counselor is unaware, or an unrecognized, unhealthy interaction between counselor and counselee. The counselor need not be condemned or judged for perhaps intensely disliking the counselee, perhaps wanting to give up on the case, or even suddenly having an intense physical attraction. Rather, the counselor needs first to be aware of these reactions as they arise and then to listen to, scrutinize, and plumb these reactions for the fresh information they may offer about what is going on within the counselee or between counselor and counselee.

Consciously held opinions are one potential cause for a break in empathy. Adherence to church doctrine can result from a lifetime of indoctrination and hence be a culturally determined mental set. To interact with someone who violates or disagrees with those opinions can stress one's ability to listen objectively and dispassionately. It was to this point that Jesus stated,

> "Judge not, that you be not judged. For with the judgment you pronounce you will be judged, and the measure you give will be the measure you get. Why do you see the speck that is in your brother's eye, but do not notice the log that is in your own eye? Or how can you say to your brother, 'Let me take the speck out of your eye,' when there is the log in your own eye? You hypocrite, first take the log out of your own eye, and then you will see clearly to take the speck out of your brother's eye" (Matthew 7:1-5).

The history of Christianity is so littered with massive violations of this saying that we must look for an explanation for its existence. In this book, judgmentalism is considered to be a stage in the spiritual growth cycle (see Chapter 8). Early in our spiritual walk, we believe and commit ourselves to what we have heard; this indoctrination of our conscious minds has not yet been balanced by a knowing of God that can only come with experience. Thus, disagreements with our position can be threatening. With maturity, the Christian not only knows church doctrine but has developed an inner relationship with God that allows the Christian to empathize.

> *Following a weekend retreat for marriage enrichment, several couples continued to meet together for some months. At one meeting, one of the most doctrinally rigid of the group told a fellow member that he could have little to do with him because his Christian doctrine left so much to be desired. Naturally, the result was a complete and permanent disruption of the relationship.*

> *In another example, a woman desperately summoned an "on call" clergyman when her 15-year-old son committed suicide. She had divorced when he was young, then remarried; the boy had gone to live with his father about a year before his death. Having introduced himself, the clergyman listened to her story*

*for a few minutes, then interrupted by admonishing her,
saying, "Well, now it is time to pay the piper." With that, he
implied that she was getting what she deserved. Both cases
demonstrate drastic breaks in empathy.*

Negative self-images held out of awareness by the interviewer in
response to an interviewee's behavior have the potential to interfere with
empathy in the interviewer. Unrecognized emotional reactions to an interviewee based on some hidden aspect of the interviewer's heart is
termed countertransference (Kernberg, 1984). For example, a counselor
raised in a family where sexuality was considered dirty or sinful might
react to a counselee who has a sexual problem with consternation, confusion, or anger. Another counselor, perhaps raised in an atmosphere of
rigid discipline, might implicitly delight in the rebellious escapades of a
counselee.

*Dolores, a 36-year-old deeply religious woman, had been
divorced for several years. She was approached by a man
from a religious order; attracted to her, he made sexual advances. Upset and confused, she sought counseling. The
woman counselor that Dolores consulted thought that she
wanted to have an affair, but religious values interfered.
Dolores stated, "She was projecting; I think she was the one
who wanted an affair."*

These reactions point to an excessive identification with or projection to
some aspect of the counselee, resulting in a loss of objectivity by the counselor. In such cases, the counselor becomes blind to the authentic needs of
the counselee, thereby losing empathy.

Countertransference reactions can also be precipitated by interactions
with a counselee that propel the counselor into a behavior inconsistent
with the stated objective of the interview. For example, the counselee
might play a bratty child, encouraging the counselor to scold him. Or a
masochistic person might act so as to get the counselor to behave sadisti-
cally. Frequently, "helpless" people can induce a counselor to take care
of them, rescue them, or direct them, actions that are the last thing a
counselee truly needs.

A woman in her 30s sought help for depression. Her father and brother had exhibited themselves to her when she was a child. Having long since repressed the memories of these traumatic experiences, she maintained a little girl's need to be taken care of. Markedly inhibited sexually in her marriage, she sought counseling from her pastor. He wound up seducing her. She was able to repress this incident for a time, but she finally broke down and was hospitalized for depression, at which point her history came out. Why had she been so helpless in her relationship with him? Why had he acted in a manner so inconsistent with his office? Most likely, she projected a wish to be taken care of to her pastor, who found her stimulating. If he had perceived his sexual arousal, then thought it through instead of acting on it, he would have averted the disaster.

The key to the management of such temptations, then, is not to eliminate countertransference feelings but to be aware of their emergence. The counselor who is aware of his feelings is able to weigh them as evidence, to use them to help get to the heart of the matter with a particular counselee.

Techniques of Empathic Interviewing

During an interview, fully or partially hidden currents of emotion course through the counselee, often springing from the heart of his difficulty or from some situation that symbolizes or metaphorizes an aspect of his heart. Empathy as a technique involves stating the observed emotion; it is a response that recognizes or names the counselee's feeling without criticizing it, accepting the feeling in the counselee even though the interviewer may believe the feeling to be wrong (Benson, *et. al.,* 1985).

I was asked to see Joan, a 34-year-old woman who had just been hospitalized with a pulmonary embolism (blood had mysteriously clotted in a pelvic or leg vein, then traveled to and lodged in the lung, causing chest pain and the coughing up of blood). The referring M.D. stated that the woman was quite upset and depressed.

A.: *(after talking about her acute illness with her)* You look upset, maybe over and beyond the illness. *(Here, I state the emotion I observe, but I underplay it a bit. Actually, she looks angry as well, but I stay away from words she might not accept.)*

J.: I am! *(glowers, bites lip, eyes moisten)* I feel like I'm falling apart!

I perceived her to be struggling for control. I decided to reassure her by communicating understanding of her emotions. Reassurance so defined is a type of empathic response.

A.: Falling apart, losing control, can be frightening, huh? Nobody likes to lose control.

J.: *(starts to sob uncontrollably)*

At this point, Joan needed further empathic responses to her uncontrollable crying, those of support and partnership.

A.: I am here to help you. Let's see if we can figure out what's going on that has you so upset.

J.: *(between sobs)* Two days ago, my husband left me for another woman. Yesterday, I started getting chest pain and spitting up blood.

We talked at length about the circumstances of her husband's departure, her rage and helplessness, and her subsequent illness. At this point, I considered confronting her to raise the ticklish question of her role in her husband's departure. A confrontation points out to the counselee an aspect of feeling or behavior that she might be unaware of or avoiding. I find it helpful to phrase a confrontation as a question. I was about to ask Joan if anything in her behavior could have contributed to her husband's departure when she volunteered the information.

> **J.:** I wonder if my pushing my husband around had anything to do with his leaving.

Joan went on to describe in graphic, painful detail how she had driven and dominated her husband; she reproached herself as she related the story. At this point, I expressed respect and offered a reframing of the total situation. Respect and reframing look for some positive aspect of a person's actions; they assume that people, however disordered, are desperately trying to make the best possible choices for their lives.

> **A.:** We could go on to beat you up some more *(a twinkle in my eye, empathizing tongue-in-cheek with her self-reproach),* but maybe you had some good reasons for treating your husband that way.

> **J.:** I did it for my kids. They mean everything to me, more than anything in the world. I drove him to provide for them! *(speaking with intensity)*

> **A.:** How do they mean so much to you?

> **J.:** *(explodes)* I had nothing growing up. Treated like dirt. I swore my kids would have the best!

> **A.:** Sounds like you have some unfinished business with your parents.

This case study illustrates several of the responses available to the counselor in handling the counselee's emotions. The goal is to facilitate the expression and comprehension of the cornerstone experiences and cognitions that constitute the heart. Let us review the maneuvers covered so far.

Empathy

Empathy names the observed or most likely feeling extant in the here and now, without regard to whether that feeling is justified or reasonable; it merely acknowledges an aspect of a person's existence in the present. Empathy can be communicated directly or indirectly through metaphor, the latter going more directly to the unconscious mind and hence to the heart; for example, I empathized with an 11-year-old boy's reluctance to see me by telling him a story of a tiger who was captured and dragged by force to a zoo.

Reassurance

Reassurance allows the counselor to convey understanding of the emotion so named, thus furthering the empathic link between the two people. Again, this can be done directly or indirectly. In the above example, I could have spoken of how understandable was the apprehension of the tiger when approached by the zoo's doctor.

Support and Partnership

Support and partnership are empathic statements that follow the above and further the therapeutic alliance. Direct statements, such as, "Let's work together to work this out" or "I can assure you that God is on your side and wants to see you well" can have an immensely beneficial effect. To illustrate the indirect approach, I might have told the boy how the zoo doctor reassured the tiger, telling the tiger that the doctor wanted to see the tiger return to the jungle feeling stronger.

> *On several occasions, I have been able to share the gospel with the sick using the principle of empathic support and partnership. I once did a physical examination on a man with amyotrophic lateral sclerosis (ALS, or Lou Gehrig's disease), a spinal cord disease that leads to muscle wasting and eventually to death. During the examination, I asked if he had ever thought that God was doing this to him. The question struck him, and he replied very solemnly, "I've done some bad things in my life, but I never did anything bad enough to deserve this!" I paused, then replied, "I know God isn't doing this to you; everything we can know of God we can see in Jesus Christ, and he never made anyone sick. On the contrary, he healed the sick whenever possible, even on the Sabbath, when it got him in trouble. God is on your side." When I saw him the next day, he looked happier, and he remarked that he was less depressed and felt more like going on. I have found that many who are severely or terminally ill feel in their hearts that*

God is snuffing them out, and I have told them this story as a
way to reach and change that heartfelt conviction.

Respect and Reframing

The counselor can show respect by attempting to empathize with a
person's intentions, however misguided, to do good in life. A direct example, such as, "I'm impressed with how you are dealing with this," is
an example of showing respect. A reframing (Watzlawick, 1974) is a
more complex, indeed paradoxical, kind of empathic response that
redefines actions or thoughts, previously suggested to be crazy or mali-
cious, as having a constructive motive.

On a psychiatric unit, an 18-year-old man ran up to me and
announced emphatically, "I'm Jesus Christ!" I replied, "Tell
me how long you've been the savior of your family." We
proceeded to discuss quite rationally his family difficulties and
his feelings of responsibility for them.

How does one go about selecting what to say in an empathic interview or, for that matter, in any situation calling for empathy? There are
six discernible steps:

- The counselor must detect that the person is expressing a
  need. This is a given in a counseling situation. In casual
  human interchange, one can detect need in a person's verbalizations and/or in voice inflection and body language.
  Expressions of need may come quite unexpectedly, like "a
  thief in the night."

- Pray silently and incline an ear to the Lord. He is close
  during such times and can guide you. Then, trust your in-
  tuitions.

- Mentally project yourself into the person's situation: how
  would you feel in like circumstances?

- Listen to the voice inflections and body language of the
  person as well as to the implications of what the person
  says. These three items—implications of speech, voice in-

flection, and body language—will always reflect the person's basic feelings.

- Verbalize what you perceive to be the basic feeling expressed. Do not worry that you may be wrong.

- Look to the person for feedback. Again, body language and voice inflection will tell you if you are right. Or, the person might indirectly confirm your empathic statement with a metaphoric statement. Usually, if you are right, the person will agree and go on to elaborate further; if you are wrong, your attempt will nonetheless be appreciated and the counselee will continue to explain.

As a practicing psychotherapist, I am struck by the number of times that deviant, neurotic, psychotic, and antisocial behavior is traceable to the empathic failure of another person. Whole-personality distortion occurs regularly from a parent's repeated failure to empathize with a child. But we do not have to look just to childhood experiences: in daily life, in schools, families, business organizations, churches, anywhere where there is a hierarchy, superiors may fail to perceive the existential and emotional positions of those under them. And how often do we, wrapped up in our pursuits, fail to notice a covertly expressed need of a friend, acquaintance, or someone who just crosses our path? Indeed, often we elect not to notice, as some did who preceded the Good Samaritan. Furthermore, empathic breaks may be gross and massive, constituting an assault on another person. Sexual and physical abuse of children is epidemic: those who commit it were generally victims themselves. In such manner, the sins of the parents easily pass to the children, and so on. Humanity thus perpetuates sin by repeating such vicious cycles. The next chapter describes specifically how the counselor can cooperate with God to help empathize with a counselee, thereby beginning to break destructive patterns that may have existed for generations.

Exercises

1. Divide into pairs. Using the vignettes generated by Exercise 3, Chapter 3, have students role play cases, their partners playing the counselor. Practice the use of empathy, reassurance, support and partnership, and respect and reframing. After the role play is completed, the counselee should give the counselor feedback. Let the instructor then ask for feedback from the entire class.

2. Divide into groups of four and practice using empathic responses, one student simulating a case proposed by students or the instructor. Try to use empathy, reassurance, support, and respect in sequence.

Suggested Reading

Wicks, Robert J., "Countertransference and Burnout in Pastoral Counseling," in *Clinical Handbook of Pastoral Counseling*, edited by Robert J. Wicks, *et al.*, Paulist Press, 1985.

5

Praying Without Ceasing

(5:17 I Thessalonians)

During an interview, the counselor will sooner or later begin to feel the grip of the counselee's impasses. The counselor, particularly if inexperienced, will also feel at impasse with a lack of knowledge and ability to help. At this point, most counselors will either start to panic, or tolerate this sense of helplessness and begin to pray. Although every counselor should maximize experience and knowledge, the Christian counselor has an additional resource, in fact the ultimate resource, Almighty God, who is keenly interested in the problems of those who suffer. The presence of our Lord and the avenue to him, praying without ceasing, can be of profound help to both counselor and counselee. Praying without ceasing is a mental or silent calling to God in the heat of the counseling exchange. It is a suspension of one's self and ideas, a listening with the third ear, a hope for and expectancy of inspiration, guidance, and progress in the interview. It is a literal listening for the voice of Providence in the midst of the clamor and confusion of many thoughts, voices, emotions, memories, and images. Such access to the presence of God is reassuring as well as inspiring to the counselor. Praying without ceasing engenders courage, hope, and propels forward the search. Many in the Old and New Testaments used praying without ceasing, for they knew that to tap into the creative power of God was to promote radical change.

Praying without ceasing calls on a God who knows the hearts of people. The Scriptures abound with references to God's knowledge of the hearts of his people, his desire to help, heal, and communicate the specific ingredients for change. For example, the Lord says to Samuel of Saul, "Do not look on his appearance or on the height of his stature, because I have rejected him; for the Lord sees not as man sees; man looks on the outward appearance, but the Lord looks on the heart" (I Samuel 16:7). Likewise, Jesus knew the hearts of men, as he knew that Judas would betray him (John 6:64), and how Peter would deny him (Jn 13:38). It remains for us as counselors to hear, and to pray for our counselee to hear, our Lord's promptings.

> *A 27-year-old Christian man came seeking relief from pain resulting from a back injury suffered at work. He had no identifiable surgically correctable lesion, and physical therapy had failed to provide relief. Depressed, he hoped that hypnosis might help. I diagnosed a chronic muscle strain that caused intermittent painful spasms. I suspected an emotional element as well, as he clearly was very passive. (Hypnosis creates an altered state of consciousness by attenuating the conscious mind while inviting the expression of the unconscious. The resulting disorientation, dissociation, and deep relaxation can provide considerable pain relief. Also, because the unconscious is more available, so is the heart.) While in a trance he remarked, "I had a dream last night; in it I was yelling and screaming." He then ceased to speak and fell back again into a passive state. I suddenly remembered the presence of God and began to pray silently, in effect asking God for guidance and inspiration for the two of us. In turn, I kept a receptive attitude, listening with an inner ear to my thoughts as they occurred to me. I focused also on the sense of God's presence. After a pause, I commented that he sounded angry in the dream and suggested that his unconscious could continue to work on the problem the dream implied. He then appeared to struggle with his thoughts. When he awoke from the trance, he described a bombardment of memories from around age five, stating that his mother had given him up for adoption at that time. "I don't know how it all fits together," he said, "but a voice, a thought really, kept saying, 'that is where the problem lies.' "*

We as counselors can develop a sensitivity to God's voice. Though the Lord speaks to all humanity, only some hear. In the Old Testament, he chose who he would visit with his Holy Spirit, but since Pentecost, he has poured out the Spirit on the world, giving every person the potential to hear him. Abraham heard him in the words of his thoughts (Genesis 12:1-3), while Jacob perceived him in the visual images of imagination and the kinesthetic images of action (Genesis 32:24-30). God can have a dialogue with our unconscious minds, so that we experience meaning as intuition or, more complexly, as a vision. The Lord had a dialogue with Moses, first through a theopany, the burning bush (Exodus 3), but then in verbal thought (Exodus 7). Moses frequently *cried to the Lord,* who always answered with direction or action to fit the need. Samuel frequently talked with God in the thoughts of his mind (I Samuel 3), but worldly Saul was deaf to God, insisting upon doing things his own way (I Samuel 14:37); this led to his rejection. David could hear God's voice within his own thoughts (I Samuel 23:2), but he ceased to listen when he became embroiled with Bathsheba. God then spoke to him through Nathan and the story of the ewe lamb (II Samuel 12). When Solomon was crowned king, he talked with God in a dream and subsequently chose wisdom over riches, certainly the result of fruitful dialogue with God, as a gift from God (I Kings 3). So inspired, Solomon directed the two women claiming a child to divide the child in half, thus coming to discern the rightful mother by scrutinizing the reactions of the two. Many others in the Old and New Testaments talked thus with God. The relevant point for today's counselor is that many perceived the events, personalities, and situations around them, then had a dialogue with the Lord, probably more unconsciously than consciously, from which they gained an essential meaning not otherwise attainable. This wisdom is available to us today; Christ, who is Lord, through his life, death, and resurrection, has secured for us an access to the Holy Spirit, the mind of God, available to only a few before.

Attaining this kind of wisdom, the ability to hear God during a counseling session, requires the spiritual preparation and discipline expected of any earnest Christian. The counselor should work toward knowing the Scriptures in a way that grasps essential meanings and the personalities therein. That means working to face failings, acting to get one's personal life in order. Personal sins of pride, dishonesty, fornication, addiction, avarice, envy, *etc.*, will deafen one to God's voice; individual morality, or at least an actively working toward it, is essential to acquiring the ability. Similarly, working toward faith and commitment and the honest admission of the lack of same are necessary. Perhaps the essence is to have a willingness to learn; an open-endedness, a humility toward one's knowledge, maturity, and competence, combined with an active asking, seeking, and knocking.

In practice, I generally experience the presence of God in the counseling session in the following sequence; you may find yourself developing a different style. Early in the interview, I call on God to help me in the assessment, later to plan or carry out maneuvers for change.

- I may start the session by silently calling on God, remembering to pray simultaneously to any interaction with my patient. Or, I may suddenly recall his presence. I feel a little like Winston Churchill, who loved cigars. Friends would notice that, at times, he would be without a cigar, then suddenly remember their availability. His face would light with pleasure as he reached for one. In like manner, I experience the Holy Spirit reminding me to call on God.

- I have learned to recognize early the appearances of impasses during counseling sessions, those frequent times when I do not know what is going on or I recognize that my patient is stuck. Praying without ceasing is especially important at such times.

- I hold a posture of open-endedness, an expectant attitude, a waiting for what is next, both in my thoughts and in the body language, voice inflections, and metaphoric verbalizations of my patient.

- My prayers are open-ended and perhaps not even verbally expressed. "What's going on here, Lord?" or "Can you help this person out, Lord?" or a simple, silent request for direction.

- In meeting the psychological, social, or spiritual needs of
  the patient, the Lord can be called on in various ways.
  Subsequent chapters cover some of the many possibilities.

What can the counselor expect to happen when using the presence of God?
Should there be signs and wonders, miracles, ecstatic utterances? More
likely, the still, small voice Elijah heard in the fire (I Kings 19:12). In my
experience, the miraculous is usually quite subtle, as follows:

- I experience an immediate sense of confidence and comfort; I can relax and need not try so hard. I am not alone.

- Enter the spontaneous. Soon both my speech and that of
  my patient become less stilted, more authentic, with more
  feeling. Our thoughts become more free, more spontaneous. I pay particular attention at this time to the spontaneous thoughts entering my mind. Specifically, I attend
  to the sudden flashes of thought, image, or memory, no
  matter how ridiculous, obscene, or irrelevant these may
  seem at first.

- I also give close attention to my patient's spontaneous utterances. They often contain important clues to the crux of
  a problem. These spontaneous utterances may be
  metaphoric or pertain to family relationships; whatever
  their expression, the counselor can recognize them as
  metaphors for the patient's life. It is the interaction of the
  Holy Spirit and the unconscious mind that prompts a person to express these casual comments and the counselor to
  hear them. A metaphor for life is a metaphoric statement
  of a life script, a blueprint for one's life based on some
  earlier, perhaps very early, decisions about life and the
  self.

- I usually then begin to see movement, gradual perhaps, and
  an enlivening of the session. I get more insight, as does
  the patient, a kind of deepening awareness or understanding of the problem. One or both of us begin to ex-

perience aha's. This creates further energy and, hence, movement.

- Sudden spontaneous actions might occur. For example, a seminarian, at the end of a stilted and lifeless conversation with a stroke victim, noted that the man's face was bathed in perspiration. The student asked if he could mop the man's brow. He then did so. Such an action sounds inspired, and might be very beneficial to the patient.

Praying during a counseling session often affects the interaction in two discernible ways. It can propel the dialogue toward the illumination of fixations or destructive life scripts. It can also bring to the awareness of the counselor the body language and voice inflections of the counselee. Because prayer often seems to precipitate such focuses, let us consider scripts and body language. Transactional analysis is a school of psychotherapy that explicitly addresses scripts. Allen and Allen (1972) write:

> Scripts, as Berne pointed out, are designed to last a lifetime. They are based on continually reinforced parental programming and on firm childhood decisions . . . From infant and child observation in nursery and child psychiatry settings, the authors have been struck by two factors which have not been sufficiently stressed in the literature of transactional analysis. First, a child does not necessarily pick up the permissions and injunctions of parenting figures. Some children actively seek alternative programming from nursery school attendants, the parents of other children, or even a fantasied parent. Secondly, as Piaget has made clear, the cognitive style of a child is distinctly different from that of "a miniature grown up." One three-year-old girl, for example, became progressively more agitated by the comfort adults tried to give her as she went about pointing to the cast on her arm and wailing, "It broke." For her, the word "broke" was very concrete; she expected her arm to fall off.

> On such bases as these, each of us decides how life is to be and then selectively interacts with and screens the world to support

and reaffirm this decision. To change one's script, a person needs to re-decide earlier decisions. Permission is important in this process.

Clinical experience has led the authors to hypothesize that the permissions each child and each parent needs can be gathered together into a hierarchical series. Each level is necessary and important in its own right, but it is also dependent upon the solidity of the preceding levels:

1. Permission to exist.

2. Permission to experience one's own sensations, to think one's own thoughts, and feel one's own feelings, as opposed to what others may believe one should think or feel.

3. Permission to be one's self as an individual of appropriate age and sex, with potential for growth and development.

4. Permission to be emotionally close to others.

5. Permission to be aware of one's own basic existential position.

6. Permission to change this existential position.

7. Permission to succeed in sex and in work; that is, to be able to validate one's own sexuality and the sexuality of others, and to "make it" in work.

8. Permission to find life meaningful.

In child rearing, parents and other caretakers nurture or poison inner decisions by the degree to which they approve or disapprove of their offspring's emerging individuality. Furthermore, these permissions are hierarchical, each level depending on the adequacy of the previous level. These permissions form the basis for the self's capacities for self-activation, self-assertion, and self-regard, which in turn affect the ability to love and to work and to give or deny self-permission. A person seeking counseling will often have deficits in these capacities and abilities. The counselor's inner prayers often seem to create a direction in the interview that leads to scrutiny of these basic permissions.

A 40-year-old woman presented such emotional intensity that I instantly began to pray. She was unhappy in her marriage and attracted to another man. She quickly jumped to a discussion of her mother, whom she described as alcoholic and inadequate. A variety of lacks of permission became quickly apparent. She had been given the name of a sister who had died shortly after birth. This impaired her ability to give herself permission to exist! When very young, she had been caught looking at the genitals of another child and had been severely punished. Now sex both over-stimulated and repelled her. Lastly, her mother had determined what man she would marry. Small wonder that she had difficulty committing herself to her husband.

The choice between life and death (Deuteronomy 30:17-20) is an even more fundamental script than those alluded to above. People are faced with this choice constantly, though many act as though the final decision had been made years ago. The Bible, again and again, documents our choice of death over life and God's action to reverse the trend. Freud was aware of the conflict; he postulated two instincts, Eros, the life instinct, and Thanatos, the death instinct, competing within each person. Many people blind themselves to the inner struggle between good and evil and rationalize away their intentional, subintentional, or inadvertent choices of death over life. The choice is clearest in suicide and homicide but is more subtly acted out every time a person smokes a cigarette, gossips, lies, or wishes or seeks revenge, to name just a few. Prayer sensitizes the counselor to these issues in a counseling session.

The counselor's silent, open-ended, receptive prayers hasten the grasp of another source of information about the counselee's heart. With such prayer, the counselor becomes more intensely aware of the body language and voice inflection of the counselee and hence more in touch with the nuances of the person. Body language and voice inflection betray the heart, regardless of how studiously one tries to conceal it. For example, Jesus, having become flesh and limiting himself to the perceptions and cognitions of any human, still knew the hearts of those around him. "But Jesus, knowing in himself that his disciples murmured at it, said to them, 'Do you take offense at this?' For Jesus knew from the first who those were that did not believe, and who it was that should betray him" (John 6:61, 64). How did he know? Did he read minds? Since he was limited, as any mortal man, he must have read the body language and voice inflections of those around him and, aided by his continuous dialogue with the Father, come to some accurate conclusions. Hence, the same source of insight is available to us today.

Body language and voice inflection are metacommunications. They add depth and color to people and conversations. The messages of these metacommunications can be divided in two categories: those that comment on the being, the intrinsic, existential position of the person and, interrelated with the first, those that comment on the ongoing relationship engaged in at that instant. The first category reflects the person's innermost thoughts and feelings at that point in time. As examples, body language and voice inflection:

- May communicate the mood of a person. For example, one evening I greeted a man I had never met before. Although the office was dimly lit, I sensed the man's intense inner rage. I soon learned that he was battering his wife and had himself been battered as a child, an experience he had not dealt with at all.

- Invariably transmit the character of the person. Our language is rich in adjectives, such as *aggressive, competitive, fawning, obsequious, haughty,* and *respectful,* which more than anything else denote the body language and voice inflections of a person.

- Faithfully communicate the self-image of the person: how he sees and would like to see himself, and how he would like others to see him. Clothing and grooming are examples.

The second category of body language and voice inflection is related to the first and is that of their role in commenting on the process of a person relating to another person at a point in time. All counselors should recognize how important they are to their counselees. The counselor can note, through body language and voice inflection, how the counselee is responding in the relationship. In the following examples, body language and voice inflection can:

- Point to the degree of intimacy or distance in the relationship. Intimacy carries with it warmth and postures and facial expressions depicting openness. People relating at a distance have a coolness and closed expression about them. Because the counseling relationship is so crucial, the counselor can monitor rapport and the acceptance or rejection of counseling through a sensitivity to the counselee's body language and voice inflections.

- Show differences in the relative power of the participants in a given interchange. In counseling a family, the counselor might note that a parent has all the power, the children none. Such an imbalance can harm the children.

- Convey the amount of rapport in a relationship. A high degree of matching of body language and voice inflection of participants indicates high rapport among them. The levels of animation and responsiveness of the participants to one another likewise depict rapport. The counselor can actually use this principle in reverse, deliberately approximating the counselee's body language and style and speech to hasten and deepen rapport.

- Mirror the agreement or disagreement between two people. The counselor can constantly monitor the effects of questions, interpretations, or interventions, by noting facial relaxation versus tightness, head nodding versus head shaking, and the like.

- Indicate how responsive a counselee is to stories or anecdotes that the counselor might tell during assessment and therapy. The counselee's response to stories can be used to gauge how close to the mark the counselor has been. This is a helpful tool in reaching the heart of another.

In summary, the counselor can use prayer to come to know the heart of a counselee. This is one of the six avenues to the heart of another presented in this book:

- Interviewing (Chapter 3)

- Empathy (Chapter 4)

- Praying without ceasing (this chapter)

- Understanding metaphor (Chapter 6)

- Assessing the self, spiritual development, and family system (Chapters 7, 8, and 10)

- Interpreting dreams (Chapter 9).

Prayer is foremost among the six: prayer enlivens the counselor's grasp of the other's metaphors, dreams, and body language and provides the guidance to know what to ask and say and the inspiration to put it all together. Prayer propels both counselor and counselee toward healing, learning, and creative change. I place prayer third in order only because I wanted the reader to have some feeling for the bewildering complexities of the interview. It is prayer that forms the foundation and internal structure for any effective Christian counseling.

This chapter concludes with a brief vignette illustrating the unique ability of prayer to get to the root of a problem quickly:

A 34-year-old woman brought her 11-year-old daughter for the first visit on an emergency basis. The child had just returned to school after summer vacation. On the first day, she had become frightened after seeing a movie in which the ghosts of two pilots who had died in a plane crash visited the passengers of other planes. She subsequently hysterically refused to attend school, becoming physically ill if made to do so. The urgency of the situation and the panic of both parties strongly reminded me to begin to pray without ceasing. The mother had left her husband, the child's stepfather, the previous June. There was abundant interesting detail with which to speculate about the situation, but two observations of body language really helped the most. First, the mother appeared harassed, tired, and a bit unkempt; but I reacted to her by becoming sexually aroused. That surprised me and I prayed, "What's going on here?" The prayer and the subsequent answer spanned only an instant. The thought flashed into my mind that she was having an affair or was at least sexually active. Next, I wondered in prayer if her daughter had seen her with a lover. (There are, of course, many reasons why a counselor might become aroused during a session, reasons perhaps personal, perhaps interpersonal. To get the correct message, the counselor needs to focus on self, and to gain experience, as well, as to pray.) With the daughter out of the room, the mother revealed that she was confused, defiant, and involved sexually away from home. When I asked if she had considered receiving comfort and guidance from God, she defiantly replied, "I don't want anybody telling me what to do." I next saw the daughter alone. The child's demeanor gave an impression of considerable strength. Prayer helped me integrate the observations of a chaotic, rebellious mother and a fundamentally strong child. I asked the girl, "Are you worried about your mother and afraid to leave her alone?" Her emphatic "Yes" told me that this was the crux of the situation.

Exercises

1. Learn to learn to practice the presence of God. To do this, every morning set aside time for worship, reading the scriptures, relaxing deeply, and praying without words, rather picturing or imagining various metaphors of Christ's being. For example, Jesus says, "I am the way and I am the door." Let a way or door come to mind, then focus on that image, having first asked God to supply a picture. Imagine some of the episodes of Christ's life, putting yourself in the picture. If it is hard to do this without words, relate the event, including your participation in it,

in the first person present tense. Such an *eyewitness account* brings the narrative into focus as an event that you experience. If you are a student, perhaps an instructor can lead you in some of these prayers.

2. Practice the presence of God at a point in the day; then, for the remainder of the day, focus on the body language of those around you, asking for the wisdom to see and understand. Utilize the categories explained earlier in the chapter. At another time, concentrate on voice inflection with the same intent. It helps to close your eyes when studying voice inflection.

3. Practice *praying without ceasing* while counseling and interviewing during simulated cases.

4. Divide into groups of three. Using a vignette generated from exercise 3, Chapter 3, let one student role play the counselee, a second the counselor. The third person can *play* God. The counselor should freely consult *God* for help throughout the interview.

5. In your own meditations, be alert for times when you particularly sense God's presence and voice. At such a time, deliberately make a circle with thumb and forefinger. In a simulated or actual counseling session, make a circle again. There is nothing magic about this. Rather, the circle becomes a cue for a desired and previously experienced mental state.

6. Divide into groups of four. Let one person tell two autobiographical anecdotes or accounts, one true, the other false. The other three members are to guess which story is true, based on their observations of body language and voice inflection.

7. Spend a week observing the body language and voice inflections of friends, classmates, and instructors. Retain your conclusions and utilize them when you work exercise 1, Chapter 6.

Suggested Reading

Reik, Theodore, *Listening with the Third Ear*, Farrar, Straus, New York, 1949.

6

Metaphor in the Interview

A metaphor is a figure of speech in which a term or phrase is applied to something to which it is not literally applicable, in order to suggest a resemblance, as "a mighty fortress is our God." In this book, metaphor is the use of the double or multiple meanings of words or anecdotes to denote or comment on a person's relationship to God (life, meaning), neighbor (important others, past or present, and the counselor), and self. In other words, each one of us communicates on two tracks: one comments on external reality; the second comments on one's internal reality (the reality of the heart), where one postulates what seems to be true at a given moment. The fascinating thing about speech is that it abounds in multiple meanings that describe events or memories of one's external life that in turn imply one's existential reality. Used in this way, metaphor can be a single word to describe someone's character (rat, for example), a complex story to describe a pattern of behavior, a highly symbolic dream to dramatize a concern or conflict, or a parable to convey a universal truth. To perceive this rich, psychological level of speech, the counselor must be trained to listen both literally and figuratively, deliberately making concrete every word, weighing possible double meanings, in the hope of grasping some essential aspect of a counselee's heart.

> *A 26-year-old man recovering from a schizophrenic break was coerced into coming to see me by his brother, who was concerned about him. No longer psychotic, he was living at home and doing little. Although reluctant to come, he did talk with me, describing playing basketball. He talked about feeling stiff and cold as he tried to make baskets, and mentioned that the ball did not have a lot of life in it. I concluded that the man felt dead. I communicated back using metaphoric speech, as*

he had. Using the scheme of "permissions" described in Chapter 5, this man fit in the category of needing permission to exist, to be alive. So, I described a friend of mine's venture into the funeral parlor business and the care he took in embalming and dressing the corpses. Later, I closed the hour with a narrative of Ezekial's vision of the valley of dry bones and how the Lord brought them to life (Ezekiel 37:1-14). He seemed quite interested and thanked me for a profitable visit.

Metaphor and God's Relationship to Humanity

The Bible abounds in historical and biographical sketches, stories, interactions, parables, visions, and dreams. Christians of all persuasions have long sensed that the narratives carry multiple meanings, describing on the one hand historical events of God's dealings with specific people and peoples, and on the other implying much for today's reader. Thus, I have identified deeply with the story of the Exodus, grateful that I am being led out of my own personal slavery. And when Nathan (II Samuel 12:1-7) comes to King David with the story of the ewe lamb, ending with the punch line, "you are the man," I am led to face and admit my own sins. And when the man runs up to Jesus and confesses, "I believe; help my unbelief!" (Mark 9:24), I find a solution for my present doubts. The metaphors of the Bible speak to each of us.

Furthermore, much of the Bible deliberately communicates on multiple levels. Marsh (1968), in an elegant commentary on John's gospel, points out that much of the book is deliberately ambiguous. For example, Jesus' healing of the man born blind (John 9) is on one level an account of the healing of a blind man. But on another level, the level of the heart, it is a cosmic parable of the congenital blindness of mankind, who, through Christ's healing actions, can come to see, particularly to see him and so ultimately to come to worship him. Thus, this use of ambiguity with the potential for multiple meanings, promotes a mental search to those open to learning. In reading the Bible, the believer reads the historical accounts with the mind, while perceiving the truths God intends, God's love for the believer.

Furthermore, the stories of the Bible lend themselves to various uses in counseling, where they can be used as vehicles to make important points. The following personal example illustrates one of the limitless uses to which the metaphor can be put.

> *I consulted Milton Erickson, M.D., for personal difficulties. After listening for perhaps ten minutes to my story, he paused, stared at me intently (thus securing my attention and anticipation), and began to tell me the story of Belshazzer's feast (Daniel 5). At the feast, Belshazzer and his party arrogantly drink from the cups taken from the temple in Jerusalem, toasting their gods with them. Immediately, the fingers of a man's hand appear and begin to write on the plaster wall. As the king sees this, he changes color, and his knees begin to knock together. At this point, Erickson looked at me and asked, "Do you know what the finger wrote?" As I paled, he said, "You have been weighed in the balances and found wanting." Terrified, my mind was a blank, but later I realized he had struck at my firm belief that in my faith and psychiatric and medical training I had all the answers. He went on to tell me dozens of anecdotes at a pace and in a manner that had me frantically searching for meaning. Later, I deduced that the stories all pertained to people who never changed, who were content with their realities and hence not open to learning. He closed the hour saying, "Take everything you think you know, and throw it away." "How could that be?" I replied incredulously. He smiled and said, "The good will stick." That encounter was crucial for me, because it destroyed my self-satisfaction and opened me to a lifetime of learning. I am now convinced that humility is not thinking little of oneself, but rather thinking a great deal of God, viewing one's strengths and weaknesses realistically, and always being willing to learn.*

This chapter focuses on how counselees may communicate crucial aspects of their being via metaphor within the interview. Subsequent chapters deal more fully with metaphor as a means of helping people change. Specifically, this chapter considers how the counselee's metaphors may describe the self, be vignettes of current life, or comment on the counselee's relationship with the counselor and how the counselor can use metaphors in the assessment phase of the interview.

Metaphors and the Self

The anecdotes a counselee relates may seem to be random and insignificant and yet carry important aspects of the counselee's being, relationships, and lifestyle. At the simplest level, this should be obvious, since everything we say must in some way comment on our being. For example, Samuel (I Samuel 9:21), in preparing to anoint Saul king, speaks highly of Saul. Saul replies,

> "Am I not a Benjaminite, from the least of the tribes of Israel?
> And is not my family the humblest of all the families of the
> tribe of Benjamin? Why then have you spoken to me in this
> way?"

On the surface, Saul appears diffident and humble; yet the statement actually is a comment on Saul's image of himself, a statement of his lack of self-esteem. Such an interpretation is born out of Saul's action when chosen king (I Samuel 10:22)—he hides in the baggage—and by Samuel's comment (I Samuel 15:17), "Though you are little in your own eyes, are you not the head of the tribes of Israel?" Saul's subsequent decline and madness dramatize just how poor his self-image was. This points out that another's metaphors, stories, and symbols must be considered in the overall context of that person's life. To jump to a conclusion about a person from one or two samples of speech without careful attention to the gestalt of the person's life is to invite disaster. The counselor must first inwardly collect a variety of data about a person from the interview, empathy, prayer, body language, metaphor, direct questions, and dreams, then *cluster backwards* to reach a valid conclusion about another's heart.

A counselee may describe any number of anecdotes about the past; some may be recent, others remote, even to the childhood limit of memory. All, but particularly those mentioned spontaneously, should be carefully noted. For that reason, I often take notes during an interview, recording such recollections as they occur. This helps me in the subsequent task of clustering backwards.

> *A 36-year-old recovered alcoholic complained of panic attacks while driving and of fears of crowds, heights, and flying. His earliest memory was of being terrified of going to kindergarten at age 5. Such an early memory points to a lifestyle characterized by separation anxiety, a frequent finding in those suffering from panic disorder and related phobias.*

Late in the first or second session, I may ask several direct questions about early memories, moving from early to late; the answers often yield valuable clues to self-images arising from family interactions. Likewise, anecdotal memories of parents can be sought out directly or indirectly. While listening to a counselee's verbal autobiography, one question to consider is why those particular experiences, out of a myriad of life events, were the ones the counselee chose to relate. My experience supports the idea that early memories indicate a person's lifestyle.

> *I counseled a man in his late twenties, suffering difficulty in getting along with women. I asked him to let his imagination take him back to a time when he was with his mother. His face registered shock as he pictured himself at age 15, helping his mother wash dishes, telling her that his friends did not like her. She cried. The revengeful image pointed to a need for forgiveness and reconciliation.*

Favorite stories and jokes often contain vivid metaphoric descriptions of aspects of the self; the counselor may inquire about stories and jokes at any point in assessment or therapy.

> *A deeply isolated, unmarried, friendless man in his 40s described a science fiction story that stood out in his mind. An astronaut is marooned on an alien planet that has an atmosphere of gaseous ammonia. The inhabitants of the planet are long extinct; the man lives in one of their homes. One day he finds himself taking an ammonia shower, only then realizing he has mutated to the alien environment. The man's preoc-*

> *cupation with this graphic picture of isolation and alienation,*
> *coupled with the intimation of irreversibility, was startling.*

Favorite jokes may likewise metaphorize key aspects of how one sees oneself.

> *A man tending toward masochism, with a desire to please, an*
> *inability to say "no," and an inability to assert himself or*
> *speak up for his needs, thought the following joke particularly*
> *funny. "A man walking along a country road came to an out-*
> *house. As he stood to urinate, he looked down the hole and*
> *saw a man with only his head above the feces. Horrified, he*
> *ran out, exclaiming to a passerby, 'There's a man in there!'*
> *To which the passerby replied, 'Oh, that's only old Pete,*
> *everybody shits on him.' "*

Metaphoric statements may reflect the *mood* of a person. A counselor may gauge a counselee's progress by noting comments as both walk from waiting room to office. Simple statements, such as "Isn't it a nice day!" or "At last they are making progress freeing the hostages!" point to an improved or more optimistic mood. Of course, facial expression and body posture can convey the same information. In the same vein, metaphoric comments at the end of a session convey a heartfelt expression of the counselee's view of the hour.

Metaphors in the Counseling Relationship

Because a person seeking counseling is often desperately hoping for help in resolving difficulty, the relationship with the counselor is particularly important. The counselee can be expected to be unconsciously monitoring the counselor's words and actions to evaluate relevancy, helpfulness, and style. The counselee will be especially sensitive to breaks in empathy, being talked down to, or being related to from a superior position. During a session, the counselee may respond metaphorically to any of these events. Indeed, metaphors are a sensitive indicator of the effectiveness of the interview.

> *I suggested to a phobic man that we contract for eight ses-*
> *sions, aiming to complete our work in that time. He seemed to*

agree to work in that time, but he began the second session by observing that he had been nervous for the past two days, "probably because I've been working with a guy who is a little pushy." His anecdote indicated that I had been overdirective and furthermore suggested that I perhaps should restrain him to some extent as we worked to help him conquer his fears.

The counselee may also respond metaphorically to interpretations made by the counselor. The tenor of this metaphor tells the counselor how acceptable or accurate the interpretation was. Such metaphoric replies to statements, advice, or interpretations are, in fact, common in all types of human interchange.

In a lecture on suicide to a group of seminarians, I described Everstine's (1983) interpretation of suicide as an act of aggression toward another person, in effect a grim retaliation for a frustrating lack of closeness in life by joining with the survivor forever in death. A student immediately replied with a description of a television drama of a teenage suicide, the play climaxing with just such a statement by one of the characters. I took this to be an affirmative metaphor on the part of the student.

On another occasion, I interviewed a severely disturbed girl before a group of physicians, hoping to demonstrate something of Kernberg's (1984) structural interview. In other words, I had my own agenda. The girl really started to open up, but, sticking to my purpose, I interrupted her train of thought to ask if she was feeling persecuted, an irrelevant question. She fell silent, her head bowed, for perhaps two minutes. Then she began to inveigh against her unit physician, who was in the audience, and the hospital, comparing it unfavorably with a hospital she had been in previously. Only later did I realize that her criticism of her doctor and the hospital was really a metaphor for her sense of mistreatment at my hands during our interview. I happened to see her the next morning and apologized, describing my break in empathy and her now un-

derstandable response.   Her body language indicated a favorable response.

Sequential Metaphors

In everyday life, people frequently relate one or several anecdotes or recollections, often prompting the listener to reply with anecdotes, recollections, or opinions of their own.   Indeed, trading stories is a typical mode of communication.   We become so accustomed to this that we routinely fail to pay close attention; instead we are content to relay the stories that have occurred to us when the other stops talking.   Or, we may become quite bored, giving the polite appearance of listening while actually thinking of something else.   In this commonplace interaction, stories and anecdotes of our experiences often convey our masks, the externals of our lives, how we would like others to see us, in addition to our desire to entertain.

A counseling session does, of course, differ from the commonplace. The counselee may partially mask personal feelings, knowing, however, that to get past a difficulty, some revelation must be made. Therefore, the metaphors shared may be quite germane, although their meanings may not be apparent.   The counselor should listen carefully to every seemingly casual statement and weigh a counselee's metaphors separately and collectively in the search for ultimate meanings.   To this end, the counselor should inwardly mark and file each anecdote, in a sense memorizing their occurrence and sequence, all the while clustering backward unconsciously, until meaning precipitates.   The following case exemplifies a sequence of anecdotes, successfully interpreted, that led to marked change within the counselee.

> *George was an engineer who was inept at his work and had survived for a considerable period by successfully manipulating his way through various civil service branches. But his ineptitude eventually became obvious, and he became depressed, and then was fired. He subsequently suffered a psychosis and required hospitalization. After six therapy sessions with little accomplished, I had the feeling we were getting nowhere. But in the seventh session, in a seemingly desultory fashion, he*

talked about a friend named Gene, one of his bosses, with whom he used to surf. They had started out friendly and ended up not so friendly. George said, "I took advantage of him, I goofed off at work." He then went on to talk about a dream of a psychiatrist with a florid face, a big nose, and a receding hairline. He followed this vignette with a comment about an incident at work when another technician had been unable to set up a certain kind of equipment, but George had been able to. "After that, I was a fixture on expeditions involving equipment of that sort." After a pause, I ventured the interpretation that these anecdotes and dreams had to do with me. I told him that apparently, in our relationship, he saw himself as able to take advantage of me, as able to goof off, as able to accomplish work that I could not. He had little to say, except to deny my interpretation. When he came, quite late, to the next session, he said he had experienced a vivid dream the night before:

"I dreamed I either got captured or found out. I was some sort of spy. This group of armed men caught me and threatened to torture or kill me if I didn't talk. I broke down and told them I would talk, that they had successfully coerced me. I was pretty cowed at that time. Then I made an escape. I ran a little way before they knew I was gone, and then they started to shoot at me. First pretty spotty and inaccurate, but then they started to get the range. I dove desperately to the ground, managing to come up behind some rocks. Bullets were splattering all around me as I crouched behind the rocks.

I interpreted the dream directly, stating that the dream again pertained to me. I told George he was feeling cornered by me, that I was the "armed" man. I interpreted his passive resistance and lateness as constituting his escape. The shooting symbolized the interpretations I was offering him. I remarked that he saw them as gunfire, and the fact that they were getting close was provoking anxiety. As I told George these things, he vehemently denied that I was right, but beads of perspiration *stood on his forehead and his hands visibly shook. At this point, I reassured him that I was on his side, that I wanted to see him live. This series of interpretations marked the turning point in George's therapy, and he went on to recover completely. He obtained training in another field and today is quite successful.*

The Counselor's Use of Metaphor in Assessment

The *listening process* involves comprehending a counselee's metaphors either as presented or as synthesized by the counselor (Langs, 1985). However, the counselor can go beyond just listening for metaphors and speak to the counselee in like manner, thus bypassing the conscious mind by communicating *heart to heart*. To this end, the counselor can enrich the communications with metaphor, thus indirectly inviting the counselee to detail more fully any concerns or attitudes. For example, I might *empathize* indirectly or metaphorically with a counselee who was brought in to see me under duress by describing how Agag (I Samuel 15:32) must have felt just before Samuel hewed him to pieces. The laughter elicited by such an image would break the ice. Alternatively, a metaphoric *interpretation* might be offered. In the following sequence, Harold, a 40-year-old single man, complained of a chronic depression of long duration, for which he had sought a variety of therapies.

H.: Hypnosis was so dramatic. For a year I felt fantastic. Then, a shattering incident. Nothing big, really, some daily trivia, just thrown back.

A.: You realized you hadn't changed. *(An empathic interpretation.)*

H.: I felt like the emperor with his new clothes. *(A metaphoric affirmative to my interpretation.)*

A.: So you gave up having real clothes. *(Sticking with his metaphor for the elusiveness of change.)*

H.: I can't orchestrate my life. I get one thing going, another falls apart. Such a long process. I keep winding up at square one.

A.: Sounds like Sisyphus. *(I explain the myth.)*

H.: Yes! An excellent analogy.

A.: Like Sisyphus, it is ordained that you suffer. *(Harold nods his head affirmatively.)* You feel your fate is sealed. Why?

H.: My mother came to such a bad end. She died a chronic alcoholic. I'm a chip off the old block. *(The heart of the matter, his fixation on his mother and his alcoholic family system.)*

In the assessment phase of counseling, metaphors are extremely useful in asking questions indirectly. Questions asked metaphorically elicit a more spontaneous, authentic answer. Thus, to learn something about a counselee's mother, I might talk about my mother; if I were curious about dreams, I might tell one of my own or someone else's. Such a maneuver takes advantage of the universal tendency to recall one's own experiences when listening to another recount theirs.

A wayward, delinquent girl of 15 was struggling to conform to rules, but a recent misdemeanor made a term in juvenile hall appear possible. This constituted a grave crisis to the girl and her mother. As we talked, I noted the cross around the girl's neck. Rather than ask her directly about her relationship with God or jump to the suggestion she pray about her crisis, I told her a story of a boy sailing around the world alone, how he encountered a fierce storm, and how he prayed. She replied forcefully, "I don't ask anybody for anything."

Zeig (1980), describing Milton Erickson's use of anecdotes in psychotherapy, defined anecdotes as short narratives concerning an interesting or amusing incident. These could be fairy tales, fables, parables, or allegories that chronicled true life adventures and experiences. He noted that most of the anecdotes told by Erickson were factual descriptions of events from his own life and from the lives of his family and patients. He used anecdotes in assessing, establishing rapport, empathizing, and treating. In treatment, anecdotes might be used to make or illustrate a point, suggest solutions, get people to recognize themselves, seed ideas and increase motivation, control the relationship therapeutically, embed directives, decrease resistance, or reframe and redefine a problem. Subsequent chapters deal with metaphor in the treatment phases of counseling.

The Christian reader will quickly recognize just how often metaphors are used in communicating and learning the gospel. It is no accident that metaphors abound in the Scriptures, in sermons, and in missionary movements such as Cursillo and Marriage Encounter. Metaphor is the language of experience, the universal language of the heart, the language through which God communicates love, wisdom, and will to us. The Christian counselor should learn to understand and speak this language. The ways in which the counselor can put metaphor to use are summarized below:

- Listen carefully to the anecdotes, stories, memories, and descriptions of activities the counselee recounts. Weigh them as metaphors for the person's life. Consider them as typical or symbolic for the person's life and problems.

- Look at the counselee's actions, symptoms, and dilemmas in the same way.

- Listen carefully for sequences of metaphors. Remember them, pray about them, and add them up.

- Listen to metaphor in its various forms as an indirect comment on the counselee's relationship to you, the counselor.

- When you say something to your counselee, look to body language and metaphor as a comment on the accuracy, acceptance, or effectiveness of your intervention.

- Use metaphor in its many forms to convey empathy, to ask for information indirectly, or to try out an interpretation, again looking to the body language and metaphor of the counselee as an indirect reply to your intervention.

Exercises

1. Spend a week noting the anecdotes and metaphors that friends, classmates, and instructors use. Coordinate this with your conclusions from exercise 7, Chapter 5. You should now be in a position to better understand your contemporaries' needs. Use your evaluations to empathize, compliment, or pray with them.

2. Using a video camera, write and enact a comedy in which the counselor violates as many interviewing methods as possible. Surprise the class with the production.

Suggested Reading

Marsh, John, "Saint John," *Pelican Gospel Commentaries,* Penguin Books, Baltimore, Maryland, 1968.

Langs, Robert, *Workbooks for Psychotherapists: Understanding Unconscious Communication,* New Concept Press, Inc., Emerson, New Jersey, 1985.

7

Assessing the Self

Four aspects of self must be assessed during an interview. First is the mask, that collection of maneuvers, defenses, and styles with which people meet the world. Feelings, the second layer of the self, are the underlying emotional responses to past and present interactions with that world. Third, and at the core of the self, are the fundamental capacities that each person needs to function effectively, both individually and corporately. Masterson (1985) calls this core of essential functions the real self. The Christian self is the fourth aspect of self. This self springs into being with the acceptance of Christ as Lord.

In Christian counseling, the counselor supports and taps into the Christian self to confront masks, heal feelings, and resolve impairments in the real self. Understanding these aspects of self requires examining how the self develops and maintains itself. This chapter deals with the healthy development and maintenance of the self, the emergence of the real self, failures in development and maintenance, feelings stemming from such failures, and the masks that hide these feelings.

Development of the Self

For healthy development, the two basic drives of the self must be fulfilled: the needs for communion and individuation. Communion refers to the inner sense of validation and strengthening that comes from relationships of trust, faith, openness, intimacy, respect, and self-sacrifice. Empathy is necessary to communion.

Freud theorized that children wished to possess sexually the parent of the opposite sex and to dispense with the parent of the same sex. Biddle (1957) argued that Freud had misunderstood the fantasies of adults and children, that

> *children's sexual fantasies were in reality metaphors or wishes for communion, the child communing with both parents by imagining entering into their bodies.*

Communion is best understood as an event. Everyone can recall specific, special moments of closeness, intimacy, and attachment to a parent, spouse, friend, or child. Mary's moment with Jesus (Luke 10:38-42) is an example. Communion is thus a feeding of the soul. Fantasies of communion, which may have a sexual aspect, are metaphors for these moments. These metaphors are cornerstones of the healthy self. It is no accident that the chief sacrament of the Church is one of feeding. Without the experiences and metaphors of communion, people create bizarre fantasies that are the germs of madness. Such nourishment benefits all that is crucial to children, particularly those under three, since it is in early childhood that the foundations of the self are laid.

Individuation springs from communion but requires, in addition, the active support of authority figures. (The permissions listed in Chapter 5 detail this support.) The developing child needs parental identification and encouragement of efforts to initiate action, explore independently, create, think, and make decisions. Children will develop solid, real selves only if adequate provision is made for communion and individuation. Masterson writes:

> This real self emerges and develops under a combination of nature/nurture forces; in a combination of constitutional endowments, genetic biologic pressure, and the mother's and father's capacity to acknowledge, respond and give emotional support to the unique characteristics of the emerging self during those important first three years of life.

> This mirroring or matching process seems vital to the development of the real self. It is important to keep in mind that I do not mean physical caretaking such as feeding, clothing, *etc.*, but rather the capacity of the parents to perceive the unique characteristics of the child's emerging self and to respond to these in a positive, supportive manner, to identify, acknowledge and treat with respect his or her unique temperament, to

encourage the unique style or manner in which the child's individuation is expressed in his exploring, experimenting, self-assertive adventures with reality. Failures in this parental function make an important contribution to the failure of the self's development.

The Real Self

The self is in essence a group of functions. The man who says he identifies with his father is saying that he in some way functions like him. Those core functions that enable a person to deal realistically and effectively with the world constitute the real self. This real self springs from satisfactory communion and individuation. Exercising these capacities in turn reinforces the inner sense of communion and personal freedom. The following chart illustrates these actions and their relationship to communion and individuation.

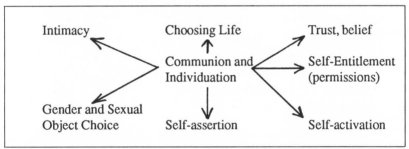

In fixated people, the functions of the real self are impaired. Those who succeed in counseling will be those who become increasingly able to exercise these functions. Let us examine these capacities in detail.

Trust and Belief

Learning to *trust* is the first crucial lesson and is a cornerstone of the real self. Strupp (1972) argues that any successful psychotherapy has been effective primarily because the person has regained a capacity to trust another. In my experience, a person loses basic trust (a belief that life is inherently friendly), through the empathic failures of authority figures possessing power over the person. Having lost basic trust, the person then reactively heightens a need to control, thus creating a desire for self-sufficiency greater than ordinarily seen in the first stage of spiritual development (Chapter 8). The counselor's empathy and willingness to listen without criticism or judgment go far in helping the counselee regain basic trust. Yet, mistrust may often be appropriate: the counselee needs the flexibility to trust or to question, depending on the situation.

Self-Entitlement and Self-Activation

There are appropriate labels for the permissions listed in Chapter 5. Children internalize the permissions of family and culture. They also extend entitlement to themselves as they master the challenges of life. *Self-activation* involves the ability to focus on and commit oneself to an idea, to implement it, and to defend it if criticized. Getting started, decisiveness, and taking responsibility for oneself are corollaries.

> Kaufmann (1973) postulated that humanity suffers from "decidophobia," the fear of making decisions. He listed a variety of dodges used to avoid making decisions, including joining a political party, joining a movement, joining a religious order, and getting married. The decidophobe can then get the party, movement, order, or spouse to make decisions. Kaufmann noted that those German monks who joined the Nazi party scored in all but marriage.

Self-assertion

Self-assertion is the ability, indeed the permission within the self, to say "no" confidently. Both aggressive protest and passive acquiescence belie a fearful uncertainty of self. The ability to assert oneself comes from a sense of security within, a permission growing out of love relationships with others where some degree of choice is allowed. The passive or aggressive person continually reinforces a poor self-image by capitulating or exploding; the resulting decrease in self-esteem further perpetuates the lack of assertion, forming a vicious circle. Furthermore, the person's inability to say "no" erodes the ability to commit to something; instead, the person will constantly assent to tasks but feel ambivalent toward them and hence perform them poorly at best. The ability to truly commit oneself grows out of an ability to say "no." In other words, you can say "yes" to something only when you permit yourself or are permitted to say "no."

> *Martin Luther King, while standing before a judge in Montgomery, Alabama, and arguing for a woman arrested for sitting in a white section of a bus, is said to have noted with chagrin that he was clutching his hat in his hands. As he left the courtroom, he remarked, "I now see that the first thing we need to overcome is the slave within ourselves." I have often told this story to people who are struggling to permit themselves to assert.*

Gender and Sexual Object Choice

The choice of maleness or femaleness and the choice of sexual objects are crucial decisions within the self. These choices are often made very early in life and are difficult to change, but they are not irreversible. Gender confusion shows up in a person's mannerisms, expressions, dress, and voice inflections. The most common departures from the norm are a sexual orientation toward members of the same sex or toward children. Although the origins of gender and sexual object disturbances are hotly debated, it is clear that these choices usually occur in families where dominance, submission, and power are big issues. I see gender confusion and unusual sexual object choice as the defensive postures taken by small children to deal with the anxieties and deprivations inherent in such families. The problem compounds as the child grows: to deal with the earlier difficulty in development, the child must make further compensations. Exaggerated cultural stereotypes and male-perpetrated violence are examples.

Steven, 27, almost hysterically complained of obsessions about homosexuality; he could hardly look at a man without having obsessive thoughts of sex with him. His job as a welder, heavy drinking, deep involvement in sports, and preoccupation with "making it" with women highlighted his pursuit of the "masculine" stereotype. We could trace his hypermasculine efforts to early childhood. His mother had always dominated his father, who in turn had acquiesced. Steven felt contempt for both and, perhaps because of divided loyalties, could identify with neither. Hence, he suffered from gender confusion. Subconsciously, he equated gender confusion with effeminacy, and effeminacy with homosexuality. This could be termed pseudo-homosexuality. Recognizing his characterological problems and his resentment toward his parents allowed Steven to forgive them; a gradual resolution followed.

At the heart of gender confusion and sexual object choice is the issue of domination and submission in the parent's marriage.   The male is dominant in most but not all cultures. But regardless of the cultural norm, too great a disparity or a power struggle between mates begets hostility. This engenders anxiety and defensiveness in the offspring and leads them to embrace stereotypes of masculinity or femininity, to enter into power conflicts of their own, and thus perpetuates conflict.

Christ's followers can interrupt such vicious circles by imitating his humility and his willingness to submit to the will of the Father and to shun domination and force in favor of love and patience. God's power lies in creativity, not in control. Partners, in turning to Christ, can further a communicative style marked by openness, patience, a sharing of feelings, acceptance of the other's feelings, and a willingness to compromise or submit to each other. To be intimate is to share with, be open with, and seek out another. Intimacy requires developing those aspects of the real self discussed above plus setting aside concerns about abandonment, engulfment, and control.

Choosing Life

A crucial cornerstone of the self is the ongoing choice of life or death. St. Paul (Romans 7:21-25) describes the choice as an inevitable conflict within the self. It is seen clinically as micro or macro suicidal or homicidal behavior. On a more subtle scale, each of us is constantly tempted to stop, withdraw, give up, self-destruct, or die. Pathological self-sufficiency can be a factor: "If all else fails, I can always kill myself." Better to say, "If all else fails, I can turn to God."

> *Carol, 45, complained of depression and a history of two suicide gestures. Sexually molested as a child, she grew up to suffer mistreatment from men. Her misery drove her early into a relationship with God. In our initial session, she reported dreaming of a huge cobra that came down from the sky, passed by other houses, and crashed through the roof of her house. The cobra reminded her of death. I speculated that God and her unconscious mind had given her a metaphoric warning about her dangerous personal temptation to choose death.*

Failures in Development

A newborn knows little of these facets of the real self. Each capacity, indeed the real self as a whole, develops over time. Given adequate communion and support for individuation, the child realizes these potentials. Being deprived of these core needs will lead to intense negative feelings. Just as the fetus develops mostly in the first three months of gestation, so the real self develops mostly in the first three years of life. Because small children have little capacity to cope with deprivation or lack of support, their psychological growth can easily be impaired. Faulty parenting is the most common cause of difficulty.

Older children and adults also can make choices that arrest their own development. Those who had good enough parenting can still interfere with the twin drives of communion and individuation. People with well-developed capacities for self-activation, self-assertion, self-esteem, commitment, *etc.*, can succumb to the temptations of self-satisfaction, judgmentalism, materialism, or power. Such actions can damage an already established real self and interfere with the development of the Christian self (as described below). When the satisfaction derived from these pursuits wanes, as it sooner or later will, many may seek a spiritual awakening.

Feelings

Feelings are physical reactions, felt inwardly and visible outwardly, that mirror a person's satisfaction with relationships with God, neighbor, and self. People experience strong negative feelings when the drives for communion and individuation are interrupted. Although unpleasant feelings are most obvious when they arise from traumatic events, they most often stem from the small daily interactions of life. Here they may pass unnoticed. All of us have at one time or another suffered guilt, loss, abandonment, engulfment, shame, or victimization, and many seeking counsel will be at an impasse with one or more of them.

Small children are more vulnerable than adults to all these feelings but especially to those of abandonment, engulfment, shame, and victimization. And the child who experienced these feelings will as an adult be susceptible to their resurgence when similar events occur. Although feelings of shame and loss are common to older people, they also most affect those scarred as children. These feelings can undermine the capacities of the real self and lead to feelings of inferiority. Because people find these feelings and impairments so painful, they often defend against them with fantasy, denial, acting out, and the like. These defensive maneuvers can become part of the character of the self. They are then called false selves, or masks.

Masks

Masks deal with appearances, not a person's true potential. Masks are meant to help gain security, safety, or self-esteem. Masks begin as defense mechanisms designed to protect against the pain of anxiety, inferiority, or shame. We all sometimes resort to these solutions to the negative side of life and ourselves, but some settle on one solution and use it repeatedly. The defensive maneuver then becomes a character style. But there is a price to be paid for the use of these masks. When a person tries to avoid suffering, the implication is that the suffering is unbearable, which it then in fact becomes. Only when the counselee can face the pain does it become finite.

Certain specific defense mechanisms underlie these outward appearances. In other words, at the heart of a character style is a particular defensive maneuver, a specific action repeated over and over. The counselor who grasps these defense mechanisms can point out their cost to the counselee. Consider a few defense mechanisms that form the essences of masks.

Acting Out

People may take action to avoid feeling. In acting out, the external action supplants feeling, so that the person literally does not feel. Contrary to sublimation, where a person consciously chooses to act because, at the time, there's nothing to be done about a feeling, the decision to act out takes place totally out of awareness. Sexual acting out (including infidelity, homosexual activity, perversions, and promiscuity) and antisocial or self-destructive acting out (such as illegal acts, substance abuse, and violence toward others) are examples of actions that serve to conceal unpleasant feelings about the self or others. When a Christian chooses to forego acting out because of moral concerns the person is then thrown into a confrontation with his or her own feelings. The same is true when a person in psychotherapy responds to the therapist's confrontations about the destructiveness of these behaviors.

> *A nominally Christian man absorbed himself in pornography. One day he awakened to his faith and decided to put aside his acting out. He immediately became paralyzed with anxiety and sought psychiatric help. Therapy helped him resolve his basic problem, a feeling of shame pertaining to his obsessively fearful and clinging mother.*

Clinging

Clinging to another is a common way of trying to avoid the unpleasant in life or in oneself. When the people of Jesus' time begged for signs and miracles and wanted him to be their temporal king, they were clinging to him, hoping that he would take care of them. Because Jesus knew that we must learn to take care of ourselves and one another, he gave himself and the Holy Spirit to show us the way; now, he is always ready to assist us if we ask in prayer. But the clinging person wants someone to take over, not just assist. Many seeking counsel appear to want the counselor to take charge and dictate what to do or how to think. But if the counselor takes the bait, the counselee will then resist or fail to carry out the advice. Better for the counselor to recognize clinging and confront it. Techniques for confrontation are discussed in Chapter 13.

Projection

Attributing to another the unwanted or despised aspects of oneself is called projection. Responding to that projection, usually by withdrawal, attack, or overgratification, is called projective identification. Using a child as a scapegoat is a convenient way for a parent to avoid dealing with a feeling or an area difficult to control. For example, a woman in her 40s tearfully told me of her father's harsh, accusatory, and moralistically religious treatment of her emerging adolescent interest in boys. She learned after his death that in his youth he had fathered a child out of wedlock! Projection can be a pernicious element in child rearing and is a common cause of neuroticism in the future adult.

Pride

We have struggled with pride since the beginning of time, needing to replace illusions of self-sufficiency and hubris with a sense of humility and realistic interdependence. But some, particularly those who suffered damage to their self-image through faulty parenting, elevate selfishness to an art, utilizing inflation to defend against feelings of humiliation, shame, abandonment, and depression. In other words, arrogance is a front. In this narcissistic defense, one sees an excessive interest in appearance, physical attributes, power, wealth, clothing, and manners; perhaps a tendency to show off, a sense of superiority, and envy. Devaluing the work of others is common, as are greed and exploitation. In interpersonal relationships, the prideful person may try to intimidate others. In its mildest form, a narcissistic defense against a poor self-image might be simply a trend toward excessive sensitivity, reading into other's gestures unintended affronts.

Denial

The preference for a limited world view, one that excludes uncomfortable perceptions, is called denial. The Jews in Isaiah's time (Isaiah 6:10) denied that their lifestyle and subsequent departure from God made them vulnerable. Jesus encountered the same denial in the people of his time (Matthew 13). The maneuver is particularly common in alcoholics. Furthermore, whole families may conspire to deny the presence or implications of alcoholism, child abuse, or incest. When denial becomes an aspect of character, it is likely to lead to severe consequences. Denial is ubiquitous and ultimately spiritual in nature: "As he passed by, he saw a man blind from his birth" (John 9:1).

This list is not comprehensive; each item boils down to a sense of control, the belief that to survive one must always be in control of oneself and the reactions of others. Unfortunately, such control defeats creativity, smothers spontaneity, harms intimacy and commitment, and may destroy the person or others. Masks are common. But those who face their masks and put aside their immature defenses will reap enormous benefits. With the birth of the Christian self, such resolution becomes both possible and necessary.

The Christian Self

Baptism, the child's introduction to the Christian community, plants the seed of the Christian self. It springs to life with the personal confession of Christ as one's God. It is nourished through worship, fellowship, prayer, and study. The Christian self differs from the real self. The real self is the equipment acquired from one's biological makeup and the support of emerging individuality by parents. Ultimately, the real self comes to be an instrument of the Christian self. For example, Saul of Tarsus had a powerful real self; he had tremendous capacity to commit, assert, and activate himself. His conversion and subsequent belief both channeled and further nourished his real self.

The real self involves self-activation, most commonly activation for self-interest. Those unable to mobilize themselves for their own welfare have a big problem. How much more difficult to activate oneself purely for someone else's interest. Our Lord's essence lay in his humility, his ability to listen to and do the will of the Father, and his willingness to act purely for the benefit of others. The good samaritan acted for the benefit of the victim by the road; those preceding him had chosen to give priority to self-interest. The ultimate in activation for another is to die for the other. "Greater love has no man than this, that a man lay down his life for his friends" (John 15:13). The fulfillment of the Christian self lies, then, in the willingness to die on behalf of another, if that is God's will.

As our Christian selves grow, we often become aware of the need for the healing of our real selves. We all are troubled with impairments of our real selves, due to unrecognized masks, repositories of negative feelings, and various fixations. Skilled pastoral counseling and spiritual direction and/or competent psychotherapy can be of great benefit.

All aspects of the self, from the foundations of communion and individuation to the various capacities to feelings to masks, are seen clinically as enduring patterns, repeating sequences of thoughts, affect, and/or action. The counselor can optimize the therapeutic process if minimal change can be brought about in some aspect of these patterns. A change in the counselee's processes of communion, individuation, or in the derivative capacities or masks can begin a continuing beneficial movement.

Exercises

1. Make a one hour appointment with yourself in a setting where you will not be distracted or interrupted. Pray for a time, then begin to confront any masks that you may harbor. Have pencil and paper available for clustering. Are you acting out in any way? Are there aspects of your relationships, past or present, that you are denying? Do you devalue other people or religious groups? Do you habitually distance yourself from others? Look also at the components of the real self as they apply to you. Should you become aware of problem areas, by all means speak with your spiritual director or pastor.

2. In the classroom, divide into groups of two. Share with your partner a concrete experience, recent or remote, that for you was a communion.

3. As a class, discuss forms of ministry that could support and further the development of the small child.

4. Chapters 6 and 7 describe several aspects of assessing a person. To practice assessment and interview skills, divide into groups of two. Interview each other along the following lines:

a.) Ask about the current climate of the counselee's life, including both strengths and struggles.

b.) Enlarge the understanding of the present by asking about current relationships, interests, troubles, and work.

c.) Ask, "What is your earliest memory?" "The one after that?" In this manner, sample memories through the teenage years.

d.) Ask for a thumbnail sketch of the counselee's mother and father, their relationship, and of important others. Ask for anecdotes in the following manner: "Let your imagination take you back to a time when you were with your mother, good, bad, or indifferent. Tell me about it." Do the same for the father and for the parents' relationship.

e.) Ask for a thumbnail sketch of the counselee: "How would you describe yourself as a person?"

f.) Ask about sex life. Preface this by saying, "I know this is a personal subject. Please feel free to decline to answer."

g.) Ask about dreams.

h.) Ask about spiritual life.

i.) Now, work with the counselee to integrate this material, keeping in mind the chapters on metaphor and the self.

Suggested Reading

Masterson, James F., *The Search for the Real Self,* The Free Press, Macmillan, New York, 1988.

8

Assessing Spiritual Development

If the heart of a person involves his world view, then the heart of that world view, the heart of hearts, is a relationship with God. In other words, how someone relates with God will govern all aspects of any relationships and, ultimately, the person's self-image. And, like personality development and family development, a person's relationship with God develops over time. The evolution of that relationship is the *spiritual life development cycle,* where *development* implies growth. Growth, in turn, is a form of constructive change. Spiritual growth can be the foundation for marked beneficial change.

The Scriptures are rich in biographies of people who changed radically, who developed spiritually over time. From a detailed examination of the lives of such people, a counselor can discover a scheme of spiritual development that is eminently useful in modern Christian counseling. Let us begin our examination with Jacob.

> Jacob (Genesis 25:31) was an opportunist who saw a chance to preempt his brother Esau's birthright and later, with the direction of his mother Rebekah, his brother's blessing. Fleeing Esau's wrath, Jacob had his first encounter with God in his dream of the ladder, receiving assurance that God was with him. Thereafter, he dealt successfully with the cheater Laban, becoming exceedingly rich in the process. He then fled Laban, talking his way out of a conflict with him, and headed for his homeland where, of course, Esau resided. Although he sent messengers with conciliatory words to Esau, he received word that Esau was approaching with four hundred men (Genesis 32:6). He was unable to cope with this grave crisis.

> Frightened to the core, he prayed to God, confessed his unworthiness, and asked for deliverance. At this point, he was fundamentally open to God, and that night he wrestled with him, receiving the name *Israel,* a symbol of his transformation. Then, instead of a confrontation with Esau, a reconciliation took place, an inevitable consequence of yielding to God.

The impending confrontation with Esau, in essence, stripped Jacob of his sense of self-sufficiency, of being able to manipulate and survive any situation. Once fully aware of his ultimate helplessness, he did what God had been preparing him for some time: he threw himself on the mercies and promises of God. Freed from a fixation on a grandiose self, he could accept the Almighty, with transformation and reconciliation resulting.

Joseph changed radically during his exile in Egypt, spiritually maturing to the point of saving his family from starvation (Genesis 47:12). Moses likewise changed after killing the Egyptian and fleeing to the desert (Exodus 2:11-15), where he grew to the point of being able to meet God on the mountain. David changed markedly after his affair with Bathsheba and Nathan's pronouncement of God's judgment; he poured out his brokenness, his repentance, and his appeal for God's mercy in Psalm 51. The sequence of self-sufficiency, breakdown, the wholehearted seeking of God, and subsequent spiritual maturation is a common one throughout the Scriptures. Even madness is described as fixation on a grandiose self, with deliverance occurring following repentance of one's past or intended action or thoughts:

> *Nebuchadnezzar was a ruler of Babylon who struggled with grandiosity. As he surveyed his kingdom, he said to himself, "Is not this great Babylon, which I have built by my mighty power as a royal residence and for the glory of my majesty? While the words were still in the king's mouth, there fell a voice from heaven, 'O King Nebuchadnezzar, to you it is spoken: The kingdom has departed from you, and you shall be driven from among men, and your dwelling shall be with the beasts of the field; and you shall be made to eat grass like an ox . . . until you have learned that the Most High rules the*

kingdom of men and gives it to whom he will.' " The king
repented subsequently and recovered, saying, "I, Nebuchad-
nezzar, lifted my eyes to heaven, and my reason returned to
me, and I blessed the Most High, and praised and honored him
who lives for ever" (Daniel 4:34).

This story repeats the common biblical theme that God lifts up the
humble and abases the proud, that people are the most sane when they
acknowledge the Lord's sovereignty. And Daniel, who knew this and
who was trusted by Nebuchadnezzar, undoubtedly helped the king
recover his sanity. This story is interesting in that it accurately describes
a fundamental aspect of some forms of madness. That is, madness is
basically the escape of the grandiose self from the organization of the
self; the resulting mania then leads to a disintegration of the self and to
psychosis. Love can cure madness, and I wager that Daniel loved
Nebechadnezzar, and through him the king could experience something
of God's love and thereby repent.

The New Testament dramatically records the radical change of many
who responded to the ministry of Jesus Christ. An ever growing army of
believers attests to Christ's power in their lives. Although a detailed examination of Christ's ability to bring about remarkable change is beyond
our scope, let us summarize a few of the changes he has wrought. The
New Testament recounts his healing of others by touching, praying, or
calling them out. Some were transformed through the forgiveness of
their sins, others as he confronted them. Many changed as they received
his teachings and heard his parables. All who decided to follow him
changed radically. Salvation was not something attained after death:
rather, it was a progression that flowed from one's faith in Christ.
Anyone who comes to know him undergoes a change of attitudes: old
negative attitudes about life and the self give way to a fresh new view
that God is love and in charge, that the self in union with him is something beautiful. The coming of the Holy Spirit produces yet greater
changes.

Saul of Tarsus (Acts 7 and 9) was a man who changed radical-
ly. Deeply committed to serving God as he understood him,

his ministry culminated in his participation in the stoning of Stephen. The subsequent breakdown of his convictions was evidenced by his fanatical war against the Church. Thereafter, Saul encountered the Lord on the road to Damascus. One can imagine that Saul, a man who desperately wanted to do right, was filled with conflict from having seen his efforts culminate in the savage execution of a man who died praising God. This crisis filled him with doubt and confusion, a mental state in which he could receive the simple thought, "Saul, Saul, why do you persecute me?" As with Jacob, his breakdown opened him to experience the Lord; and as with Jacob, he received a new name as a metaphor for his new self, a self borne out of a new relationship with God.

These examples from the Scriptures stimulate in us our own memories of our particular spiritual development. Although the spiritual development of each of us is unique, there are common recognizable experiences and states of being that allow the mapping of a general scheme of that development. A general scheme of spiritual development is valuable to the Christian counselor, for it enables him to recognize and accept where his counselee is and then to begin to move to the next step. Of course, people may not follow the sequences outlined below; instead, skipping steps or remaining fixated at one particular step for a lifetime. And each of us can recognize parts of ourselves at each stage and realize that we will be working on and through each stage for a lifetime. The value of this scheme lies in noting that some need help moving to the next stage.

Stages of Spiritual Development

Self-sufficiency => conversion => fear of God, fear of self => breakdown => acknowledging God as essential for control of the self => Thy will be done => love, the fulfillment of the self.

Self-sufficiency

The stage of self-sufficiency is characterized by the fundamental need to control. The person seeks power through manipulation, domination, competitiveness, and the need to win. Since success is defined as doing these things well, failure is inevitable for some, perhaps most. For many who have had a taste of excessive childhood helplessness and shame resulting from faulty parenting, these traits can be exaggerated, with a neurotic need to control apparent, a grandiosity that constitutes a defense against hurt, feelings of rejection, helplessness, shame, and ultimately against the internalized images of those who hurt the child in the first place. This neurotic pride expresses itself in statements such as, "I don't need anybody telling me what to do!" or, "I don't depend on anyone but myself"! The subsequent, illusory sense of having all the answers compromises the ability to learn. In other words, self-sufficiency is a defense. Furthermore, the person seeks perfection and is critical of the self when the inevitable lapses from perfection occur. The person tries so hard that tension and stress build up. Feelings are repressed, for they are viewed as signs of weakness. The repression of feelings causes the creativity of the unconscious to be overshadowed by the obsessive action of the conscious mind as it *tries hard*. Feelings of dependency are despised, and the internal struggle nourishes psychosomatic conditions such as migraines, ulcers, and heart attacks. What one fears in oneself may be projected onto and hated in others (an example might be a young man's hatred of homosexuals).

In the stage of self-sufficiency, those less well endowed struggle for success and may develop an obsessive fear of failure or of making mistakes. Others drop out of the game altogether but retain their envy of the success of others. Many seek others to take their responsibilities and go on welfare or disability. Weakness, illness, or neurosis can dominate the strong, and a strong person can end up as a reluctant slave of a weak one. The heart of this stage is the person's relationship with God. The person is consciously indifferent to God but inwardly views God as weak or a crutch for the weak (Marx's *opiate of the masses*). He may reject God as punitive and intimidating, qualities again projected from the self-image or a bad parental image. Materialism is a symbol of the exercise of control and a means of hiding the emptiness resulting from alienation from God.

However, it is not always easy to recognize a person stuck in the stage of self-sufficiency. Such a person may be an upstanding, churchgoing, hardworking, successful citizen, one who characterizes the American ideal. But this person only pays lip service to God, and in reality he depends on innate abilities and is satisfied with them. This person does not know God, for to be dependent on other than self-centered resources is a foreign idea.

Conversion

Conversion, the next stage of spiritual development, is the emotional acknowledgement of God as a power and the dawning awareness that God possesses the power to create and sustain. With this insight, the person *chooses* to defer to God and *decides* to follow him. A child raised in the Church may have made this decision so long ago that it may seem that following Christ is a natural occurrence, not a definite choice. Another may have fallen away and experienced the new commitment as a dramatic event, like being *born again*. Every Christian must at some point, perhaps repeatedly, decided to follow Christ in order to pass out of the stage of self-sufficiency. To put it another way, each of us must own the religion given to us by others. . . . "It is no longer because of your words that we believe, for we have heard for ourselves, and we know that this is indeed the Savior of the world" (John 4:42). *Conversion* can be a trying, even convulsive event, for it may carry with it a separation and individuation from one's peer group or family of origin and their beliefs. Often, as in the cases of Jacob, Joseph, Moses, and Saul of Tarsus, some event that calls into question the illusion of self-sufficiency precedes that decision.

> *My own conversion occurred at age 25. Raised in the Church,*
> *I recall sitting during the Eucharist and wondering why I had*
> *to be there. I left home at 18 and stopped attending church. I*
> *had vague but rather grandiose fantasies of making lots of*
> *money, but at 25 I found myself working in a tedious job that*

would lead nowhere. Finally understanding that I alone could not change my situation, I began to pray for guidance. The result was an immediate relief and an evolving sense of the presence and reality of God. Although resolving my vocational crisis took another 18 months, my life took on an unmistakably different course.

Fear of God, Fear of Self

The person next enters a phase of spiritual development marked primarily by the effort to live up to the ideals surrounding the object of the commitment. "Since I now know that God is real, I shall attempt to keep God's rules." This stage, the fear of God stage, is really the stage of spiritual childhood. People need to experience this stage, just as a child needs to be trained by parents, for here the bad, internalized image (the god within) formed by the combination of the sins of the parents and the projection of the child's anger, grandiosity, and talion impulses, should be encountered.

Teaching a third grade Sunday school class taught me something of the origins of the fear of God. I taught the love of God in Christ, but the children repeated, through their questions and anecdotes, themes of God's punishment if they were bad. Where did they get those ideas? My own children were in the class and agreed with the rest, yet they had not been taught that way. Discipline yes, intimidated no. This exemplifies the presence in the hearts of children of the talion impulse, eye for an eye type thinking, which persists into adulthood and expresses itself in people's interpretations of Christianity. But Christ never operated by this principle: His ministry was rather one of calling and offering choice. His parables, frequently containing such extreme opposites as the rich man and Lazarus (Luke 16:19-31), were not meant to threaten but rather to portray choice. God does not punish us for our transgressions; rather, bitterness is an inevitable result, a logical consequence, of sin. "The measure you give will be the measure you get" (Matthew 7:2). In counseling, the counselor can draw, lead, offer choice, and predict the consequences of behavior, but if the counselor tries to control the counselee, all can be lost. On the cross, Jesus gave up all control, but in the process drew us to him.

So, as spiritual children we must learn the love of God, but we need discipline as well. For example, my sons need to learn, among other things, table manners, respect for their elders, the value of following instructions, and how to limit the expression of aggression. Similarly, the Jews spent a thousand years with the Law before Christ came. I think this parallels our own development. That millennia allowed the Jews to become well acquainted with what was expected of them, and it also demonstrated amply that their own efforts to please God by keeping the Law would, in the end, prove futile. In like manner, we must each learn that regardless of our efforts, we must ultimately depend on God's grace for salvation.

This stage has its pitfalls, however. In conjunction with fearing God (on whom is projected one's own talion impulses), a person may come to regard sins, doubts, sexual impulses, *etc.*, with a terror that can lead to their repression rather than their resolution.

*I view the current cultural trend toward sexual license as, in part, a reaction to the Victorian attitudes of earlier generations. Many of my 40 and older patients were taught to view their spiritual doubts, their sexuality, and even pleasure with suspicion or as feelings to be completely suppressed. These patients have suffered from guilt and the marked **inhibition** of emotion, spontaneity, and creativity or have rebelled and in the process, rejected God.*

Thus, in a misguided effort to please God and avoid going to hell, a person may heighten the maneuvers of self-sufficiency, striving even harder for perfection, resulting in more stress in the self. One person might attempt to get rid of doubt by rigid adherence to the Bible or doctrine or attempt to bolster spiritual self-esteem by criticizing, judging, or condemning other denominations or religious groups. Another might become judgmental, critical of faiths of others or its lack. Parents, in striving to keep up a spiritual image while suppressing *unspiritual* behavior or thought, might overcontrol or intimidate their children, perhaps making them rebellious in the process. I have worked with many who had been damaged or had resented having had religion or morality forced upon them. To threaten a child with the wrath of God for misbehaving is both poor theology and poor child-rearing.

Another pitfall is to adopt without thought a given doctrine or teaching. Because such doctrine or teaching has not been thoughtfully integrated into the person's being, it can only be applied by rote and hence may prove ineffectual or destructive in governing behavior. Such a rote adoption of the beliefs of a church may be done to avoid looking at oneself or, out of fear of making a mistake, thinking for oneself. True Christianity confronts the person with critical decisions, not pat answers. Yet some belong to *mother church* but in essence only exchange mothers, thereby avoiding growing up. Success in this stage comes partially from learning to *think through* critical questions, where thinking through means the process of deducing the basic premises of a belief or church teaching and then deciding if one agrees or disagrees with that premise. As discussed in Chapter 10, many of our basic premises may actually be the unspoken scripts of our families of origin.

> *A 45-year-old Army colonel had attended Mass every day for years, yet found himself embroiled in an unhappy marriage and a tempestuous affair. Neither he nor his spouse had integrated their religious practices with their emotional lives.*

> *In another case, a 30-year-old woman was referred to me after complaining to her family doctor that she sometimes would slap her children uncontrollably. Referring to the teachings of her church, she explained, "Spanking leads to salvation. It has been deeply ingrained in us that spanking can lead our children to salvation." She stated that she and her husband spanked their 3-year-old weekly. She admitted that her husband would at times get carried away with the spankings. Although I have not heard her church's version of this teaching,*

I have heard this kind of discipline advocated before. What impressed me was her propensity not to think for herself.

This stage should, therefore, properly be a period of study and learning, coupled with an exercise of one's own intelligence. Those who have kept to their commitment in the conversion stage really are eager for study and guidance. Study should center on coming to know intimately the Father, Son, and Holy Spirit through the Scriptures, worship, prayer, fellowship, and service and on coming to know oneself in relation to God. The student should think through and critically weigh doctrine, teaching, and the Bible rather than simply accept everything offered. Pastors, in particular, have a responsibility to provide this kind of guidance. It is, I believe, the failure of the large denominations to provide substantial teaching that has led many to move to sects where much teaching is offered. Ideally, this stage should produce a knowledge and love of the Lord from which one can say from the heart, "Thy will be done." Life is far from ideal, however. Many people break down, thereby embracing change whether they like it or not. In this stage, the person's efforts to control destiny by maintaining *the god within* begin to falter, bringing about a confrontation within the self with grandiosity's polar opposite, helplessness.

Breakdown

Breakdown stems from events that call the illusion of self-sufficiency into question. Breakdown does not necessarily imply psychiatric disorder; rather, it is an inward experience to life's events that has as its first step a sense of losing some level of control over oneself, one's destiny, or one's relationships. For example, Jacob broke down as he faced Esau; Moses lost his sense of being in control of himself when he killed the Egyptian. Saul of Tarsus lost his vision of who he was and the value of his actions at the stoning of Stephen. In each case, what was lost was a sense of the validity of one's world view, thus opening each to a new world view with God as head. Events that lead to breakdown are quite familiar: death or other loss of a loved one, disaster, moral failure, marriage or family problems, financial loss, aging, and even simple things such as moving are common causes.

> *A member of the clergy told me this story. Raised in the church, he became successful in business and a committed churchgoer. Although happily married, he became involved with his secretary. He quickly broke off the affair, but the experience changed his life. For the first time in his life, he thought deeply about his faith and began to pray in earnest. The effects eventually led him to the ministry.*

> *The motion picture The Cardinal dramatizes the breakdown of a man and his subsequent passage to a more mature level of spiritual development. A cardinal in an iron curtain country is arrested for "crimes against the state." The cardinal is forced to confess to these false charges by a KGB man who breaks into and utilizes an area of the cardinal's private life, his relationship with his mother. As he is forced to acknowledge the sad state of this relationship, he breaks down, is filled with guilt and remorse, and finally signs the "confession" his inquisitor has prepared. The picture ends as the cardinal leaves prison, not broken any longer but strengthened by a sense that he is a better man for having dealt with something previously too painful to face. I felt that I had witnessed afresh the crucifixion, followed by the joy of resurrection.*

The pain and loneliness that arise from the feeling of being out of control can sometimes be too much to bear. To avoid the pain, the sufferer may turn to drink, depression, or exaggerated self-sufficiency. Some seek psychiatric help; others may consult their pastor. Breakdown is an exciting and rewarding field to work in. People seek help when stripped of the illusions of control and self-sufficiency. Some erect elaborate defenses that require expertise to penetrate; others simply drop their masks and bare their souls. However such people present themselves, they are primed and ready for growth.

> *The Bible describes Jesus' ministry to those in the breakdown stage. In Matthew 9, Jesus heals a paralytic after forgiving his*

sins, calls the outcast tax collector Matthew, and says "Those who are well have no need of a physician, but those who are sick . . . For I came not to call the righteous, but sinners" (Matthew 9:12-13). He then heals several others. The chapter closes with "When he saw the crowds, he had compassion for them, because they were harassed and helpless, like sheep without a shepherd. Then he said to his disciples, 'The harvest is plentiful, but the laborers are few; pray therefore the Lord of the harvest to send out laborers into his harvest' " (Matthew 9:36-38).

The Christian can then come to regard every loss, every impasse, every failure as a fresh reminder to seek and depend on the Lord and hence to draw closer, for in such events we again learn to acknowledge God as essential to our self-control. And, following Jesus' example, we need to pray that we recognize others, especially those close to us in our daily lives, who are breaking down so that we may effectively minister to them, for it is them that Jesus is calling.

Acknowledging God as Essential for Control of the Self

The twelve steps of Alcoholics Anonymous epitomize the power for creative change inherent in acknowledging God as necessary for control of the self. First, the alcoholic must admit to having no power to control the drinking. Second, the aloholic must turn over the struggle to a *higher power,* thus admitting a need for dependence on a greater power for recovery. Every Christian should regard these steps as a powerful metaphor for life. From this *submission* comes humility, and from humility comes a willingness to listen to God and an eagerness, indeed a craving, to learn from God and from those around us. Learning becomes an exciting, rewarding adventure that leads to further seeking, asking, and learning. One comes to know God, to feel a part of him, and to trust him as the ultimate friend. But we can only know God as we know Christ, so that knowing Christ is the final fulfillment of this phase.

"Thy Will Be Done" (Matthew 6:10)

Knowing God in Christ leads to and intertwines with an attitude of the heart called *thy will be done,* a constant attitude of looking to God—a waiting on him; a willingness to follow; a constant asking, seeking, and knocking. One inwardly and constantly refrains from reaching one's own conclusions, instead submitting to the answers resulting from a creative and often subconscious dialogue between God and one's own unconscious mind. Neither God nor the unconscious can inspire a person who tries to control them or tell them what to do. In this phase, there is also a willingness to submit, to suspend wants, opinions, or ideas around others, especially around one's spouse or close friends or relatives. *Thy will be done* forms the foundation of Jesus' prayer; through it he shows us how to live life, demonstrating how he does it. The attitude generates the creative and healing acts so characteristic of the life of Christ. As a person begins to live this way, there is a feeling of being plugged into the eternal, a discovery of the way things work. At the same time, the person can further let go of cocksureness; further feeling weakness and further seeking God's voice and presence leads to more of *thy will be done.* True creativity, of which love is the chief manifestation, can only spring from the source. And the only way to tap into the source is to say from the heart, *thy will be done.*

Love, the Fulfillment of the Self

Love leads to fulfillment of the self. But love and fulfillment are not the destinations of the journey, but rather our companions on the way. Fulfillment lies in the process of *becoming,* and in the process, the action of *loving.* I can best express it in a poem.

Love and Fulfillment
by a psychiatrist in his 50s

Lord, am I loving?
I don't feel it.
The old negativity clings to me like grease.

Fear too. Am I slipping?
And the *What ifs!* They never bothered me before.
Too many phobics and 50-year-old disableds?

I'm a psalmist like David
Age clutched him like a frost
But I'm too young to get old!
Getting old—damn, the 40s were comfortable.

But this I know:
Everything passes away.
The young who seem so fresh and early will look like me
And I like my Dad, bent and blind.

My hope is in the Lord
And I love his people and his book,
Which is about his people
And my family, who reflect him.

Deer and waterbrooks, longing for you,
Filled by your presence in my friends;
I praise you for this.
Your Church is my fulfillment.

The usefulness and applicability of the scheme of the spiritual life cycle in both assessing and counseling a person is illustrated in the transcript given below.

> *Betty was a 65-year-old widow, referred to me by her physician because of a protracted severe depression. In the first visit, Betty told me of her depression, nervousness, insomnia, and self-imposed isolation. A Christian, she had ceased going to church or visiting friends months before. She said the depression had started about the time of her husband's deterioration, three years earlier. Also, she had cared for a time for her terminally ill mother, who had died several months before Betty consulted me. The following transcript is of our second visit together.*

B. I feel better.

A. Perhaps because you talked with me.

B. I agree.

A. Have you ever talked with friends about your depression?

B. No. I don't want to burden them.

A. I read about a study of depression in the elderly. They regularly found that the depressed person had isolated herself. If they could get her to share her difficulty with someone, her depression would lift. Would you tell your friend about how you are feeling?

B. I'll do it. But I feel so frozen, so unable to express myself, unable to paint.

A. That sounds like a strong feeling. Go back to when you started feeling frozen.

B. It was when we moved to the Avenue *(a low-rent district)*. My front window looked at the trash bins behind the Santa Cruz Market. I would watch people rummaging through them. I couldn't leave because I had to answer the phone for my husband. I had time to paint, but I couldn't do it.

A. Sounds like you despaired, gave up, and you feel it still.

B. Yes! *(pause)* There's more I need to tell you. My childhood home was cold, my parents not affectionate. Mother always criticized me; I was never good enough. I left home at 18.

A. That was a poverty situation of the emotional sort. You weathered it. But the second situation, symbolic of the first, got to you, and you despaired. Then, add on your husband's alcoholism and death, and your mother's dementia, and you get a vicious circle of helplessness, despair, and withdrawal, leading to depression, which in turn led to more withdrawal, and so on. *(At this point, considering the spiritual life cycle, I sense she is stuck in the breakdown phase, so I inquire about moving to the next stage,* *dependence on God.)* When you feel so stuck, can you pray, can you turn it over to God?

B. I can't! Though I believe, I can't seem to ask, or let go. If I try to pray, my mind drifts away.

A. *(now thinking that maybe she is actually or basically stuck in the self-sufficiency phase of the cycle)* Could you say that it is in your make-up to not ask others for help?

B. Definitely! I should be able to manage on my own!

A. Sounds like you feel very strongly about that! Go back in your life to an incident at which you began to feel that way.

B. Oh, my whole childhood! My parents raised me that way! To be self-sufficient! They were perfect. They told me they always got straight As. They ridiculed me because I didn't.

A. What a conflict! To feel helpless on the one hand, as on the Avenue, but also to feel you must always be in control on the other! *(we both laugh) (pause) (I think maybe she is now ready to consider depending on God)* You know, God was with you all along. He imperceptibly moved you from the Avenue. And it was no accident that you came to see me. *(Tears come to her eyes. Sharing her depression with her friend would be a good metaphor for opening herself to God.)* Going and talking to your friend will be a good exercise.

B. My friend is a Christian who prays and gets answers.

A. We all have the receptors in our brains to hear the inaudible and see the invisible. As you practice, you'll do so too.

B. I've been reading John Powell; that's what he says, too. *(An affirmative to my suggestions and comments.)*

Betty went on to recover completely from her depression. Her frozenness proved to be of fundamental importance: it was a lifestyle deriving from her relationship to her family of origin. Yet her resources of affability, willingness to face problems within herself, curiosity, intelligence, and basic goodwill (particularly toward God) were easily accessed, and she thawed rapidly.

People subjected to mistreatment, deprivation, trauma, or extreme (for them) disappointment earlier in life may react by exaggerating their sense of self-sufficiency and the need to control. They may thus become quite rigid, and if they awaken to their Christian faith, may prove rigid in their practice of faith (*i.e.,* become judgmental). Breakdown, occurring as it does out of one's inability to control some aspect of life, is particularly difficult and fraught with symptoms for such people.

Humanity's traversal of the spiritual life cycle may not, of course, occur in such an orderly, step-by-step fashion. Those able to begin to experience the *love and fulfillment of the self* stage will nonetheless continue to work and rework each of the preceding stages. And one may occupy several stages simultaneously. Nonetheless, the counselor will repeatedly encounter people who are mired in one of the negative stages and will need help to move on. This scheme can be quite useful in deciding the direction the counselee needs to be led.

Exercises

In groups of three, discuss personal anecdotes that describe your presence in one or several of the stages of spiritual development, or your traversal from one stage to another. Pick two or three to present to the class.

Suggested Reading

1. Osmer, Richard, and Fowler, James W., "Childhood and Adolescence—A Faith Development Perspective," in *Clinical Handbook of Pastoral Counseling,* edited by Robert J. Wicks *et al.,* Paulist Press, New York and Mahwah, New Jersey, 1985.

2. Tyrrell, Bernard J., *Christotherapy—Healing Through Enlightenment,* Seabury Press, New York, 1975.

9

Dreams

Research into the phenomenon of rapid eye movement (REM) sleep indicates that the average person dreams for perhaps two hours a night in discrete periods lasting 10 to 20 minutes, each period accompanied by marked electroencephalographic and physiologic changes that far more resemble alert waking than normal sleep. Dreams are a reality to which we react as we would in a like event in waking life. But, of course, they are an internal reality. Dreams represent our internal reality to ourselves and to anyone who might be interested. The average person spends a twelfth of the life span participating in the internal reality of dreams.

The metaphors of dreams dramatize our internal realities just as the metaphors of the unconscious convey meaning in art, drama, and literature. Just as a person may use anecdotes or memories of past events to portray a point, so dreams use symbols in sequences to denote or communicate aspects of the relationships with God, neighbor, and self. In dreams, people, places, or things can dramatically illustrate such varied themes as relationships with parents, fixations, past events and their implications for the dreamer, and various aspects of the self (including struggles with guilt, conscience, intimacy, grandiosity, current misbehavior, and sexual identity). Dreams can be viewed as constructs of the unconscious pertaining to the heart, that centermost part of us that relates and represents those relationships to us.

But before giving some illustrations of dreams, their language, and how they dramatize our crucial relationships, a word of caution. This chapter approaches dreams with the same theoretical bias that is found in the rest of the book. The remarkable thing about people receiving counseling is that they tend to pick up the counselor's frame of reference and to reflect it in dreams. A client of a Jungian begins to produce archetypes and shadows; of a Freudian, symbols of sexuality; of Daim's, symbols of fixation; and so forth. The idea that *we are who we follow* shows up in our dreams. This is not hard to understand. A counselee who is disoriented, confused, and perhaps defeated may well look up to and want to please a counselor, particularly if the counselor is impressive. For that reason, the Christian counselor should think through theological and theoretical orientations and have them congruent with personal make up. Furthermore, although we all have biases in approaching dreams, it is a common mistake to attempt to fit a counselee's dream into a theoretical framework, to interpret a dream according to a preconceived idea. Better to suspend opinions and allow an unfolding of the dream's meaning as the counselee sees it. Techniques to allow such an unfolding are discussed in this chapter.

In practice, the distinction between weighing a dream for assessment purposes and working with it therapeutically is blurred. In the model of counseling described here, that of assessing another's heart and then speaking to it, the dream may occupy a crucial position, for, as the REM sleep research indicates, in a sense dreams *are* our internal reality. Thus, if a Christian counselor learns another's heart and handles it in a God-directed way, that must be therapeutic. This chapter describes not only the language of dreams and their value and assessment, but also their use in therapy. Dreams easily fall into the categories of relating to God, neighbor, and self, so we deal explicitly in this chapter with these three categories.

Dreams and Relating to God

The dreams of those seeking counsel repeatedly pertain to the sequences of fixations to impasses discussed in the introduction. For these counselees, salvation is in part a freeing from objects, feelings, defenses, *etc.*, to which the personality is tethered. Dreams about God are unusual; dreams usually point to fixations on a parent, a family system, feelings, a depressing event, or aspects of a self-image or an attitude. However, in those counselees with a strong spiritual bent or quest, dreams pertaining to God usually deal with fixations or maladaptive attitudes that interfere with closeness to him.

My own spiritual search is a case in point. Raised in the Episcopal Church, I became a praying, seeking Christian at 25 over a crisis in vocational direction. Our Lord graciously helped me find the right track, and at 28 I entered medical school. By this time I was aware of impairment in my real self. I had difficulty with self-activation, decisiveness, commitment, and intimacy. I was prone to sexual acting out, activities that I came to see were exploitive of others. At 29, I sought counseling from the Rev. S. Dunham Wilson, an Episcopal priest with a gift for dream interpretation.

Early in counseling I dreamed I was kneeling at an altar rail, praying. As I prayed, I tossed a bag of coins over the rail, praying "Lord, please help me." A loud and frightening noise filled my ears, and I woke up.

The picturesque language of this dream can be paraphrased as "pay my money, pray for help, and get noise in reply." To understand a dream, the counselor must know the context within which the dream occurs. The context of this dream, the fundamental direction and concern in my life around the time of the dream, had to do with seeking change from God. I was told that I was trying to buy change from God. I knew this was right: I took pride in giving and felt it ingratiated me with God. Father Wilson directed me to give nothing to the church for a time. It was a good lesson: Our Lord cannot be bought. And on a transference level, my task to not give told me that Father Wilson could live without my pledge.

Sometime thereafter, I dreamed I took an elevator to an upper room where I was greeted by a Roman Catholic priest. He told me that Christ was the answer to my problem with lust. Later, seated with others, a basket of bread was passed. I noticed that the priest was smoking a cigarette.

The priest was the central figure of the dream. On the face of it, a Catholic priest is a convenient symbol of one's ability to live without sex. But this man was unique in his own right, ul-

timately masculine, vividly human, yet supernatural. His front teeth were slightly crooked, a detail that attested to his humanness. To this day I do not understand the significance of the cigarette. Although all dreams are probably a dialogue between the Holy Spirit and our unconscious, I believe that in this case our Lord generated the preponderance of the dream.

A month or two later, I dreamed I was in a village when the electrifying news that Jesus was in town was announced. I pushed through a crowd to find him in a room, sick in bed. I knelt beside his bed and prayed for him.

In this dream, a person is used to symbolize an attitude or feeling within the dreamer. At first blush, the sick figure seems to represent my anemic comprehension of the real person at that point in time. But the dream also says I was doing something right: I was praying.

These examples illustrate several points about the language of dreams, methods of grasping their message, and their value in a spiritual pilgrimage. The language in each is that of a little play in which the actions of the dreamer or the characters of people in the dream represent heart-level characteristics of the dreamer, those personal characteristics tending to interfere with a full relationship with God. A helpful technique in understanding the implications of the little drama of the dream is to paraphrase it, then look to the counselee for confirmation as to how that paraphrasing applies to this person in the present. Thus, the second dream might be paraphrased, "God's spokesman is powerful beyond my comprehension. Perhaps he comes from God, not from my unconscious. I feel fed in his presence. Yet, he is not perfect (the cigarette)." A positive paraphrase of the third dream might say, "I will find Christ as I care for the sick," certainly a prophetic statement for a young medical student. Note that although these dreams dramatized the deficits in faith, understanding, and action, they also pointed to improvement and growth: in the first and third dreams, I was praying. The counselor should receive and respond to not just the negative in dreams, which represents the problem, but also the positive, which represents the solution.

Dreams and Relating to Others

Dreams can pertain in various ways to relationships with others. Examples include fixations on others, unresolved grief over the loss of a loved one, powerful feelings toward others, transference toward the counselor, and traumatic incidents (which almost always involve another party). Daim (1963) focuses extensively on dreams that symbolize fixations on another person; consider the following example from Daim:

> The analysand* finds himself inside a cathedral of extraordinary height. He looks upward from where he stands, and he suddenly becomes aware that outside a thunderstorm is raging; the church is being struck by bright flashes of lightning. Simultaneously he feels that the building is being shaken by an earthquake of rapidly increasing strength. The church begins to collapse, and while he saves his life by fleeing into the open, the church remains in ruins beyond repair.
>
> The church reminds the analysand of his mother; he always looked up to her—she is for him "Mother Church." He further remembers that he was taught by his mother "Catholic principles" (actually, he had been indoctrinated with Manichaean rather than Catholic principles), and he is "locked up" in these principles. But now a thunderstorm bursts over this entire edifice; the building collapses, and the unconscious in the form of successive shocks of an earthquake demolishes the structure. The time has come to flee into the open to avoid being crushed and buried under the ruins.
>
> This dream reveals that the analysand suffered from a mother fixation. The mother is represented symbolically by the cultic-sacred building. She has indoctrinated him with rigid Manichaean principles, hostile to his human nature. And now this entire system of idolatry collapses. The idea which the analysand (under his mother's influence) had formed of Catholicism was obviously incorrect and distorted. This dis-

*one undergoing psychoanalysis

torted image, including the mother who was the cause of the distortion, must be disposed of.

One can well imagine that this kind of "breakdown"—an event which is a regular and necessary occurrence in the course of every psychoanalysis—is an extremely tormenting and yet at the same time also a very salutary experience (in his desire for liberation the analysand flees into the open!), an experience which analysands try to evade as long as possible. Its effects are revolutionary in a very radical sense and are thus indicative of a far-reaching and enduring transformation of the individual.

First, note the language in this dream. A cathedral represents a person and also the attitudes and teachings of that person. The raging storm may represent developing doubts about his mother's teaching or perhaps his anger at his awareness of his fixation. Again, objects and natural phenomena symbolize relationships, mental attitudes, and emotions. Fixation is discussed in Chapter 2 as a positing by the personality of a false absolute, one that stultifies the growth of the personality. A person centered on God is whole, free, open-ended, free to think deeply and to learn; to be centered on something other than God is to find oneself sooner or later in a finite system that ultimately enslaves and prevents the development of the personality.

Unresolved grief almost always finds its way into dreams; in such cases, the loved (or perhaps not so loved) one, perhaps long dead, makes recurrent vivid appearances, usually looking alive and well. At the same time, the bereaved obsessively remembers the departed, cannot cry, or cannot stop crying, and feels prolonged guilt and remorse, often far beyond the three or four months usually needed to finish grieving.

A 47-year-old African-American gentleman complained of periodic depressions lasting for two weeks at a time. These mood swings rarely had clear precipitating events; the depressions were marked by obsessive and suicidal thoughts, withdrawal, and emotionality. His depressions dated back to his teens: his father had also suffered bouts of depression. He recalled being an only child, very protected from racism and "everything else," sleeping in the same room as his parents until age 13. "They put me on a pedestal," he stated. When asked about his dreams, he became tearful, saying "I dream often of my dead aunt Maud, and of my mother who died 16 years ago." He wept as he expressed regrets for not having visited both more frequently before their deaths. "I've never told anyone about this, about my grief and regret, because in the South we kept the bad stuff hidden," he exclaimed. I told him I was glad he was sharing his grief with me, as it is very hard to resolve grief by oneself.

Another way that dreams represent the essence of relationships with others is the symbolization of traumatic experiences involving those other people. Although psychic injury can result from natural catastrophes, most post-traumatic neuroses result from the actions (whether deliberate or accidental) of one or of a group toward another, the victim(s). The real injury in traumatic experiences is the victim's acceptance of negative attitudes toward the self. Also notice that in the following example and in all the previous examples, various aspects of the self are richly illustrated. Most dreams represent the heart of the self, but always in terms of God or others. Dreams prove that the heart never exists in isolation.

Joe, in his 30s, suffered mild but chronic depression and poor self-esteem. He reported a recurrent nightmare dating back many years. In his 20s, the dream consisted of a night terror, a sudden surge of anxiety from which he would awaken screaming. Over the years, the night terror evolved into a vivid nightmare. He would dream he was in a room, perhaps in bed; he would become aware of a sinister, terrifying "presence" in the room. Although he had often tried to stay in the dream, in an attempt to face this presence, the anxiety would awaken him.

A.   Imagine that the "presence" is sitting in that chair in front of you. Have a dialogue with it.

J. You terrify me. You haunt me, returning again and again.

A. Use your imagination to pretend you are the presence and reply.

J. I am the presence. I am here to intimidate you, to accuse you, to beat you up. *(He goes back and forth a few times, first playing one part, then the other, until recognition begins to appear on his face.)* I think the presence is my dad. He is about to jerk me out of my sleep and whip me with a belt. He whipped me with a belt on several occasions.

A. Tell your dad how being jerked out of bed and whipped makes you feel.

J. You make me feel like a criminal! *(He goes on to describe several minor delinquent activities, pervasive feelings of guilt, and much self accusation.)*

In this dream, it is the conclusion, the imprinting of a feeling of criminality, that terrifies the dreamer. The traumatic incident is the vehicle for the transmission of the negative script.

The emotion (the *affect*) present in dreams symbolizing traumatic experiences usually is or relates to the emotion felt at the time of the traumatic experience itself. Thus, the emotion felt in dreams can be a bridge to the original experience and is therefore called an affect bridge. In the above example, the counselor might have said to the dreamer, "Let your unconscious mind take you back to an incident where you felt that same terror." The end result would have been the same: the uncovering of the traumatic experience and the negative life script derived from it.

Dreams Relating to the Self

Various pathological aspects of the self are richly represented in dreams, and all dreams pertain in one way or another to the self. Examples of the possibilities include guilt, fear, what if's, sexual identity, divisions within the self, self-criticism, perfectionism, and grandiosity. This section considers dreams illustrating several of these categories, starting with guilt. When the self is burdened with guilt, dreams will be used as a signal and problem-solving device as the self attempts to rid itself of guilt.

Sam, a Vietnam veteran in his 30s, had been traumatized in an industrial accident. A drop press had crushed both hands. We successfully worked through his posttraumatic anxiety, depression, and nightmares, but no sooner was he feeling better than he began to have nightmares of " . . . snakes everywhere; I'm running every which way trying to avoid them."

   A.   What pops into your mind when you think of these snakes?
            What do they remind you of?

   S.   *(Mentions several associations, then starts to tremble.)* They
            remind me of the snakes that used to drop on us from the trees in
            the jungle. *(With intensity and an expression that conveyed his
            nausea.)* Now I remember killing my first Viet Cong soldier.
            I emptied my carbine into him as he rushed me, screaming. He
            wouldn't go down. Finally, I hit him across the head with my
            empty weapon. He fell dead at my feet *(starts to cry)*.

   A.   You feel terrible about killing him.

   S.   Yes, I do! Up until that moment I thought I was a good man.

   A.   Since that moment, you've been stuck with the realization that
            you have it in you to kill, something you didn't realize before.
            The snakes in the nightmares then stand for the guilt you've been
            struggling with and trying to avoid ever since.

   S.   That's right!

   A.   You've told me you were raised Catholic. Let me explain how
            God in Christ can forgive you and rid you of your guilt.

This man arrived suddenly and forcefully at the realization he was a sinner. This was an important step in his spiritual development, but he was unable to integrate and progress beyond that realization until I helped him to look to his neglected religious faith for the answers.

False guilt often makes its appearance in dreams. Many people demand perfection of themselves and will criticize, accuse, and punish themselves when they fail to live up to their own expectations. Feelings of guilt pervade such people. Consider the following case, in which dreams played a crucial role in assessment and recovery:

Jan was a lovely, open child of 12 who complained of trichotillomania (a compulsive pulling out of her hair), nervousness, tension, and frequent headaches. She was accompanied by her mother, a sympathetic and understanding woman who tried hard to be a good mother to her. I had treated the mother earlier for depression, when Jan was about three years old. After two sessions for evaluation and getting to know one another, Jan came to the third session complaining of increased anxiety and hair pulling. She related several nightmares in which her mother appeared as a demon to inflict numerous, small cuts on the back of her legs with very sharp scissors.

Using techniques described in the next section, we deduced that the mother in the dream was a symbol of her own conscience. Each wound inflicted was a punishment for some minor misdoing or omission. Such judgment and condemnation came out of a need to be perfect. Assembling together my knowledge of the mother, the child's story, and the dream, I suggested that Jan had felt deeply abandoned and guilty during her mother's deep depression and that now she needed to be perfect to please mother, both to pay her mother for Jan's guilt and as a means of keeping mother from "going away" as before. Jan gave strong nonverbal assent to this interpretation.

I then talked with Jan about how God is our father and mother and how God can be depended on to not "go away." I told her of God's love and mercy for imperfect people, such as her and me, and how he does not require us to be perfect, but rather to have faith. And if she could have faith, she would indeed have

*an "ultimate" father and mother and would not be so vul-
nerable to her mother's moods.*

Self-recrimination is a consequence of the need to appear perfect
(Horney, 1950). As with Jan, those who build a colossal apparatus to
maintain this appearance are anxious about impending disaster (although
they may not be aware of such fears). Perfectionists find it hard to face
life's ups and downs. Unable to reconcile themselves with life as a risky
adventure, they cling to the hope that life is ultimately calculable and
controllable.

Four Methods of Dream Interpretation and Utilization

Dreams are often another metaphor for the counselee's difficulty.
They contain the points of interview cones. A counselee might volunteer a dream, or the counselor could indirectly ask for a report of the
dream by describing the dream of another person with a similar problem.
Having been presented with the dream, the counselor must decide how to
respond to the dream's content. There are four options:

- Ask for associations to the dream or figures within it.

- Summarize the content and either hold it or share it.

- Proceed with a direct method of plumbing the dream's message.

- Make no comment on the dream but later use its content.

Praying without ceasing for direction to the next step is necessary here.

1. Associating to Dreams

This is the simplest way to respond to reported dreams. Questions
such as, "What do you think about this dream?" or, "What does that particular image in the dream remind you of?" send the counselee into deep
thought to face crucial issues. People will often dream of another person. A request such as, "Tell me something about that person," inevitably expands the metaphor of the dream.

*A man reported a lengthy dream in which a coworker named
Don repeatedly appeared. "How would you describe Don;*

*what kind of person is he?" I asked. The counselee blurted
out, "He's an egotist!" After a long pause, he said, "I can see
that in myself."*

2. Summarizing Dreams

A good summary can often capture the essence of a dream. An example is my dream of seeing Jesus. The summary,"I will see Christ as I care for the sick," rounds out the manifest dream content and provides enormous confirmation for my efforts. Summarizing a dream is a trial and error process, a paraphrasing that takes into account life circumstances surrounding the dream and the dreamer's attempts to respond constructively to life. An exercise at the end of this chapter will give the reader an opportunity to practice summarizing dreams.

3. Interpreting Dreams Directly

This section gives a step-by-step method of interpreting dreams directly. The method, taken from Downing (1973), requires a cooperative and not too disturbed counselee to be successful. As noted above, timing is important. The approach can use the techniques of associating to and summarizing dreams. This method is pragmatic; invariably bears on the heartfelt at-the-moment concerns of the counselee; and avoids arcane intellectual debates, which usually are not effective in producing change. The approach consists of 12 steps, but in a given dream, one or a few of the steps might lead to an interpretation.

1) Pray silently as the counselee begins to recount the dream, and pray without ceasing throughout the dialogue regarding the dream.

2) Keep in mind the context of the dream: What are the pertinent issues or tasks the counselee currently struggles with? What statements, anecdotes, or memories did the counselee relate immediately before describing the dream?

3) Listen to the dream, then summarize it to yourself and perhaps to the counselee. To summarize a dream, try to paraphrase the essence of the dream in a single sentence.

4) Ask for clarification of any part of the dream that is obscure or ambiguous to you. You might ask the counselee for an interpretation, but regard the answer with caution.

5) Ask what the various figures in the dream remind the counselee of. Pay attention to the first words regarding any particular figure.

6) Ask about the counselee's feelings during the dream. Can the counselee recall a time in life that evoked the same feelings?

7) Ask the counselee to dream the dream again. Have the counselee do this with eyes closed, narrating the dream in the first person, present tense. Verbalizing a memory in this way makes it immediate.

8) Close your eyes and picture the dream as the counselee relates it; be aware of your own impressions, associations, and feelings.

9) Depending on what unfolds, ask the counselee to have a dialogue with dream figures, to play-act certain figures, or to allow a guided daydream to take place.

10) Be prepared to be more active in later parts, talking to dream characters or suggesting what to say to characters. Pray all the time, and treat all the figures with Christian respect.

11) By now, the counselee will be deeply engrossed in innermost psychological processes; it may be appropriate to simply be quiet, periodically asking, "What's happening now?" Spontaneous realizations, the sudden recall of forgotten memories, or spontaneous utterances of phrases that point to life scripts are common at this time. The counselor's repeated question, "What's happening now?" implicitly urges the counselee's unconscious to keep observing and to keep working.

12) The previous steps will have given the counselor a great deal of data. Integrating these data yields at least an approximately accurate

interpretation as to what is going on. Essentially, the counselor clusters in reverse to make these guesses or interpretations.

The following situation illustrates these 12 steps. I taught a course in Ericksonian hypnotherapy to a group of marriage and family counselors, psychologists, and clergy. During a session on dreams, one participant volunteered to work on one of her dreams.

An attractive 40-year-old woman, Judy was very talented, motivated, and intelligent. She reported a dream in which she discovered that a pet snake had an infection rimming its mouth. In the dream, the snake looked at her with pleading eyes. She reported that the dream disturbed her. We agreed to work with the dream in front of the group:

1) *My nervousness in front of the group made me especially motivated to pray for our Lord's help.*

2) *The context of the dream was clear to me. Judy was deeply committed to learning and practicing psychotherapy; her enrollment in the course was an example of that devotion.*

3) *As I listened to the dream, I summarized it to myself. "Something I am supposed to take care of has fallen ill, and it accuses me."*

4) *Clarification of dream content furthered the idea that she was supposed to be taking care of the snake.*

5) *Inquiry into what the snake reminded her of led to her describing the snake as a pet of her daughter's but with the care falling to Judy.*

6) *Judy reported her feelings in the dream as anguish and concern for the snake, laced with guilt at letting the creature get sick.*

7) *I asked Judy to close her eyes and dream the dream again, making the dream a current experience by relating it to me in the first person present tense. She replied, "I am in my kitchen. My daughter brings in her pet snake from the garage. I am appalled to see that its mouth is rimmed with an infection. It pleads with me with its eyes for help. I feel I have failed it."*

8) *As Judy dramatized her dream, I closed my eyes and pictured it. A vivid memory came to my mind of the sinking feeling I experienced when I discovered that my son's goldfish were dead.*

9) *I asked Judy to speak to the snake, to have a dialogue with it to tell it how she felt. "I've failed you; I haven't given you everything you've needed." Then she burst into tears.*

10) *At this point, I felt I knew what was going on and could offer an interpretation.*

11) *Essentially, I had clustered in reverse to put it together. I said, "I think you are*

12) *feeling very responsible for the well-being of your clients, so much so that you blame yourself when they don't do well. Really, all you can do is do your best and pray. The rest is up to your client and God." She relaxed, dried her tears, said, "I can see I've been pressuring myself too much, losing sleep over my clients. I'm sure that I can now keep a better balance." Later, she reported feeling more at peace, with a sense that God was in charge.*

4. Using Dreams Indirectly

The direct method of working with a dream is not always necessary or desirable. The counselor might simply note without comment the report of a dream, instead using the dream along with other data to *cluster in reverse*, thereby coming to some conclusion regarding the counselee's heart. Or, the counselor might choose to work within the metaphor the dream portrays, as in the following dream:

I admitted a 28-year-old woman to a psychiatric hospital. Married and a mother of four, she was involved in a lesbian relationship that was disrupting her marriage. Her frame of mind was one of chaos. At the end of the initial interview, she reported a dream in which she was "drowning in a universe of blood." I was struck by such a graphic image. Later that week, I happened on a print by Klee, a surrealist painting that showed a small boat floating on a sea of red. I bought the

print and hung it on my office wall. At the woman's next ap-
pointment, I pointed to the picture and asked what she thought
of it. She gasped, and as she stared at it, I pointed to the boat
and said simply, "That's Christ." Months later and improv-
ing, she remarked, "I'm keeping close to Christ."

I did not know the meaning of her dream. Rather, I simply used her symbolism to make a point. She could be trusted to supply meaning to the intervention.

In summary, dreams are internal representations of our crucial interpersonal relationships. They are problem-solving devices in which difficulties in these relationships can be dramatized. Dreams often contain statements of core conflicts. A knowledge of and skill with dreams offer the Christian counselor a marvelous opportunity to first know and then speak to the heart of the counselee.

Exercises

1. Create a dream, then ask a partner to interpret it. To create the dream, pray for a moment, then select an aspect of your relationship to God, to others, or to yourself. Choose a word or phrase that characterizes your choice and cluster around it. From somewhere in your cluster or from an intuitive flash, create your dream. Your partner can then plumb your dream.

2. Exercise 5 in Chapter one asked you to keep a journal of your dreams. With a partner, select several dreams, then practice summarizing them succinctly.

3. In summarizing dreams, note struggles or tension between figures. With the aid of your partner, play the part of opposing figures, staging a dialogue between the two of you. In addition, be each object, creature, or person in the dream: in a sense, *write a script* for each figure. Remember to pray constantly.

4. Select several dreams from your journal. Summarize them, and with summaries of other observations in your overall journal, make a list. Do not try to add up or synthesize your data; rather, submit the lists

prayerfully to God and your unconscious mind. Remember to consider your dreams in the context of your life and remember too that a particular context of your life is this book and your interest in Christianity and Change.

Suggested Reading

Peruse the various titles on dreams available at your local library. Read six, selecting a variety of theoretical orientations.

10

Assessing Interactional Systems

We tend to relate to one another in patterns, rather than randomly. When people meet, they quickly establish patterns of interaction, patterns that with time may become increasingly rigid and ingrained. If these patterns of behavior are fulfilling and reasonably open-ended, allow for individual expression, and enhance self-esteem, they produce peace and contentment. But if they are unfulfilling or negative, the result will be symptomatic thinking or behavior. Our selves are partially predicated on these sequences with important others, past and present, and they in turn influence these sequences. Our Lord makes clear that the particular behavioral sequences that comprise love, described for example in the parable of the good samaritan (Luke 10:25) and attitudinally in Paul's letter to the Corinthians (I Corinthians 13:4) are the behaviors commanded of us (John 13:34), for they lead to life. People seek counsel because their past or present patterns of interaction have frustrated the quest for life.

If we become who we follow, then it follows that those we interact with influence how we behave and, hence, what we become. In other words, if our identity or our genuine love for self rests on our relationships with God, neighbor, and self, then in working out our salvation we must attend to those relationships. The model of counseling presented here depends, in part, on rapidly diagnosing the key attitudes, premises, and relationships of the counselee: *the heart of the matter*. The core difficulty of the counselee will often pertain to interaction with *neighbor*. This chapter will consider seven aspects of family and other interactional systems:

137

- Circular causality in interactional systems

- Patterns in interactional systems

- The dialectics of family systems

- Intended solutions in family systems

- The struggle with uncertainty

- Uncertainty and undifferentiation

- The differentiation of self

Circular Causality in Interactional Systems

"Who is my neighbor?" asked the lawyer of Jesus (Luke 10:29). Certainly, the neighbors we know and contact most intimately and frequently are our families, past and present; our families of origin and our present families, parents, spouses, and children. Family systems theory describes the family as an operational system comprising individuals standing in consistent relationships with one another; the behavior of the family system is best understood as a product of its organizational characteristics. In other words, individuals within the system are not entirely free to behave according to their individually determined drives, motivations, and personality attributes; rather, the nature of the relationships they have with each other may constrain, encourage, or shape their behavior:

> *Bill, a 34-year-old Navy chief, was referred because of problem drinking. He admitted drinking, but cockily asserted he could quit anytime; he refused to go to Alcoholics Anonymous, and his drinking continued. Since Bill clearly did not plan to change, I talked with his wife, who had complained to me over the phone. Her appearance surprised me—a more passive person I had never seen. She described a pattern that had prevailed for years. Nearly every evening, Bill would come home drunk and she would complain, whiningly and ineffectually. She and I visited a few times, and we enabled her to resolve some of her masochism and formulate an effective*

response. In a climactic confrontation, she said to Bill in a
tiny voice, "Honey, I have some news for you: I'm training for
a job." The chief turned white; he had gotten the message in-
stantly. Shortly thereafter, he entered an AA program.

Thus, symptomatic behavior can be seen as the product of the various in-
teractive relationships and organizational characteristics of a family (or
even a culture as a whole) rather than of some linear, casual chain of
events. However that may be, in the above example I failed to move Bill
by appealing to his sense of responsibility, while his wife succeeded at a
different level.

Patterns in Interactional Systems

The patterns of interactional systems are living patterns comparable
to organisms. A central dynamic fuels the pattern, while the participants, through their efforts to foster or resist change, create a circular
process, a dissatisfying equilibrium. Examples are found in those disorders that occur at about the time a young adult should be leaving home.
Outbreaks of symptomatic behavior or thinking are very common during
that age range, approximately from 17 to 22. Haley (1980) postulates
that such disruptions as antisocial behavior, psychotic breakdowns, in-
volvements in cults, anorexia nervosa, and the simple refusal to leave the
home to work all have in common an intentional element to occupy the
family's attention and to divert it from strife in the marriage.

Tim, 19, had done well in high school but had shunned college
to work for a soft drink distributor. He did so well that he was
promoted to route deliveryman. After several successful
months at this job, he chanced to take out a young woman,
who, during the date, said, "I'm going with Joe. Watch out,
he's mean; if he knows we're together he'll get you." Since
Joe worked at a liquor store on Tim's route, Tim became panic
stricken. The next day, during a delivery to Joe's store, Tim
had a full-scale panic attack even though Joe never said a
word about the date or implied he knew of it. As time went by,
Tim experienced increasing panic attacks, quit his job, began

to stay in his room, became depressed, and finally attempted suicide. Only then did he consent to see me. He suffered from agoraphobia, with anxiety attacks occurring in crowds, in closed spaces, and while driving. Tim avoided such places and situations, instead preferring to stay at home.

We worked in early sessions to help him cope with his anxiety. During one of our meetings, he remarked that shortly before the event with Joe, an incident involving his parents had shaken him. A friend had suggested that they share an apartment, but his mother had strongly opposed this plan, causing him to abandon the idea. Soon thereafter he broke down. In a subsequent meeting with the whole family, I observed what proved to be a typical interaction. Father opened with a long pep talk, telling his son he could do anything, that he was very talented, etc. Tim listened impassively. Mother finally interrupted, with irritation, to state that she understood Tim's phobic condition since she too had broken down some years earlier. Father then angrily accused her of overprotecting Tim and of undoing his efforts, to which she retorted that he was insensitive and harsh. Tim finally interrupted to say that he was trying. All were then silent. They agreed that they had played this scenario numerous times. In a later session, Tim reported another conflict with his parents: at Christmastime, his parents had insisted he go with them to visit his grandmother, but he had wished, instead, to visit his girlfriend. His anxiety mounted with this conflict, a conflict I saw as metaphoric of the family's problem.

The cases of Bill and Tim illustrate several characteristics of troubled family interactions. Each showed a kind of arrested development of the family unit: a fixation on maintaining recurrent although dissatisfying patterns of interaction. Each communicated verbally and nonverbally in a circular, repetitive fashion, with each participant's actions or reactions cementing and polarizing the other's position until the limits of tolerance had been exceeded.

In both examples, at least one family member sought change, yet the very attempts to change tended to worsen the situation. Watzlawick, *et al.* (1974) discuss two levels of change—first and second order change. In first order change, alterations occur within a system while the system itself remains intact. The chief's wife attempted to change her husband or their relationship by being *more* giving, more loving, more helpful, more submissive. Her first-order attempt at change was linear, a change in quantity, not quality; she used the same problem-solving strategy repeatedly, trying harder and harder over the years to be a *good* wife. The attempt was first-order because the structure of the interaction between husband and wife remained constant.

The second example, involving three people, is more complex. Elements of first order change are seen in the parents' attempts to change themselves and to resist change, and in Tim's attempts to help in their marriage. The possibility of second order change appears as Tim breaks down. Weeks and L'Abate (1982) refer to second order change as a change in the system itself, where the system is transformed structurally or communicationally. Such change can be sudden and unexpected, radical, discontinuous, and not logically predictable. In Tim's family, his breakdown, occurring after he realized he was not free to leave, represented a kind of *reductio ad absurdum* that forced the family to get help. Opening the family system to outside help and learning new information constituted another form of second order change. With help and new ideas, each family member in the system at large can initiate novel and successful attempts at change.

The Dialectics of Family Systems

Watzlawick, *et al.* (1974), describe the systems basis for dysfunction, its relationship to first and second order change, and how their theory of change is related to dialectics. They summarize this relationship as follows:

> An *Event A* is about to take place, but *A* is undesirable. Common sense suggests its prevention by means of the reciprocal not-*A*, but this would merely result in a first order change solu-

tion. As long as the solution is sought within this dichotomy of *A* and not-*A*, the seeker is caught in an illusion of alternatives and he remains caught whether he chooses the one or the other. It is precisely this unquestioned illusion that one has to make a choice between *A* and not-*A*, that there is no other way out of the dilemma, which perpetuates the dilemma and blinds us to the solution which is available at all times, but which contradicts common sense. The formula of second order change, on the other hand, is not *A* but also not not-*A* . . . philosophically the same principle is the basis of Hegelian dialectics with its emphasis on the process that moves from an oscillation between thesis and antithesis to the synthesis transcending this dichotomy.

Polarization, such as seen in Bill's case, is of particular interest. Even as the relationship deteriorates to the point of rupture, one person comes or continues to dominate completely while the other submits completely. Or one may come to overfunction while the other suffers dysfunctions. Every counselor should be wary of a person who comes complaining of the dysfunction of another since it may be that it is the relationship that is dysfunctional, as well as its participants.

Liz, 30, complained of her husband's recurrent depressions, pleading that if he could be helped with medication he would be easier to live with. Her husband, Mark, agreed wholeheartedly that he was depressed, adding that many in his family had also suffered from depression. I placed him on antidepressant medication, and he improved markedly. But Mark returned in three months to report that, in spite of his improved outlook, his wife had left him. In another case, Dan dutifully brought his agoraphobic and almost totally disabled wife to me. Helen responded beautifully to treatment, whereupon Dan left for another woman. Apparently, when it is the dominant partner who has the symptoms, moving the relationship to a more equal footing reduces stress and improves the relationship. But when it is the other way around, improvement can increase the stress in the relationship.

Intended Solutions in Family Systems

The intended solutions that those within a family system adopt form the matrix of patterns in families and contribute in circular fashion to the problems that necessitated the solutions. Intended solutions are each person's contribution to the dialectics of the system. People and groups habitually rely on particular responses or strategies to meet challenges. Bowen's reciprocity (Hall, 1983) is an example: the relationship of the overadequate with the inadequate. In a flexible system, such differences can provide balance. But with those who too rigidly adhere to one solution, a polarization of overfunction and dysfunction can predominate.

> *The Johnsons had fought bitterly for years. In a couples' group, the husband passionately described his efforts to make his wife happy. A woman in the group angrily challenged him, asserting that he could not do it, that his wife would have to find happiness on her own. When he subsequently gave up this "benign" domination of his wife, her functioning improved and the fighting lessened.*

The Struggle with Uncertainty

Conflicts inevitably complicate the relationships of those who marry. Young people bring to their marriages the styles of conflict and reconciliation they learned in their families of origin. Whatever balances they achieved, the turmoil created by inner and outer uncertainties will stress those balances. *Inner uncertainties* arise as a person begins to experience the myriad complexities of mental functioning, such as doubt, impulses, fears, compulsions, aberrations, addictions, and the like. *External uncertainties* pertain to such life complications as loss: loss of health, loved ones, spouse, job, youth, *etc.*

People in the *self-sufficient* stage of spiritual development will attempt to utilize various methods of control to manage conflict and dispute. The emergence of inner or outer uncertainties will heighten those maneuvers and probably be combined with a *denial* that the maneuvers are taking place at all. These maneuvers will have a remarkable effect on children and on the family system. They will produce what Bowen calls the *undifferentiated family ego mass*, a term describing the overwhelming and confusing emotional climate that envelops each participant in the system, a kind of fixation *en masse*. This can enmesh all members with one another or can lead to detachment and alienation. Either configuration can contribute to various symptoms in the offspring.

From the struggle with uncertainty, parents and then the family as a whole may generate solutions or ways of coping with the stresses of everyday life. Of the many possible coping patterns that families might adopt, a few are listed below as examples:

- Banding together as a solution, or the *us against the world* approach. Boundaries between the family and the outside world are emphasized. Loyalty is prized. Individuality and leaving home are discouraged.

- Keeping the rules as a solution, or the *legal* solution. Legalism is prominent. These families may use religious systems or doctrine to attempt to control self or children.

- Lying and deceit as a solution, or the antisocial solution. The view is to bend the rules when necessary since it's a dog-eat-dog world. This approach is guaranteed to produce progressively more antisocial offspring.

- Blame as a solution. In this solution, a scapegoat is sought to blame for the family difficulties. This often produces a symptomatic child who is the family's *identified patient*.

- Pride as a solution. *I'm always right!* is what the parents convey. This will lead to strong feelings of guilt and frustration in the offspring.

- Isolation as a solution. With this approach, feelings are concealed, conflict is avoided, and communication is sparse and superficial.

A relatively normal family probably resorts to one or more of these daily but in combination with the healthy solutions of confronting and working through conflicts; admitting guilt where appropriate; seeking outside help; and submitting to and calling upon God in Christ, both in prayer and in the church.

> *At a church retreat, we were asked to graph our spiritual growth, noting the critical junctures. As I graphed mine, I recalled the chaos and stress of the early years. Then I vaguely recalled being baptized when I was about seven. I had the distinct impression that my family had stabilized after that event, which marked the beginning of the family's spiritual life.*

Uncertainty and Undifferentiation

Families just beginning their spiritual development have not discovered the resources of faith and belief. Without such resources and faced with uncertainty, such families may tend to cling to or manipulate one another, blurring the boundaries between members and leading to the family coming to function as an *undifferentiated ego mass*. In other words, family members cease, to some extent, to think for themselves. Rather, each reacts according to the prevailing emotional climate of the family. Bowen uses the term *undifferentiated* to describe a person's propensity to be absorbed or dominated by the emotional forces that spring from the family's aggregate system of *intended solutions*.

Family systems, in times of uncertainty, may resort to three particular intended solutions that will increase the degree of undifferentiation: *triangling, emotional cutoff*, and *family myths* or *secrets*. These solutions all blindly attempt to avoid the pain of change. They are short term solutions that in the long run predispose families and offspring to more uncertainty and anxiety. Each is examined below.

Married people normally relate to each other, but in times of conflict might irrationally involve a third person. *Triangling* is an intended solution to conflict which temporarily reduces tension but at the cost of avoiding any confrontation that could lead to creative change. The extramarital affair is a prime example. Husband and wife are at impasse. Either's involvement with another can create peace for a time.

Other combinations of triangles are possible. Husband or wife could involve friends or extended family who might offer advice, usually *derogatory* to the absent party. Children are available for triangling. A parent might seek solace in a child or target a child for abuse. Or, parents might avoid conflict by focusing on some defect in the child, the child becoming the symptom-bearer of a problematic relationship. Parents together might idealize another child, who then becomes the family hero. Children can quickly adapt themselves to such roles as hero, rescuer, entertainer, or troublemaker, thereby diverting tension from the marriage. All these maneuvers allow for the avoidance of issues between husband and wife.

Gossip is a relationship between two people built around discussing a third person and derogating that person in some manner. A dysfunctional family could have several shifting triangles, allowing the gossipers to avoid their own sins and uncertainties about themselves and create a pseudo-intimacy with each other. But since true intimacy, built on love, openness, and truth, is negated, the result is stultification. Racial and/or religious prejudice is yet another example of triangling. Triangling can be seen as a family maneuver to avoid the anxiety of some particular uncertainty; it is an intended solution to a problem of life that will ensnare its users. Triangling can become a chronic, dysfunctional pattern that prevents the resolution of marital difficulties and makes it difficult or impossible for children to leave home.

> *Kevin, 35 and married, had complained for years of homosexual impulses that conflicted with his religious beliefs and interfered with his sexual adjustment within marriage. As we discussed his family of origin, it became clear that his grandmother, mother, and aunt had regularly confided in him their opinions about the others while his father had been a peripheral, usually absent figure. Furthermore, this multiple, shifting triangling had continued to the present. When I described the pattern as triangling, Kevin asked me to explain. I replied, "You've been the recipient of gossip from the women in your family." He blushed and replied, "For years I've prayed for relief from my own compulsion to gossip!"*

Emotional cutoff is another approach to solving or coping with a lack of differentiation or individuation. In this solution, a person deals with unresolved fusion to the family of origin by cutting himself off emotionally or physically. The person might physically leave for good or might just minimize contacts with family members. Such emotional withdrawal can achieve the same distance as a physical one. The more intense the emotional fusion the person experienced while growing up, the greater the likelihood of a significant cutoff later on.

Emotional cutoff in an interesting paradox: it simultaneously reflects, solves, and creates a problem. It reflects the problem of the underlying fusion between the generations. It solves a problem because, by avoiding emotional contact, it reduces the anxiety of the moment. It creates a problem by isolating and alienating people from each other. Furthermore, once cut off from one another, people are vulnerable to equally intense fusions into other relationship systems. Those subsequent relationships, complicated by the preset thrust for fusion, would then be subject to the same maneuvers as the family of origin: triangling and/or cutoff.

Lastly, families may try to conceal their uncertainties, particularly those arising from the deviant actions of one or more members, by establishing *family myths* or *family secrets*. This solution often comes into being in families where there is spousal abuse, physical or sexual abuse of children, or alcoholism, or a combination thereof. Thus, an entire family might try to function by letting father's incestuous activity or mother's drinking problem go unnoticed or uncommented upon. The family functions as if it were normal. Significant pieces of reality must be corporately denied, however. For example, in a family where a parent periodically becomes intoxicated and violent, two rules might pertain: there is no problem in this family and do not comment upon it. Such unconscious denial or conscious deception can profoundly affect the offsprings' ability to perceive reality.

The Differentiation of Self

The differentiation of self involves both growing up and transcending the artificial limitations imposed by the expectations of family and culture. According to the Scriptures, our Lord grew up (Luke 2:52) and refused to be bound by the limiting patterns of nationalism (Matthew 22:21), materialism (Mark 4:19), conventional religion (Luke 6:6-11), egocentrism (Matthew 18:4), the wishes of the crowds (John 6:15), and family (Mark 3:31-35). He broke through any fear of rejection (John 8:28) and the fear of suffering and death (Luke 22:42). He found ultimate fulfillment in setting aside self will for the Father's will. He accomplished his absolute differentiation of self through his oneness with the Father.

Growing up is the working through of immature intended solutions—pride, denial, acting out, clinging, triangling, cutting others off, *etc.*—that hope to control others and deny one's brokenness. St. Paul said, "When I was a child, I spoke like a child, I thought like a child, I reasoned like a child; when I became a man, I gave up childish ways" (I Corinthians 13:11). It is possible to grow up without being a Christian; it is possible to be a Christian and not grow up. Those willing to work at their belief (John 6:27) will discover their capacity to learn (Matthew 7:7-8). The growing capacity to communicate with the Father will maximize growth, enhance creativity, and deepen the capacity to love. God in turn changes people in innumerable ways, among them by providing communion and strengthening love between couples and families far beyond their own abilities.

Suggested Reading

1. Bradshaw, John, *Bradshaw On: The Family,* Health Communications, Inc., Deerfield Beach, Florida, 1988.

2. Guerin, Philip J.; Fay, Leo F.; Burden, Susan L.; Kautto, Judith Gilbert, *The Evaluation and Treatment of Marital Conflict,* Basic Books, New York, 1987.

3. Palazzoli, M. S., Cirillo, S., Selvini, M., Sorrentino, A. M., *Family Games: General Models of Psychotic Processes in the Family,* W. W. Norton and Co., New York, 1989.

11

Assessing Resources

What is within people that can aid them in changing their hearts and world views? As Christians, we may find it all too easy to focus on the negative, on our struggle and the struggles of others with sin, evil, loss, and death in their various forms. The world, the flesh, and the devil represent an unholy trinity, a compelling one to fix on. Emphases on confession, contrition, and self-sacrifice all carry implications of the struggle with the darker side of life. Jungian psychologists remind us of our *shadows,* while Freudians tell us our ids boil with lust and aggression. Lent, as a penitential season, reminds us to prepare and cleanse ourselves, the season culminating in the shining forth of Jesus Christ. So far in this book, the techniques for coming to know the heart of another lead usually to the heartache, loss, doubts, misery, and defenses that complicate people's lives. And, although assessing people along the continua of their spiritual, personal, and family developmental lines emphasizes the value of learning and the hope of growth while discouraging judgmentalism, those same assessments still focus on the *deficits* of personal functioning.

But our counselees' hearts have another side, one that contains positive aspects, perhaps eclipsed by the negatives with which they struggle. We are basically good, though fallen, and possess constructive and creative, although often latent, qualities. Even though the road to hell may be paved with good intentions, at least something *good* is implied. In our counselees, we can easily begin to take note of their positive attributes: belief, trends toward faith, loyalty, a willingness to lead or to serve, honesty, forthrightness, ingenuousness, love, generosity, compassion, curiosity, humor, and many others. We can detect these qualities, however nascent or hidden, in the counselee's body language and voice inflection and in the implications of their stories, reminiscences, dreams, and other metaphors, particularly those uttered spontaneously. Specifically, every person desiring change has available the ability to think deeply; to believe and pray; to draw on personal experiences, interests, and strengths; to view symptoms as assets; and to take advantage of relational ability and humor. Let us examine each in some detail.

The Ability to Think Deeply

The first resource needed to promote change is one's God-given intelligence, creative ability, imagination, and ability to learn. When one begins to bring these assets to bear, the result is often the start of constructive change. Interfering with the ability to think deeply are fantasies of magically being taken care of and the pathological defenses discussed in Chapter 7.

> *A constantly unemployed man made no progress in psychotherapy. During one session, he pulled a picture out of his wallet and showed it to me. "It's a ship," I said. "Yes'" he replied, "It's my ship; I'm waiting for it to come in."*

If the counselor notices a failure to close interview cones or detects magical thinking or pathological defenses, these must be confronted if any progress is to be made. The art of confrontation is discussed in detail in Chapter 13. Confrontation often allows the counselee to set aside defenses, thereby enabling him or her to use the ability to think deeply.

The Ability to Believe and Pray

Oddly enough, *brokenness* is a remarkable asset. The broken, shorn of any illusions of omnipotence and having given up trying to survive by controlling others, often turn to God in prayer, exercising their belief, however small. Their recovery will be organized around and will in turn augment that faith and belief. In my practice, people are referred to me without any forewarning that I am a Christian; most come to me requesting help, knowing nothing about me. Yet I would estimate that ninety percent believe and, in the midst of their breakdown, have been calling on that belief. The simple conclusion is that people in trouble pray more, are more motivated to believe, and hence are more open to God. The counselor should gratefully acknowledge, accept, and utilize such offerings.

The following case history illustrates how, with the patient who believes, God, therapist, and patient can organize and direct the therapy around that belief, with healing of the heart occurring rapidly.

> *Bob, a married man of 35 with two children, had been coerced by his wife into coming to see me. He frequently exhibited himself and was a voyeur. While driving to and from work, he would pull up beside a car occupied by a woman and begin to masturbate; he had masturbated frequently since adolescence. He had peeped in windows earlier, then in recent years confined his interest to pornographic literature. He had a compulsion to undress women mentally from a distance. He had never been arrested, but he lived in terror of getting caught. His wife knew of his exhibitionism and voyeurism and resented him deeply; they fought frequently and had had no sexual relations in over a year. Although he described himself as struggling to cope with life and felt terrible about himself, he could not stop his behavior. He had converted to Christ two years before, attended church and Bible study regularly, and prayed often that he would not be attracted to women. However, his symptoms continued unabated. Before becoming a Christian, he had thought nothing of his problem and in fact had enjoyed his behavior; only after his conversion had he begun to worry.*

> *We spent three hours plumbing his background, his marriage, and his motivation for change. Although he had come to counseling under duress after a particularly bitter argument with his wife, he conveyed a wish to resolve his troubles. He had marked difficulty communicating his ideas, feelings, and imaginings, being quite shy and nonverbal. I had to work hard to discern his intentions.*

His mother had dominated his family of origin. His father's primary wish seems to have been to punish him, but his mother would not allow it. Father was allowed to sit next to him at meals, to control his eating habits, and to correct his bad manners. His mother would baby his father, but would periodically put her foot down. His father was content to spend most of his time watching television. In this bleak environment, our counselee became "a skinny kid whom others made fun of, a boy with few friends."

As the therapy phase of our counseling relationship began, I began to utilize his belief and faith by reframing his voyeurism and exhibitionism as efforts to see and be recognized. He was astonished at my ascribing some good intent to his actions; he thought of himself as merely a worthless pervert. Furthermore, reframing his actions as a wish to be recognized fit with his lifelong awareness that recognition was exactly what he sought. Since recognition is the first step in nurture, I told Bob that as he was newly adopted into a family where God is his father and mother, he could begin to internalize the nurture this new family offered. To aid him in this learning of the heart, I gave him a task to set him on his way.

I directed him to try each night to dream of eating good food. I explained that this strange sounding request had a very specific purpose. As a child he had internalized his parents and the deficient nurture they had provided him. In other words, he had from the beginning painted within his heart portraits of his parents, images depicting his interpretations of their actions. These images of his father and mother eventually became an integral part of his self-image. Since he had been adopted by grace into God's family, he could begin to change these images into images more congruent with the being of his heavenly father and mother. Since food is a convenient and universal symbol of nurture, by asking to dream of eating good food he would, in a sense, be asking his heart to accept and believe the reality of his nurture. That is, good food was to symbolize the nurture of the good mother. I told him it was no accident that the major sacrament of the church was one of feeding. Although he initially understood little of what I said, he agreed to try to dream of eating good food as I had suggested.

He returned the following week to report a series of unusual dreams. He had dreamed of trying to build an airline terminal out of a shack in a thick forest but a bear kept running through, interfering with his work. In what seemed like another dream, other men had been building a terminal and a runway in a flat area near a lake. We worked with these dreams (see Chapter 9), but he had no ability to make associations to the dreams. He did remark, however, that the men in the second dream had a more realistic plan than his. I directed him to again try to dream of eating good food.

He returned the next week in a good mood, reporting that for the first time in recent memory and for almost the whole week he had been free of any desire to exhibit himself. He had no explanation for his improvement. He then reported dreaming of being in charge of a church project for distributing food to the needy, but of being interrupted when he was about to make a delivery. Noting that the theme of being interrupted or interfered with ran through his dreams, I asked him, "What in your life interferes with your being nurtured?" He immediately replied with an anecdote of a recent visit from his mother. His mother completely ignored Bob's oldest child, a boy, but lavished gifts and attention on his baby girl. In a flash of insight, he traced the trait of preference for girls back several generations. Clearly, men were not in favor. He went on to say that it was now clear to him that the interference to his being nurtured was his own conviction that he was unlovable, which was his interpretation of his mother's actions. In other words, if he could not imagine himself lovable, how could he see love if it were offered to him. With forgiveness in his voice, he stated that he now realized that it was his mother's problem, not his. He realized that his exhibitionism was a way of crying out for recognition, but also a way of expressing anger and defiance. Now, feeling fed as a part of God's family, he could forgive his mother. In a very real sense, Bob's faith had made him whole.

Experiences, Interests, Strengths

A person's metaphors and the self-descriptions in them can convey strengths and abilities. These recollections can be from the present, adult past, or even from childhood. Because early memories indicate a person's lifestyle, memories can be scrutinized not only for their clues to a person's impasses, but also for indications of strengths. So, like voice inflection, body language, and other metaphors, recollections from childhood can point to important abilities latent within a person. Dreams may also imply talents, either by virtue of their very creativity or by their content.

In the movie Amadeus, *Saliere, an Italian composer and contemporary of Mozart's, attempts suicide and is sent to an asylum. A young priest comes to hear Saliere's confession. Saliere states that he had declared war on God and destroyed Mozart because God had graced Mozart, not Saliere, with musical genius. He goes on to describe Mozart's genius in great detail. The priest is left speechless, and Saliere exits contemptuously absolving all, saying, "Mediocrity, I absolve thee." Now, suppose that our priest, refusing to be so quickly defeated, had decided to return and confront Saliere. What might he have said that would have made a difference? I envision something like the following, "Saliere, I have heard your confession. At first thought, one might accuse you of envy, but I don't think that was your real failure. You feel God cheated you of talent, but I say you failed to utilize the talent God gave you, that of understanding Mozart as nobody else did, and thereby cheated yourself. But you can still redeem*

*yourself; just as you enlightened me with the story of Mozart,
go out now and enlighten others."*

The presence of such positives in the personality is not surprising: "And God saw everything that he had made, and behold, it was very good" (Genesis 1:31). A person can easily be blind to particular qualities of goodness in personality, by focusing instead on its deficiencies, and on solutions intended to avoid, deny, or correct that deficient self. The average counselee may have lost sight of anything positive, having reacted to impasses with sins by despairing and regarding that part which was negative as the whole self. Psychotherapy, in competent hands, has been able to help people resolve underlying depressions and unproductive intended solutions, allowing creativity to flourish. But for the truest self to emerge, the positive parts of the personality must crystallize and grow around a central core. That central core, which is within us all if we will only tap it, is the kingdom of heaven.

Assessing the resources of a counselee refers as much to our own attitude toward that person as to the pinpointing of specific positives. Reframing in counseling is an art that simultaneously involves a counselor's positive attitude; the recognition and accessing of some positive feature of the counselee; and a therapeutic technique promoting reflection, insight, and change in the counselee.

Reframing: Symptoms as Resources

Reframing is the counselor's deliberate attempt to affect a counselee's attitudes toward a relationship, an event, or some aspect of the counselee's own thoughts or actions. Remember that our hearts comprise our attitudes toward life, the world around us, and ourselves. Reframing is an interpretation or empathic statement with a twist: it transmits a sudden, surprising, positive valence to something the counselee saw in a negative light.

Winnicott (1971) describes working with a teenage boy who was stealing. The boy had lost his father some months earlier, and the stealing had begun thereafter. The family was upstanding and the boy himself had never shown antisocial manifestations before. The family became enraged at the child and threatened to expel him. Winnicott reframed the boy's stealing as an attempt to reach back and regain for himself the lost object—his father—or the part of himself that he felt he had lost when his father died. This allowed the family to see the boy as hurt rather than bad and to begin to believe in him again. The boy, now armed with an explanation that implied his love for his father but did not support continued stealing, decided to change.

Suppose that the boy's family had displayed many antisocial tendencies. Then the boy's stealing could have been reframed as an attempt to call attention to a pathological system. If instead there had been no discernible reason for his stealing, the boy might have been congratulated for letting himself get caught by yielding to an unconscious morality and asked rhetorically how many times he would wisely get caught before he *consciously* embraced his good morals.

In practice, we seldom know why people misbehave, and even the person in question is unlikely to know. But it is reflex to ascribe madness or badness to deviant thinking, behavior, or actions we do not understand. Reframing does not excuse *mad* or *bad* behavior, but rather transmits that the counselor refuses to give up on and insists on believing in the counselee. As another example, consider the following case.

Jack, a paranoid schizophrenic, told me of voices that called him "queer" and "cocksucker" and urged him to homosexual activity. I asked him if he had ever been afraid he was a homosexual. He replied that he had tried it once in response to his insistent voices but had found it repugnant. Jack's psychosis had worsened after this one homosexual encounter. I told him I did not think he was a homosexual. I speculated that he had probably felt insecure about himself as a man, felt unmanly, and had equated that feeling with homosexuality and, hence, had concluded that he must be a homosexual. But since his system rejected this, the fear haunted him in the form

> *of accusatory voices. He was delighted with the interpretation and blurted out, "I'd like to suck your cock!" Unruffled, I replied, "That means your are feeling fed by me!" This delighted him even more; with these reframings as a turning point, Jack went on to improve markedly.*

Reframing—ascribing constructive intent to chaotic thinking or destructive behavior—can surprise the counselee and cast doubt onto previously dark self-evaluations and make the counselee more receptive to further suggestions or confrontations. But such explicit suggestions or confrontations may be unnecessary because in accepting a reframing, the counselee also accepts the implicit idea that there are better ways to accomplish goals.

The counselor may use various types of reframing maneuvers:

- Reframing can emphasize a positive aspect of a person's actions while downplaying a negative one. An example is Saliere in *Amadeus*. Focusing on Saliere's strength, while mentioning his sin only to bypass it, would allow the counselor to assign a task that Saliere just might carry out, to his lasting benefit or even salvation.

- Reframing can move from a negative, concrete situation to a positive if the situation is taken metaphorically. For example, after Jesus fed the 5,000 (John 6:10-15), the crowd wanted to seize him and make him king. Although the crowd certainly misunderstood Jesus, they were on the right track, because Jesus certainly wants us to crown him king now. Reframing, then, utilizes the ambiguity inherent in most thought and experience. John's gospel is full of such ambiguity.

- The reframer can often find positives in the fundamental motivations of the counselee. For example, I frequently use Biddle's (1957) reframing of the Oedipal complex. Freud declared that children universally desire sexual intercourse with the parent of the opposite sex; with maturity, the person renounces this desire, identifies with the same-sex parent, and achieves genital intimacy with a peer. Biddle asserted that what children actually desire is *communion* with both parents, and the blessing of the same-sex parent to commune with the opposite-sex parent. The child imagines this communion, in fantasy, as an entering into the body of the parent. Freud mistook a fantasied communion as a sexual act, something that the small child does not want.

- In somewhat the same vein, I regularly reframe a parent's critical attacks on a child as attempts to hold on.

Beverly, age 40, occasionally received calls from her mother, who would proceed to ridicule her and find fault with her. Beverly followed these calls with drinking episodes and suicide attempts. She was convinced her mother despised her. I disagreed and asserted that her mother feared abandonment; her attacks on Bev were derivatives of a desire to cling to her. Of course, by her behavior, her mother was bringing about the very thing she feared the most. I gave Bev the task of interrupting her mother's attacks with the statement, "Mother, I will never abandon you." This stunned and derailed her mother, who, after receiving this intervention a few times, toned down her attacks. The two women became closer, and Beverly's symptoms ceased. The undifferentiated person almost by definition is not skilled in letting go, instead trying to control his or her own destiny and the destinies of others by dictating, criticizing, and manipulating.

- The Christian reframer has an opportunity for reframing that is not available to the secular counselor. Recalling that the heart has to do with relationships with God, neighbor, and self, the Christian counselor can reframe struggles with neighbor or self as pertaining to attempts to find God. An addiction to drugs or sex, for example, might be reframed as attempts, however misguided, to create some

kind of connection with God. The Scriptures record
numerous examples of reframing. For example, religious
persecution is reframed as something to be glad for in
Matthew 5:11-12.

Utilization, a therapeutic technique derived from assessing resources
and reframing, is the art of seizing on some positive aspect or ability,
then assigning a task that utilizes that ability to move toward a desired
goal. Utilization is mentioned here to underscore the value of recognizing a counselee's strengths. Erickson (1967) originated this maneuver,
and in his practice he regularly recognized skills, opinions, and attributes
that could be used to propel a person toward health. The following
vignette illustrates the technique and its relationship to resources and
reframing:

*At one point in his career, Erickson traveled widely, conduct-
ing workshops in clinical hypnosis in major cities throughout
the United States and the world. Before a trip to Minneapolis,
a physician friend told Erickson of his concern for his sister,
who lived in Minneapolis. A woman in her 50s, she lived
alone and had largely withdrawn from the world. Erickson
consented to call on her while in Minneapolis. In talking with
her, he learned that her only outing each week was attendance
at an Episcopal church. For the remainder of the week, she
isolated herself, occupying her time growing a myriad of
African violets. Erickson's first move was to reframe her
withdrawal as depriving the other church members of her company. After castigating her for her unfair treatment of her
church family, he persuaded her to carry out the following
task: she was to attend every baptism, wedding, and funeral in
the next month, taking with her an African violet to give to the
participants. At last report, she was deeply involved in church,
attended every function, was much revered, and was known as
the "African violet lady."*

Relational Ability

The ability to relate to others is an important resource in a counselee; the outgoing person frequently improves substantially in counseling of almost any kind. However, as might be expected, it is more often the person with some limitation in relational ability that seeks counsel. It is presumed in this section that everyone wants to relate, but that some need help in overcoming obstacles. Once such people start to relate, they begin to change within. The main obstacle to relating is the defense mechanism of distancing. The following example illustrates this:

> *Nancy, an attractive woman of 35, had isolated herself in her apartment for ten years following a divorce, leaving only to go to work. Raised by an attacking, narcissistic mother, she felt powerless and vulnerable. In counseling, she gradually improved and involved herself in activities, but the recognition of a particular pattern of withdrawal allowed us to make a vital step forward. On several occasions, I had observed her become literally unavailable during our sessions: she would actually go into a trance if threatened in some way. She perceived any situation in which she felt intellectually inferior as threatening. This behavior, which we labeled "crawling into a cave," happened repeatedly for varying periods. I congratulated her on this remarkable ability to move so quickly into and out of a trance. Once aware of the pattern, she began to renounce "the cave" and learned that she was not so intellectually inferior after all.*

Humor as a Resource

Humor is a marvelous resource that we all possess. It originates as language develops in the child: we have all observed three-year-olds twisting words around in ways they consider hilarious. From then on, most children, even disturbed ones, spend immense amounts of time making jokes, clowning around, punning, and the like. For the adult locked in grim combat with impasses, humor offers welcome relief and can help the sufferer see problems in a softer light.

Although a method for using humor in an interview cannot easily put down on paper, spontaneous quips and puns or the sudden telling of a relevant joke can be helpful. I suppose that my own humor comes from the same source as my other creativity; in other words, God can be funny. In using humor, I often accept what a person tells me and then take the idea to its logical and often ridiculous, hence humorous, extreme. Behavior taken to absurd extremes often leads to breakdown and then change. Humor often seems able to accomplish similar change before actual behavior reaches extremes. Humor points out where things are going and by so doing often makes it unnecessary to go there. But humor should never detract from or otherwise be at the expense of the counselee. Some examples are given below to illustrate the constructive use of humor.

- At times a patient may be unable to resist the attack of a spouse or boss. At an appropriate time I might say, *illegitime non carborundum*. After allowing the person to stare blankly at me for a moment, I translate, "Don't let the bastards grind you down!"

- An embattled woman told me of dreaming that as she walked up a hill she was attacked by a dog, who tried to bite her. She retreated, cowed. I replied, "Tell the dog that if it's so hungry that it'll take a bite out of you, that it should team up with you, so that the two of you can forage together." The woman laughed heartily.

- Farrelly (1974) is a master of the absurd. For example, while working with a suicidal person, he will discuss ways of doing oneself in, concluding that the best way would be to put one's arm in a vise, then cut it off with a hacksaw. By the time he has finished his recommendation, the patient is probably in stitches.

The use of humor, like the other techniques described in this text, really derives from the life experiences and creativity of the counselor. Its use will come with practice.

Exercises

1. In groups of three, share a past failure, struggle, or embarrassing moment. Let the other two reframe the event in as many ways as possible, using the guidelines on pages 157-159.

2. Pair up with a classmate you know relatively well. Interview each other to grasp as many positives as can be found in a 20-minute period. Be sure to share favorite jokes. As you note positives, try to think of ways such resources could be marshaled to help overcome a difficulty.

Suggested Reading

1. Watzlawick, Paul; Weakland, John H.; Fisch, Richard; *Change: Principles of Problem Formation and Problem Resolution,* W.W. Norton, New York, 1974.

2. Biddle, W. Earl, "Images, the Objects Psychiatrists Treat," *Archives of General Psychiatry,* Vol. 9., No. 5, Nov. 1963.

12

Spiritual Approaches to Change

People seek counsel when they are at an impasse with some aspect of themselves or their relationships with others. Impasses may involve symptoms and situations such as fear, depression, destructive habits, unproductive modes of thinking, or unchanging interactions ranging from a problem-filled mother/daughter relationship to a family fixation spanning generations. Such situations change when people change the way they see or do things.

Taken together, attitudes and actions form patterns that are to some extent diagrammable and predictable. It is in this interrelatedness and predictability that can be found the key to all change: change a strategic part of a pattern, and the whole pattern will change. Consider the following example:

> *Ted, 40, compulsively chewed his fingernails. He tried painting his fingers with a foul-tasting material, but soon acquired a liking for it. Numerous other attempts also failed. But then he noted a key aspect of the pattern: after biting off a piece of nail, he would roll it about with his tongue for several minutes. He resolved to continue to bite his nails but to spit out the fragments immediately. Within four days he had stopped biting his nails. Ted had overcome an impasse by changing only one aspect of the pattern.*

The patterned activities of personal thought, interactions with others, and interactions with God all interlock. Some patterns are life enhancing, others impede the person's walk to salvation.

Specifically, how does our Lord change us? What is our role in the process of change? God changes us through speaking to us, confronting us, and working with us through life events and our own sins. God utilizes these things to help us learn, joining us in the person of the Son and infusing us with grace. Through the church, imperfect as it is, we are taught—we participate in our transformation by committing ourselves, working at our belief, praying, asking, seeking, knocking, thinking, and learning. Through all of this, we come to know the Father and the One who was sent, and we grow to love each other the way we are loved. Christian counseling and/or competent psychotherapy should augment and accelerate this process of spiritual growth.

The Christian counselor often must choose whether to focus on a counselee's spiritual life or on the specific temporal patterns leading to impasse.

> *During a class in pastoral counseling, a seminarian role-played a man in his late 20s who was separated from his wife. The ensuing dialogue made it clear that there was an issue other than his marital difficulty that the man wished to deal with. In turning to his priest to seek ideas on how to cope with his marriage, he was turning to God. Although he did not verbalize this, his body language and voice inflection implied a new openness to God.*

The counselee's relationship with God is the ultimate frame of reference for life and the solution of problems. When a person earnestly seeks God, when someone chooses to follow and center on Jesus Christ, forces within and outside the self are set in motion that will lead to radical changes in the person's world view and relationships to others. But the Christian counselor may also offer approaches or solutions to temporal problems that are specifically spiritual. Four of these spiritual approaches—evangelism, praying, meditation, and letter writing—are discussed below. All may pertain to the frame of reference or offer specific solutions.

Evangelism

How can you help a counselee commit to God? Is counseling even a fitting place for *evangelism?* But, if a counselee can realize such benefits from an improving relationship with God, how could we think of holding back? So the real question is what is appropriate evangelism in a counseling context. There are three approaches to evangelism in counseling, corresponding to the degree of receptivity of the counselee: *receptive, possibly receptive, or nonreceptive.*

The *receptive* counselee is in the breakdown stage of spiritual development. These are the people Jesus is talking about when he refers to the harvest (Matthew 9:36-38). Many come to counseling on the verge of or actively crying out to God. They have learned that their ability to control their own destiny and the destinies of others is quite limited; somehow they have turned to God rather than to suicide as the way out. The counselor can detect a person's readiness to deepen their spiritual walk by such simple questions as: "Can you tell me something of your religious background?" or, "How do you see God fitting into your current difficulty?"

Evangelism consists here of supporting and furthering the relationship with God by explaining how God is on our side, how the son came into the world to help us, how we are loved and forgiven, how we are reconciled, one to another, and how we can communicate with God and benefit from that guidance.

The *possibly receptive* are the second category. Perhaps parents or teachers intimidated them with religion in a misguided effort to control them. They often see God as vengeful, as *the god within,* as the projection of their own talion impulses. At any rate, they are people who would react negatively to evangelism in any other overt sense. The preferred approach is to help them close their interview cones, to appreciate fully their fixations (as listed in Chapter 2), to empathize with their loss and sense of abandonment, and to allow them to ventilate their resentments. These people feel alienated, abandoned, and distrustful; no wonder they *fear* God. Their first task is to trust the counselor. As trust develops, the counselor can begin to speak to the fixations. The primary fixation would be the feeling of alienation, the lack of permission to exist, and of feeling starved and not fed. At an appropriate time, the counselor might give a witness of God's invitation to join the family of the body of Christ, with the desire that the counselee not only exist but prosper. Assuming a firm therapeutic alliance, the counselee might feel safe in revealing a view of God as angry and vengeful. This would provide the counselor a perfect opportunity to contrast *the god within* with the person of Jesus. Although the counselee might express skepticism, the counselor can know a seed has been sown by speaking to the counselee's heart. The counselor could close with an explanation of forgiveness and an invitation for the counselee to forgive those who have caused harm.

Some have been so grievously wronged that they have difficulty forgiving. These might benefit from the story of Jesus and his forgiveness from the cross. How could Christ, during his very murder, say,

"Father, forgive them; for they know not what they do"
(Luke 23:34).

It could only be that he believed that his attackers could do better, and by forgiving he was holding out for the eventual emergence of his attacker's true selves. Such a story helps counselees see that their assailants, no matter how physically or emotionally brutal, really only wear masks that bury the part that belongs to God.

The third category of counselee, those *unreceptive* to the gospel, explicitly deny any spiritual interests. It is thus fruitless to offer direct Christian witness. Better to use empathy and active listening to let them close their own interview cones. Confrontation can also help. The more active counselor can speak indirectly to the heart, using stories, jokes, or tasks. Dream work, keeping within the metaphor, as with the Vietnam veteran described in Chapter 2, can help. In this way, the counselor, by interest, support, and advice, becomes a living parable. Only God and the counselee will know the effect on the counselee's ultimate fate.

> *A man with AIDS sought hypnosis for an intolerable itch that had brought him to seek medical attention in the first place. Although closed to God, he was open to my efforts to help him with hypnosis. In four sessions, his itch was gone.*
>
> *A woman suffering from cancer came to me for depression. Defiantly irreligious, she drank heavily and enjoyed promiscuity. She responded to my confrontation, empathy, and support by giving up her suicidal bent. She joined a hospice program and volunteered actively. She became a kind of "Auntie Mame" to her relatives and friends. I think that in her heart she is close to God, something consciously she would deny.*

In reality, any approach described for the possibly receptive or the nonreceptive could benefit the receptive person. In addition, three specific spiritual approaches might help the receptive and possibly receptive: (1) praying with a person, (2) leading a counselee in a meditation, and (3) writing a letter.

Praying with Another

Praying with another is an intervention used by Christians throughout the ages. Used at the right time and place, an appropriate prayer can reach then move the counselee's heart. Furthermore, by coming to know the heart of the counselee and specific fixations and intended solutions, the counselor can pray accurately and succinctly about the counselee's needs. In addition, having noted the counselee's manner of speaking and acting, noting metaphors and body language, the counselor can include some of these characteristics, thereby *matching* aspects of things dear to the counselee. Such a prayer can have a remarkable effect. The counselor can also touch or hold the hand of the counselee, hence *anchoring* his petitions:

> *Jim (described in Chapter 7) gave up pornography and stepped closer to God, but then immediately began to suffer intense panic. We traced the origins of his panic to an over-*

whelming fear of being alone. This fear came from his neurotic mother, who would cling to him, threatening to withdraw if he attempted to separate or grow up. In this situation of being "damned if he did, damned if he didn't," he had caved in to his mother's demands. Consequently, whenever he acted from his real self (committing himself to God, for example), it triggered the withdrawal of his mother image, causing him to feel intensely abandoned and hence to panic. At a point at which the Spirit moved us to do so, we prayed together. First, I asked if I could pray with him. Next, I took his hand, lifted it slightly, and prayed (I made a point of using his name in the prayer):

"Lord, we lift up Jim to you, especially the fear he feels when he is being dropped. You promised that when two or more of us pray together, you'd be in our midst. We know you are here. Reassure Jim that he is never alone. And give him a mother image that will support him. We pray in Jesus' name. Amen."

He went on to recover completely. As he left treatment, he told me how helpful that prayer had been.

The next example highlights the value of accessing a particular fixation and then offering a specific intervention.

Jeff, a 27-year-old Christian with a wife and two children, became depressed when he and his family moved into a new house. Long before his breakdown, he had been irritable, impatient, tense, and always in a rush. He was negative, dwelling on the what if's in the future and the if only's from the past. He searched for excellence and pressured himself with shoulds. He never knew his family. He contemptuously likened himself to his mother, whom he described as "clean, nagging, and nit-picking." Using the empty chair technique (Chapter 14), I asked him to have a dialogue with his mother. In the tearful exchange that followed, he related the pain and frustration of a lack of communion with the frantically busy woman. At this point I prayed with him, asking God to heal his hurt and give him peace. The effect was remarkable, and at our next meeting he described a new-found ability to stop the what if's and if only's.

In both cases, the prayers were accurate and timely and hence effective.

Meditating with Another

A meditation can also effectively reach the counselee's heart. In a meditation, a person can symbolically or metaphorically work on problems. For example, again let us consider the case of Jim, our reformed pornographer.

Having assessed Jim's heart, we might have used meditation to help him resolve his mother fixation, his resentment toward her, and his abandonment anxiety and depression. Having explained our objectives, we might have proceeded as follows.

Jim, I'd like to ask you to make yourself comfortable and close your eyes. To start off this meditation, I'd like to say a prayer. Picture the prayer, feel it, as I say it:

O God of peace, you have taught us that in returning and rest we shall be saved, in quietness and confidence shall be our strength; lift us by the might of your Holy Spirit to your presence, where we may be still, and know that you are God, through Christ our Lord.

So, Jim, feel yourself being lifted. Notice the quietness, then the stillness. Jim, as you relax there, you can know that Jesus is with you. And you can see him! He says,

"I am the door."

Let an image of a door come to your mind. Now walk through the door. Feel its texture and weight. Next, Jesus says,

"I am the light."

I don't know what kind of light you see, Jim, but by its light you can see a path, because Jesus says,

"I am the way."

Follow that path. Walk on it. As you do, you will find that it begins to climb steeply.

A steep climb perhaps suggests his effort to overcome his problem. However, the counselee will read into the scenario meanings important to him. The counselor need not and should not be exact.

Now, the climb is difficult. You notice, too, that you are burdened by your pack. It has several heavy objects in it. As you climb, you come to a shrine with an altar. You can leave your objects on that altar, if you choose.

Again, the counselee can assign his own meanings to those objects.

Now, you climb further. You come to a curious object by the path. A creature is fixed to a board by a large nail. The creature is alive, but in agony because of the nail. You pray, pull out the nail, and free the creature.

A metaphor for fixation. The counselor should choose a metaphor to which the counselee might relate.

You climb further, then come upon another structure by the path, something that looks like a cage or prison. It reminds you to confess your sins. As you do so, the door of the cage swings open. You climb higher and next find a ledger book. It has your name on it, and within it are listed the names of those who owe you. This is a place to forgive any whom you may resent. You climb still higher. Now you pass by a gorge; it is deep, dark, and full of frightening things. As you stare into it, fear grips you, but you suddenly remember the words of Psalm 23.

This might represent fear or depression. By mentioning Psalm 23, the counselee may recall those comforting words any time he feels depressed. By introducing such a healthy figure into an unpleasant pattern, the counselor changes the pattern permanently. Minimal changes in a pattern tend to spread, changing the whole pattern.

Feeling now that you can better face whatever that gorge symbolizes for you, you climb higher. Now you feel lighter and more alive. Ahead is the peak. As you struggle to the top, you are not prepared for the breathtaking scene beneath you. Winding rivers, green woods, fertile fields. It is as though you are looking at the face of God!

That is a way of trying to metaphorize some of God's richness and grandeur. A way to try to capture a feeling of awe, wonder, surprise, and delight.

Now, after resting here, you can pray. Now, you can descend, back to the rush of the world. And you can take the experience of your climb, and what you have learned, back with you. And as you descend, give thanks. You can arouse yourself now, feeling very refreshed and relaxed. Amen.

A prayer verbally seeks change in some aspect of the heart; a meditation does so metaphorically. The form and content of a meditation need be limited only by the imagination and inspiration of the counselor. Consider the following example:

In an exercise in a pastoral counseling class at St. John's Seminary, a fellow student complained to Ray, a talented semi-

narian, that "All I ever do is take in. I find it hard to give out."

Ray asked the student to close his eyes. As a preliminary, he prayed and meditated on Jesus as the door, etc., as noted above. Then he asked the student to picture a large jar. The student was to try to imagine filling the jar. Then, when the jar was as full as he could fill it, he was to imagine giving away the jar's contents. To the student's astonishment, he could neither entirely fill the jar nor completely empty it. He took this as a vivid lesson that in life we can never take in enough to fill us, nor can we give away enough to empty us.

The metaphor of the never full nor empty jar is, though intangible, something of lasting value to the man who conjured it. Indeed, just as a grasp of metaphor helps in assessing another's heart, so it helps in moving it.

Writing a Letter to Another

Letter writing as an instrument for change has its precedents in the Christian tradition. Yet modern Christians may overlook its astonishing effectiveness in strengthening faith, providing confrontation, and the offering of specific solutions to difficulties. A letter is something tangible, something that can be held onto. Practically any idea in this book can be incorporated into a letter. For example, I wrote the following letter to a friend of mine suffering from Parkinson's disease and depression.

Dear Fred,

I've thought a lot lately about your suffering with your disease. Even though I've been over such questions before, both as a physician and a Christian, I can't help asking why you are suffering like this and why God allows it. That Rabbi that wrote about the Book of Job—he concluded that God is helpless to prevent suffering. Somehow that view depresses me more. So I've prayed about it, and I got an interesting answer. You undoubtedly understand what I'm about to say anyway, but I'll tell you what I've come to accept.

The "why" of your suffering is not important. Probably you had the flu when you were young, and this disease is a late effect. Even if we knew the cause, it wouldn't change anything. The doctors may come up with some solutions, but they are inevitably short term. But the ultimate solution lies in God's action, what will be done for you as you stick with God. So, remember Easter, my friend. I love you and pray for you.

In Christ,
Ralph

To summarize, timely spiritual intervention can bolster the all important spiritual frame for life and can change the hearts of patterns, thereby changing, over time, the whole person. The four interventions described above only scratch the surface of the spiritual resources available for change. The conversion, growth, liberation, and healing of others should be the ultimate aim of all one learns in one's Christian education.

Exercises

1. In groups of two, share with each other a personal difficulty, struggle, or feeling. Then take turns praying for the other. Give feedback to your partner regarding the effectiveness of this effort.

2. In like manner, lead one another in meditation.

3. Using case vignettes generated by Exercise 3, Chapter 3, write a letter to one of the people described. Read a few of the letters to the class for their critiques.

Suggested Reading

I make no specific recommendations here, because the totality of one's Christian training can be used in the service of change as outlined in this book.

13

Confrontation

People at impasse are not the only ones that can suffer a lack of awareness or denial of the significance of certain actions or attitudes. Even those not at impasse may deny or not recognize the significance of their actions or attitudes. David failed to recognize his sin and separation from the Lord. The Pharisees were blind; the sick were often passive; and the disciples were wrong in their estimates of themselves. Too often we deny something within that can destroy us and separate us from God. Such insensitivity springs from the assumption that our perceptions and world views are correct. But if change is to take place, it is these perceptions and actions that must often be confronted.

Confrontation, as described here, is a therapeutic technique that sticks to observable facts and is neither critical nor attacking. Used with discretion and proper timing, confrontation is an invitation to think deeply about one's heart, world view, and intended solutions. If the counselee responds by thinking deeply, it sets in motion the process of change.

This chapter first discusses what a counselor should confront, considers confrontation in the Scriptures and as practiced by the church, and describes forms of confrontation for use in counseling. These may include simple confrontations, metaphoric confrontations, "why" questions, paradoxical confrontations, interpretations for pride-based solutions, and predictions and logical consequences. Confrontation is common in everyday life. The counselor must confront in the most therapeutic manner possible.

The *What* of Confrontation

The counselor needs to confront a counselee's maladaptive, unproductive, or destructive attitudes and actions. Masks, acting out,

174

deficits of the real self, and intended solutions that will not work must be faced if impasses are to be overcome.

> For a time, San Francisco police videotaped drunk drivers at the moment of arrest; the tapes were used in court as evidence. Offenders shown the tapes were astonished at their appearance and were motivated to seek treatment.

In a sense, all good counseling is confrontation: it brings people face to face with the truth of a situation or of the self.

Confrontation in the Scriptures

Much of the Old Testament confronts the problem of sin. It is not surprising that many find this disagreeable. The story of Adam and Eve (Genenis 3) metaphorically dramatizes humanity's propensity to sin. When God asked the couple why they were hiding (Genesis 3:9), he posed a question meant to induce deep thought, not only in Adam and Eve but in all of us. When God spoke of the pain of childbirth and the sweat of earning a living (Genesis 3:16-19), it was prediction of the consequences of sin and the subsequent struggle necessary to recover lost creativity and generative potential. God's question of Cain (Genesis 4:6), "Why are you angry?" was likewise more than rhetorical. Cain did not integrate this confrontation with the choices that it posed. He acted out rather than facing his shortcomings. In the New Testament, our Lord repeatedly confronted with metaphor. For example, after driving the money changers from the temple (Luke 19:45), Jesus was confronted by the chief priests, who demanded to know by what authority he had driven out the merchants. He replied with a story of a landlord whose tenants attempted to usurp his property and were consequently evicted. Like Cain, the chief priests did not integrate this confrontation. Jesus confronted Peter's illusions about himself with a prediction (Luke 22:34). He confronted Paul with a *why* question, "Saul, Saul, why do you persecute me?" (Acts 9:4). Let the reader peruse the Scriptures with the idea of confrontation in mind.

Simple Confrontation

Counselors can use brief statements to call attention to problem behavior and the need to deal with it. Such confrontations should stick to observable facts or obvious feelings. Comments such as, "I think you ought to look at this . . . ," "You are hurting yourself . . . ," "I have noticed . . . and I'm worried about you . . . " can be helpful.

> *Mark and Phillip were partners in an auto repair shop. Phillip was frequently drunk, alienating employees and customers. Mark was coached to confront Phillip at an opportune time by staring at him intently and saying, "It's got you by the balls!" Phillip immediately quit drinking for several weeks, but then relapsed. Mark saw the impossibility of the situation and dissolved the partnership. The language of this confrontation may seem coarse, but it is important to communicate in the vernacular of the counselee.*

Sometimes a buffer statement such as, "You may not like what I have to say . . ." can precede a simple confrontation.

Alcohol or drug intervention therapy is an elaboration of a simple confrontation. In this procedure, a problem drinker is met by an assembly of people who are genuinely concerned about the difficulty. Each person points out to the alcoholic specific instances of drunken behavior. Faced with such an array of facts from well-wishers, the alcoholic often decides to seek help.

> *Velma, 50, abused Valium, acquiring prescriptions from numerous doctors. I arranged a meeting with family members. When Velma arrived at my office, she found virtually her entire family there. Each named dates and times when Velma had exhibited slurred speech, had staggered or fallen, had embarrassed herself or others, and had shopped for pills. With her denial so dismantled, Velma agreed to immediate hospitalization at a drug detoxification center. She returned several weeks later to express gratitude for her new life.*

Metaphoric Confrontation

Stories can confront. Nathan's story of the ewe lamb (II Samuel 12:1-6) and Jesus' parable of the rich man and Lazarus (Luke 16:19-30) are examples. Metaphors are parallel communications that dramatize for the listener that which needs examination and correction.

> *I posed a situation to students at St. John's Seminary, Camarillo, California. A 50-year-old man seeks counsel for marital problems. A fiercely dominating and possessive person, he can hardly allow his wife to go to the bathroom without becoming suspicious. He greatly fears losing her to another man. Stifled from years of scrutiny, the woman seeks refuge elsewhere. Our counselee, at an impasse with the situation, breaks down and seeks help. But he proves stubbornly resistant to any leading. Can the seminarians suggest a story that might move him? Beto, a talented deacon, wrote as follows:*

>> A boy loved butterflies. One day he found an especially beautiful creature, graceful and multicolored. The butterfly liked him and wished to stay with him. But in time he grew fearful that it might fly away, so he tied a thread to its legs. If it flew too far, he would reel it in, then place it in a tiny cage. One morning he found the butterfly dead, destroyed by the frustration of its captivity.

Such stories have an advantage over direct confrontation: they are difficult to rebut, dismiss, or even forget. Rather, they are intriguing, they lodge in the recipient's conscious and unconscious minds. If on the mark, they may evoke rage, as with David (II Samuel 12:5). But David was able to integrate the confrontation, and his rage changed to deep sorrow. Such emotional reactions point to the potential for a radical change of heart. If the confrontation is rejected, the recipient may withdraw or attack, as did the hearers of Jesus' parable of landlord and tenants (Luke 20:19).

The most common confrontational stories are those of another case or situation that parallels the one in question. But the more effective stories are those with symbolism, such as the four referred to above. I fabricated the following story in response to an alcoholic's reluctance to return to AA after a six-month drinking bout.

> *A man experienced a fire in his house. He thought he could put it out himself, but it got out of hand, so he called the fire department. Six months later, sitting in the living room of his rebuilt house, he again smelled smoke. Oddly enough, he told himself it was nothing to worry about. What he didn't know was that the walls were full of flames.*

The man agreed to attend an AA meeting that afternoon.

Such confrontations impel their listeners to consider the choices involved when a course of action is pursued. Since people may not like that, confrontation carries with it the risk of rejection. Our Lord can testify to this. Techniques of creating metaphors are discussed in Chapter 15.

Why Questions as Confrontations

Masterson (1983) has pioneered the use of *Why?* to confront those habitual defensive styles discussed in Chapter 7 as *masks*. He describes these defenses as efforts to avoid or palliate depressions stemming from failures to individuate. People suffer fixations when crucial authority figures fail to support efforts to create, grow, and mature. Such failures to support frustrate the drives for communion and individuation and create a sense of abandonment and stagnation. Masks defend against such feelings. Masks are ubiquitous—all of us commonly avoid or defend against feelings of hurt, guilt, loss, anger, and depression. They are solutions intended to insulate us from life's hurts. But these masks are major obstacles to change and must be brought to the counselee's attention if growth is to take place.

Masterson's generic confrontation is as follows: "Why are you (acting, thinking, wishing) when such (actions, thoughts, wishes) are so harmful to you, or not in your best interests?" Such questions, posed to the receptive counselee, inevitably encourage *deep thought* and bring the counselee face to face with painful feelings. Because a person not yet receptive will resist such confrontations and withdraw from the counselor, intervention by confrontation requires timing. Let us examine some confrontations that might be used for each of the following defenses:

Denial. My wife, a marriage and family therapist, often works with women who were physically or sexually victimized as children. She at times observes that these women smile as they relate sad aspects of their lives. A counselor confronting such behavior might say, "I notice that whenever you talk of something sad, you smile. I wonder why that is." Such confrontations eventually will enable the person to face the feelings of devastation over specific incidents of abuse. It won't be easy, but it must be done. To someone who continues to drink in spite of the problems it is causing, the counselor might say: "Why do you deny that you have a drinking problem, or refuse to stop, when it is killing you?" Such querying, systematically pursued, just might help the counselee face the addiction, rage, and suicidal feelings.

Masterson describes a mother whose children are out of control. Seeking counsel, she talks animatedly about how successful she is at her job. The question, "Why do you feel the need to tell me this now?" allows her to express her feelings of guilt, failure, and fear of criticism surrounding her failures at childbearing. By using this technique, the counselor has allowed her to control what is said in the interview. Appreciating the safety of the counseling setting, she can go on to face the underlying fixations that have rendered her helpless. As she resolves her fixations and becomes freer to center on God, she will be better able to follow his guidance and, hence, to mother better.

Clinging. The person using this defense tries to get the counselor to take over responsibility for the counselee's life decisions.

Paul, in his 40s, became consumed with anxiety when he developed hypertension. His blood pressure proved easier to control than his anxiety, and he was referred to me. In the first meeting, he persisted in obsessing about his fear of stroke, ignoring any reassurances from me. Even demonstrating that his blood pressure was normal failed to quiet him. He was clinging to me. I questioned with genuine wonder, "Why do you choose to obsess about your health when your doctors clearly tell you that you are OK?"

After hearing several such questions, he suddenly reflected, "All right, I guess I'll have to talk about it."

He then launched into a tearful account of verbal abuse from his mother from childhood through the present. He went on to do extremely well in therapy, but as the end of our sessions approached, he talked repeatedly of his desire to have a friendship with me. When I wondered, "Why is it so important to have me as a friend?" he replied, "Here in counseling I feel alive. Without it I feel dead."

As he comes to realize in his heart that with Christ and the Church he is not alone, his recovery will be complete.

Distancing. A good way to avoid unpleasant feelings is to create distance from those people or situations that might evoke those feelings.

Roger, in his 30s, described his isolation, his avoidance of contact, his difficulty in making conversation, and his quest for the perfect woman. He admitted that if he were to find the woman of his specifications, he would go into shock and withdraw. A counselor might be tempted to offer advice as to how to socialize, but I think that a confrontation such as, "Why do you distance yourself and involve yourself in fantasy when the resulting loneliness is so painful?" might lead Roger to deal with the core feelings of his life, the painful distance he felt in relation to his parents.

To the woman who talks incessantly in an interview, refusing the counselor all but an occasional nod or word, one might ask with genuine curiosity, "I've noticed how important it is to you to convey to me how you feel. Could it be also that you mean to distance yourself from me in some way? If so, why?"

Projection. A man repeatedly asks me if I'm going to give up on him. Since I have no such intention, the idea of giving up must be coming from him. Perhaps part of him, a despairing or suicidal part, wishes to quit. If he is to encounter that part I must resist the temptation to reassure him, instead confronting him with the question, "Could it be that it is you that thinks of giving up?" Projection runs strong in marriage and families. People take out their frustrations on others. A confrontation might take this form:

> "At times you can't seem to find a good thing to say about your (spouse/child). Why is that?"

Because this is obviously a potentially explosive area in a counseling relationship, timing and good rapport are requisites to success.

Grandiosity. As mentioned elsewhere, children subjected to deprivation may exaggerate their sense of importance, prowess, and self-sufficiency as protection against depression that accompanies feelings of hopelessness, vulnerability, and helplessness. Similar effects occur with children raised by narcissistic, perfectionistic, and self-sufficient parents who ignore or give mere lip service to God. Whatever its origins, it is self-sufficiency that the dark side of life beats down. To those in the process of breaking down, and to those who still retain illusions of grandeur, an explanation of the spiritual developmental life cycle (Chapter 8) in terms of their own lives will suffice. Interpretation, as discussed below, is useful with this defense.

Acting Out. Confrontation finds its most important use in acting out. Sometimes this defense is an attempt to save oneself. There is often a contradiction inherent in this behavior, as actions designed to save actually harm the actor and others. Acting out may also result from unthinkingly following others. The result is the same—harm to the self and others. Confrontation calls attention to the contradiction and harm inherent in acting out. Thus, Jesus says to Saul of Tarsus,

> "Saul, Saul, why do you persecute me (Acts 9:4)?"

The question is not rhetorical; it expresses genuine curiosity about why one would act to harm oneself and others. In short, confrontation is to ask with amazement why one would act against one's own best interests. Used in this way, confrontation is really a test of the *receptivity* of the person; the unreceptive person will ignore or fail to act on the confrontation.

> *A pastor consulted me about the following situation. A lovely 18-year-old woman, very active in his congregation, confided in him she was actively engaged in, indeed was seeking, sexual relations with her father, a derelict who had sexually molested her as a child. The pastor laid the fear of God on her, saying "You are displeasing your heavenly Father." Masterson might ask, "Why do you allow or even seek this relationship when it cuts you off from your friends, leads you to withdraw, and is an assault on your own body?" Kernberg (1984) might pose the contradiction inherent in the behavior by asking, "I wonder about the contradiction between your actions and your religious faith."*

Such an approach, pursued over time, might lead the girl to face the real reasons for her actions. She would probably begin to encounter her feelings of guilt, rage, abandonment, loneliness, and finally her own emptiness and deadness, feelings she must face if she is ever to be whole.

Paradoxical Confrontations

A paradoxical confrontation is akin to reframing. The counselor finds some positive aspect of the attitude or behavior in question, affirms the positive, then suggests continuing the behavior in slightly altered or perhaps more socially acceptable form. Weeks and L'Abate (1982) write paradoxical letters to individuals, couples, or families to help them face and work through problem behavior. In addition to reframing behavior positively, they might ask a family to escalate what they are doing to defeat one another or to congratulate each on their ability to triumph over the other or the therapist. For example, the parents of a teenager who has been acting up might be asked to ritualistically read the following letter at dinner for a week:

Dear -----:

*We [the parents] are appreciative of your protecting us be-
cause as long as you act up neither Mother nor I will need to
look at ourselves and deal with our middle age. You will also
help your brother stay the way he is.*

Consequently, we will understand that any time you blow up it
will be to protect us and your brother. We hope, therefore, that
you will continue protecting us, because we need it.

This letter confronts not only the teenager's behavior but also the parent's
reticence to face their own issues.

This section is only a brief introduction to a fascinating subject.
Paradoxes are powerful instruments for change, but they require study
and forethought to be effective. The counselor willing to pursue the
mastery of paradox will be able to offer a great deal to his counselees.

Interpretation for Pride-based Solutions

Pride is perhaps the most common mask of all. The prideful person
can be haughty, arrogant, boastful, self-aggrandizing, self-centered, ex-
ploitative, controlling, and in extreme cases grandiose, idealizing or
devaluing others in an effort to heighten self-esteem. Pride is listed as
chief of the seven deadly sins and is contrasted with love in St. Paul's
classic discourse on charity (I Corinthians 13). At the heart of pride is
the grandiose self, a self-image that is a metaphor for the conviction that
one is perfect. This core grandiose self hides a profound sense of inferiority and severe deficits in the real self. Hence, the prideful person is
narcissistically vulnerable, keenly sensitive to any intimation of failure
or shortcoming. Confrontation would be experienced as a humiliating
attack and defended against with counterattack.

The prideful are subject to depression, particularly as they age. Although often successful by the world's standards, they invariably have
marital problems and poor relations with coworkers or subordinates.
They find the breakdown stage of spiritual development difficult. To
ask for help is humiliating. Empathy is the key to reaching the narcis-

sist, for it is to real or imagined failures in empathy that the narcissist is vulnerable and to which the narcissist erects a grandiose self. This sensitivity will be painfully apparent in the minute-to-minute relationship between counselor and counselee. Inevitably, the counselor will fail to keep in perfect touch with the counselee's feelings. The counselee will react with a heightening of grandiosity or devaluing. The recognition of such give and take provides the opportunity for scrutiny of the pattern, a pattern that recurs with painful regularity in the counselee's life. Put another way, the narcissist is continually disappointed in people because others are expected to be in perfect touch with the narcissist's feelings. Reactivity will abate as the narcissist comes to understand this. The use of empathy (Chapter 4) will enable the counselee to work through a recurrent sense of disappointment.

Prediction as Confrontation

God's statements to Adam and Eve after they had eaten the forbidden fruit (Genesis 3:9-19) have been interpreted as pronouncements of punishment rather than descriptions of the logical consequences of their act. This is our projection, for all too often we attempt to control others by threatening them with logical consequences. Such attempts, by engendering resistance, run counter to hoped for change. Prediction differs from threat by the presence of empathy and the absence of judgment. The counselor who perceives a pattern of thought or interaction can be certain that it will occur again. The prediction of such a recurrence would probably be met first with denial, but then by deep thought as the prediction comes true.

The simplest confrontation by prediction is the counselor's straightforward comment on the extrapolation of a pattern. For example, I might predict with confidence that a wayward teenage girl, using drugs and missing school, will be promiscuous, get pregnant, have an abortion or two, and pretend to feel nothing about it. I might then tell her a story of how a Catholic priest, working in a Youth Authority with girls unable to find relief from guilt over undergoing abortions, would work with the girls to name the dead babies, thus arriving at a resolution of guilt and mourning. Such predictions may have a paradoxical effect, with the counselee determined to prove the counselor wrong. Therefore, a counselor might preface any potentially upsetting statement with the words "You are not going to (like, believe, agree with) what I am about to say . . ."

The wife of an extremely narcissistic man consulted me. The couple planned to attend a Marriage Encounter. I predicted that he would walk out after six hours. He did exactly that. I wish I had delivered the prediction to the husband via letter. This might have made him determined to stay. And if he had left anyway, I would certainly have gained some credibility with him. But I did gain enormous credibility with the wife, who thereafter came periodically for further advice about her marriage.

Prediction is crucial as a person starts to change during the counseling experience. Change is individuative, and such individuation is often met with resistance, both from within and from close relationships. Predictions alert the counselee to this resistance. Statements such as the following are realistic and can act as paradoxes as well:

> *"Now that you are ready to look for a job, you need to know that you are going to get turned down, and you'll get depressed and want to give up."*

> *"As you get creative or step out or prepare to leave home, you'll probably question yourself and feel disloyal to your parents."*

> *"You should get ready for setback. You know that when things start to go right, anything can happen."*

People in the environment commonly resist change, also. It is imperative that this be predicted:

> *I had two cases of women who were disabled and totally dependent on their husbands. One was housebound with panic disorder, the other a hypochondriac. Both changed dramatically with treatment. The husband of the woman with panic disorder abruptly left and did not return. I was able to predict*

to the recovering hypochondriac that now that she was not clinging to her husband, he would react with fears of abandonment and castration. I was right. The wife was able to reassure her husband and help him through the adjustment period

Exercises

Discuss several vignettes generated by exercise 3, Chapter 3 from the point of view of confrontation. What are the intended solutions and the masks, defenses, and maneuvers that each case exemplifies? What deficits of the real self were these people not facing? Try out the six forms of confrontation described above on each case.

Suggested Reading

Masterson, J.F., *Countertransference and Psychotherapeutic Technique*, Brunner/Mazel, New York, 1983.

14

Achieving Change Through Confronting Images

Images are the building blocks of metaphor. The tangible reality of REM sleep shows that the images that comprise dreams are discrete entities that exist in their own right. Our images are our portraits of key aspects of others and of ourselves. We originate them from birth on as we interact with our environment. It is to be hoped that we update them to represent our external realities accurately. But since neither we nor our lives are ideal, our images, perhaps reflecting the darker realities of ourselves or others, may now serve to perpetuate a view that life is cruel and unfriendly. Many of us, perhaps mistreated or frustrated as children, grow to adulthood fixated on infantile, hostile, or undependable images. But faulty parenting is not the sole cause of our bad images: as children we frequently misjudge the intentions of others, perhaps projecting onto them our own hostile, angry, or self-centered wishes, and then create images of them that contain that projected anger. Christians have the opportunity to confront images to update them in the likeness of God, Father, Son, and Holy Spirit. Not something that one can do alone, such updating requires help from God and others.

Once we create our images, we interact with these symbols as well as with external reality. Images thus take on a life of their own. In counseling, they should be objects of treatment in and of themselves (Biddle, 1963). In my practice, I have found images and metaphors to be important avenues to solving impasses. I quite literally address images as though they were third parties present in the room. Thus, each person constructs a story out of life experiences. The stories then become metaphors, and the metaphors contain images, each image a kind of summary about the nature of something. In that sense, images are universals

187

for us: They are the essence of our world view. The following dramatic case illustrates the point:

Carlene, a woman of 23, was admitted to a mental hospital hysterically crying that her bottom half was becoming a man's. The precipitating stress had been learning of her husband's unfaithfulness, but focusing on that had no influence on her hysterical delusions. In addition, she was obsessed about becoming a man and hated her name because of the root "Carl." She became irrationally upset when she bathed her small boys, and suffered unexplained bouts of nausea and vomiting. She experienced disquieting sensations in her genitals, and at times was unhappily certain she had a penis. During treatment, we helped her resolve her feelings about her unhappy family of origin, her distant and uninvolved mother, and her alcoholic but caring father. But in spite of this progress, the resolution of her marital problems, and the initiation of a relationship with God, her symptoms continued. She often described an awful feeling in her stomach and chest. On several occasions she was asked to focus on the feeling to let her imagination take her back to a time or incident when she had felt such feelings. Each time, she recalled an incident when, around age five, she had happened to see her father in the nude. Although the incident seemed important to her, she could not tell me what it meant to her. I asked her to cluster around her memory. As she did so, she pulled forth a remarkable admission: "I see his penis. I grab it. I swallow it. I put it in my vagina." With that, she signed, "It's out!" Her symptoms and preoccupations dramatically ceased, and shortly thereafter she declared herself cured."

This case vividly illustrates one child's interaction with external reality, such interaction leading to the introjection of an image (the penis) that came to have an independent existence in the person, exerting effects as though it were really present. The metaphor here is one in which a person seeks to be fed, such need for nurture hypertrophied by the lack of nurture in the external reality. Also note that it was the child's solution to her problem (the lack of nurture), that got her into trouble. In like manner, but usually in a much more mundane way, each of us forms images of important others in ourselves.

The Mother Image

The first image formed is that of mother. Because mother's foremost function is to nurture, the mother image, and particularly the food she gives, come to symbolize communion. Our mother images are our composites of those who nurture us. As such, they are amalgams of the character of the nurturing (or nonnurturing) other and our feelings and interactions with him or her. The most basic sacrament of the church is not by accident a feeding one, and many of Christ's most compelling actions and parables had to do with feeding. Food becomes symbolic of our permission to exist. Each of us strives to feel fed and to order our images in such a way that they nurture us. In addition, we each seek to overcome the *bad mother*, the symbol of all that refuses to nurture or allow us to exist. Consider the following case.

> *Joanne, a woman of 28, had excelled at a career. At 26 she had become pregnant and had settled down at home to mother her son. However, she became deeply depressed and developed severe pain in the shoulders, the cause of which was unknown. Her family physician referred her for treatment of her depression. She complained of feeling overwhelmed by motherhood and had no zest for the role. In turn, her metaphors added up to a deep frustration with her own mother, who up to the present ignored her or was deeply critical of her. In her dreams, hostile figures pursued her. I placed her on antidepressant medication, then instructed her to have a dream about having something good to eat. A devout Christian, she easily accepted my explanation that with God as her father and mother she now lived in a new family system that willed to nurture her; she could therefore begin to recast her images in the likeness of the God whom she knew fed her. She returned to exclaim that her depression had suddenly*

lifted; she reported dreaming of a priest giving her com-munion. I interpreted the dream as feeling fed by me through my empathy and understanding and also as a communication that she could indeed feel nurtured by God through the church. In that session, she went on to tearfully forgive her mother for her failings.

In the next session, she reported that her shoulder pain had returned. She then talked of feeling upset that her mother-in-law, with whom she was close, would not be visiting as planned. She described other instances that told her that her in-laws were pulling away. Using the empty-chair technique (described below), I noted emphatically her fear and feelings of abandonment. She acknowledged that she found the fear of loss difficult to face; yet she almost expected it. Although ac-knowledging that such a fear might be groundless, she agreed to write a conciliatory letter to "Mom" (she had thought of writing an angry one) expressing the fear that Mom was be-coming more distant. She then told of her perfectionist striv-ings, and together we came to understand that she felt she had to be perfect to avoid being abandoned. She concluded that such strivings were a great burden, and that the "burden" ac-tually worsened the pain in her shoulders.

Thus, in a brief time, this woman brought out in metaphor her view of her-self as unnurtured and of those around her as unnurturing. Furthermore, she could change those perceptions to conform more with her spiritual con-victions and could accept the possibility of her own misinterpretation of the actions of others. We were also able to help her discover her *intended solution* to the dilemma of lack of nurture, abandonment, and loss: her perfectionism. This perfectionism provided her with a whole new set of problems (*e.g.*, depression, self-criticism, and psychosomatic symptoms) and paradoxically reinforced her conviction that she was unnurturable.

The Father Image

The developing child grows apart from mother and moves toward father and, hence, toward individuation. The parents' encouragement of such movement empowers the child to explore, experiment, and invent, thus discovering what power is. The essence of power lies in creativity. If father is unsafe or unavailable, or mother cannot let the child go, the child will develop a sense of powerlessness, and power will become confused with force, domination, and/or submission. Thus, lacking a reasonable father image, the child will resort to force or slip into helplessness. In turning to the Father, he can correct the father image, become empowered, and discover latent creativity, for power is of the Father's essence (Genesis 1:1).

Mother and Father Images in Relationships

Just as a child needs parents who love and enhance each other, so the child needs mother and father images that fit together nicely. This is so whether the person is 9 or 90. Thus, the combination of father and mother images represents the person's view of relationship, and how the child relates these images will be a blueprint for relating. In this regard, Biddle (1967) made two remarkable contributions. Freud and his followers, noting the sexual metaphors of children, interpreted these sexual fantasies as an indication of the child's desire for intercourse with the parent of the opposite sex: the Oedipus complex. The Freudians buttressed their argument with observations of patients' preoccupation with the *primal scene* (*i.e.*, fantasies of the parents in sexual union), asserting that this was another proof of the primacy of the sexual drive. Biddle, after repeatedly observing primal scene fantasies in a hospitalized mentally ill population, reframed these fantasies as attempts to safely unite father and mother images or as metaphors of the relationship between the two. In other words, a child who sees parents locked in a frightening power struggle would, in fantasy, try to keep them apart and would be apt to image their attempts at union as savage affairs. Given the traumatic nature of such images and the underlying drive to try to make them good, loving, constructive, and the like, it is easy to see how a person might plunge into sexual relationships in external reality to try to make the images *good*. In the same vein, Biddle saw Oedipal fantasies as the child's attempt at imagining communion with both parents, not as a wish for sexual intercourse. Again, if the images are too threatening, communion is not possible, and the person must then either renounce the drive for communion and withdraw or work to correct the images by acting them out in ongoing relations with the world. Neither solution works: only by facing and working through unpleasant feelings, memories, bad images, or present conflicts can communion be achieved.

Self-Images

Out of the mother and father images, the child creates self images. Children and/or adults subjected to negative or traumatic experiences may evolve a developmental arrest centered around the appearance of a helpless or damaged self-image. Since the personality seems to abhor imbalance, it typically compensates for a deficient self-image by adopting a *grandiose* self-image, the outward sign of which is a heightened struggle for self-sufficiency, over and above that encountered in the average person. This posttraumatic split in the self-image is intended to guard against the anxiety inherent in the helpless, damaged self-image. It stands to reason that a child made to experience the painful reality of helplessness will counter by vowing never to feel that way again. Hence, the child creates an illusory *invulnerable* self, one that can resist pain, display no weakness, and always be in control.

> *A 23-year-old man consulted me after he had been arrested for exhibiting himself to a woman on the street. This was the first time he had ever done such a thing. He was extremely upset, not only for his legal problem, but also because this was totally out of keeping with his character. Married for about six months, the incident occurred shortly after his wife had refused a sexual overture. He had felt emasculated by his wife's refusal, and he could understand how displaying his penis to a strange woman was a symbolic way of regaining his*

loss, but he could not understand how he could have behaved with such radical inappropriateness. Such an act can be understood as a regression, a going back in time to regain something lost earlier. During therapy, he mentioned how, at about the age of puberty, his father, suffering his own difficulties, had repeatedly criticized and verbally attacked him. Now, to a boy at puberty, a penis is a remarkable thing, certainly symbolic of emerging manhood. I asked him to use his imagination, to be that pubertal boy. He wept deeply as he played the part of a confused teenager, struggling to realize his masculinity, yet feeling deprived of it by his father. His reaction helped him to re-integrate that disowned self-image; he could then go on to forgive his dad. The healing was helped along by his sense of acceptance by Christ through me.

Spiritual maturity carries with it an acknowledgement of an inability to ultimately control one's own destiny, counterbalanced with faith in God as Savior. A child's faith is centered on the parents; if that faith is lost, the child may only conclude that the whole universe is hostile. Hence the appearance of a grandiose or artificial self that will try to make up for the loss *symbolically.*

Methods for Working with Images

The first method for dealing with images is to keep in mind their concrete reality and to look for them during the counseling hour. Images are most readily apparent in dreams; in working with a dream, for example as described in Chapter 9, the counselor is working with images. In addition, the counselee's anecdotes may contain them. Stories of an overbearing boss or a critical or attacking parent suggest an image that threatens communion or individuation. In addition to dream management (Chapter 9), the counselor can resort to the *empty chair technique* and *Biddle's maneuver.*

The *empty chair technique* offers a counselee a stage on which to work toward mastering out-of-control images and the difficulties they represent. The technique occupies a middle ground between pacing and leading; it allows counselor and counselee simultaneously to further the assessment, pace, and lead. The technique consists of a counselee's imagining that a person or figure is seated in a nearby empty chair. The counselee is then invited to have a dialogue with that projected image. A favorite device of Gestalt therapists (Perls, 1970), it initially appears to be a rather contrived kind of "play acting." However, a counselee using it quickly experiences its power, a power that derives from its ability to carry the person deeply and quickly into feelings very close to the heart.

> *Mike, 34, sought counseling for depression. A very cautious person, he related in a tight, constricted, controlled, and very polite manner. In session two, he reported that his wife was pregnant with their second child but that he looked forward to the birth with mixed emotions. During session eight, he grimly related that the baby had died in utero and been delivered stillborn. He choked back tears and tensed his whole body as he described the funeral arrangements. I urged him to let himself cry: attempting to hold his feelings in was actually contributing to his depression.*

> *The suggestion had no effect, so I asked him if he would be willing to imagine that the dead child was sitting on the ottoman opposite him. He agreed, turned to the ottoman, and began to weep, although he continued to sit with legs tightly crossed and hands neatly folded. I asked him to open his posture, lean forward, and gesture with his hands as he talked with his deceased child. As he did so, he wept deeply. The physical, outward expressions of feelings that Mike had achieved through the empty chair technique left him visibly relieved, relaxed, and much less depressed.*

The empty chair technique is a method for improving empathy between counselor and counselee and between counselee and others. The technique facilitates leading the counselee: the counselor can often discern unexpressed feelings from the dialogue and then lead the counselee to express them. To bring out an unexpressed feeling, the counselor can say something like, *Try saying* . . . As the counselee follows this lead, important blocks may crumble. Consider the following example:

> *Bernie, a 37-year-old, complaining of poor self-esteem, dreamed that a leper coughed in his face. Over a period of weeks, as he thought about the dream, he began to realize that the leper was a self-image.*

> **A:** Have a dialogue with the leper, over there on the empty chair.

> **B:** You are really rude, coughing in my face like that.

> **A:** Bernie, would you mind now sitting in the empty chair and pretending you are the leper?

> **B:** I am a leper. Your leper. I'm close to you. I do what I please. *(There is a long silence, after which Bernie returns to his seat.)*

> **A:** You look thoughtful. What are you aware of right now?

> **B:** I'm feeling a sadness in my chest, one I've felt often in my life. It's a kind of loneliness.

> **A:** Let your imagination take you back to the first time you felt that way.

> **B:** *(becoming deeply meditative)* I'm 7. I'm at school. I feel different from the other kids. So I show off. I have new shoes on. I show them, but the others don't pay attention.

> **A:** Try saying, "Look at me, at my new shoes."

> **B:** Wow, that doesn't work. They withdraw from me in horror.

> **A:** Try saying, "I'm special."

> **B:** I can't believe it! When I did that, I turned into a huge, stone Buddha!

> *Bernie went on to describe a surge of warmth and well being. Together, we decided that in the meditation he had integrated a split off grandiose self-image, that particular image itself formed at a point in time in defense against feelings of low self-esteem. Thus, leper and Buddha both dissolved, leaving*

the man a little freer. The techniques of the empty chair and the empathic use of "try saying" allowed him to experience and hence discard a grandiose defense against a poor self-image.

People frustrated in their quest for communion can display various symptoms ranging from neurotic to psychotic. Biddle (1963) regularly asked his patients to try to have a dream of eating good food, explaining that such food was symbolic of the desire for communion. He taught his patients that they could change a frustrating mother image into a nourishing one by realizing that through Christ they were adopted into a new family where God was their father and mother. In essence, this maneuver asks the counselee to challenge dreams, the goal being to integrate Christian faith into the heart. The counselee's subsequent dreams typically dramatize the obstacles to such integration. The lengthy cases of Bob (page 151) and Joanne (page 189) demonstrate the application of Biddle's approach.

A Menu of Clinical Applications

Five areas of concern lead to or are symbolized by images, and all can be dealt with through working with dreams, the empty chair technique, or Biddle's maneuver. They involve frustrations around the need for feeling fed and experiencing communion; loss; intimidating images; traumatic incidents; and feelings of fear or hate. The preceding section discusses frustrations around the need for feeling fed and experiencing communion.

Loss is the second area of concern. Images can symbolize difficulty coping with loss, which can include bereavements, disappointments in love, and loss of health through illness or accident. A bereaved person might repeatedly dream of the lost loved one during sleep and constantly dwell on the person while awake. Likewise, a person unable to accept a divorce or a broken relationship might recurrently dream about the person by night and be preoccupied with the figure by day. Lastly, the depression following loss of health often is manifested as a preoccupation with the former healthy body image and a refusal to accept the damaged body and its image. In each case, the empty chair technique can be quite useful. The counselee is asked to talk with the lost image. In this manner, the counselee is brought into touch with previously suppressed feelings of abandonment, anger, grief, remorse, warmth, and love. Following such a catharsis, the counselee can usually say goodbye to the images symbolizing difficulty, thereby symbolically closing the chapter and accepting the loss. At an appropriate time, the counselor can help by consoling with the assurance of God's presence and timeless love.

> *Twenty-eight-year-old Sharon was wheelchair bound from multiple sclerosis, a slowly progressive and crippling neurological disease. A consultation was sought because she would periodically and inexplicably lapse into coma for days at a time. At the interview, she complained bitterly of inept housekeepers and of her own inability to get up and clean house.*
>
> *Sensing by intuition that she was in a rage against her illness, I invited her to have a dialogue with her sick body, projected onto the empty chair. For two sessions, she furiously berated her body and its weaknesses. At the same time, she was receptive to my expressed hope in the resurrection of the body. In the end, she apologized to her body for attacking it. She told her body that she loved it, weaknesses and all.*
>
> *With such an acceptance in place, she had a wonderful lifting of mood and again felt life to be worth living. Her strange comas ceased.*

Intimidating images, the third area of concern, may plague a person. For example, the prototype nightmare consists of a hellish phantasm that threatens the dreamer, who usually awakens in a flood of anxiety. Such images are the distillates of fear, but (as noted above) have a life of their own. People harboring these images have been intimidated or mistreated; the menacing images symbolize such treatment and the feelings of rage, hate, helplessness, guilt, and self-persecution that accompanied it and still linger. But intimidating images may also embody something the counselee *should* be afraid of. In either case, since the counselee cannot cope with these images and their attendant feelings, the counselor must intervene. The counselor can begin by instructing the counselee to face the phantasms at their next appearance, make the sign of the cross, and ask God for help. This will astonish the counselee, who cannot imagine affecting dreams, much less facing fearsome images.

Often an *intimidating image* is the memory and feelings associated with an ongoing or just ended relationship. Much as one grieves over a loss, a counselee can struggle with the memory or *image* of another who dominated him or her, often in the past. Again, it is up to the counselor to realize that the heart of the distress lies in the counselee's inability to cope with another person. For example:

> *Sarah, a Christian girl of 16, complained of premenstrual tension, emotional upset, and depression. She had withdrawn from friends and wished to change schools. Her father had abandoned the family four years earlier. During two interviews, however, she repeatedly referred to a recent breakup with a boyfriend. It became clear that this boy had possessively dominated her while carrying on with another girl. Although it had been Sarah who ended the relationship, she continued to obsess about it and had worried herself into a depression. Through discussion and the empty chair technique, she aired her fear of and attraction to the narcissistically dominating boy and was then able to more definitely break away.*

As another example, consider the following.

> *Jose, a man of 32, was referred because he was abusing his wife and children. I could sense his intense rage at the instant of our meeting. He complained of an uncontrollable temper when he was with his wife and expressed a fervent hope that I could help him change. He quickly went on to describe a childhood of extreme physical abuse at the hands of his father, who he described with a hate that glowed in his voice. He could not talk of his father without losing control of himself, so*

we changed the subject. Subsequently he told me of frequent nightmares in which a devil would attempt to strangle or smother him. I explained the origins of the figure, suggesting that when we rid him of the image he would be able to face his dad and his feelings about him. He was willing to do anything to get rid of those nightmares. Using the empty chair technique, I asked him to place the "devil" on the chair and to have a dialogue with him. He did so, and we became well acquainted with the figure. Since the counselee was a Christian, I asked if I could pray with him, lay hands on him, and drive the image out. As we prayed together, the figure evaporated, to the great relief of the counselee. He later was able to have a dialogue with his father image (via the empty chair), and forgive him. He went on to reunite with his wife and subsequently did well. Biddle (1967) has also described such "exorcisms."

Traumatic incidents, the fourth area of concern, and the conclusions the sufferer draws from them may be compressed into a single menacing image. Such images serve to fixate the personality on the feelings of fear or hate that came from the traumatic incidents. A combat neurosis illustrates the ability of a single event to imprint fear. A soldier's friends are killed and he is wounded in a sudden attack or explosion; he awakens from the incident paralyzed with fear and suffering recurrent nightmares of being stalked by overpowering and evil pursuers. The images of his persecutors embody his fear. In a parallel situation, a man of one color is beaten and robbed as he passes through a ghetto of another color; he subsequently breaks down and is overcome with anxiety and nightmares. He holds an irrational hatred for all members of the race of his attackers. He carries a gun and wishes he could kill just someone of that race. Such men see themselves as helpless and incapable of withstanding the assaults of a hostile world. They must conquer their fear and hate if they are ever to be whole. The cases of Joe (page 126) and Sam (page 128) are examples.

Fifth, *feelings of fear or hate* can be symbolized, and the sufferer then is dominated by the image itself.

Steven, the 30-year-old described in Chapter 7, continuously obsessed about sex with men. To compensate for his feelings of helplessness, he adopted hypermasculine behavior. As we discussed this, he recalled an incident when he was nine in which he had been suddenly surrounded and threatened by a gang of Hispanic youths. He recalled feeling terrified.

A.: Can you imagine that they are sitting on that sofa.

S: Sure. I'm afraid of you. I have nothing against you, though. You are just guys like I am. Some of you are my friends now.

A.: Maybe the terror is your problem. Maybe you got imprinted with fear.

S: I sure did!

A.: Put your "fear" over on the sofa.

S: I see a mountain there. It is much bigger than I am!

A.: It's a bluff. Tell it that you have God, and you won't let it bluff you.

S: Hmm. I never thought of it that way.

In conclusion, working with images often leads to the heart of the matter, fixations on relationships that have left the counselee feeling powerless. With God's guidance and the help of the counselor, the counselee faces these relationships and feelings and gains strength, the true strength that comes with the realization and utilization of God's presence.

Exercises

1. Divide into groups of two. Choose a dream from your journal (exercise 5, Chapter 1) in which there are opposite figures (evil *versus* good, weak *versus* strong, kind *versus* cruel, helpless *versus* powerful, *etc.*). With the help of your partner, use the empty chair technique to enact a dialogue between the characters.

2. Should you, while studying this chapter, become aware of frustrations around communion, experiences of loss or intimidation, traumatic incidents, or powerful negative feelings, ask your partner, a classmate, or your instructor to assist you in using the empty chair technique to deal with them.

Suggested Reading

1. Biddle, W. Earl, *Integration of Religion and Psychiatry,* Collier Books, New York, 1962.

2. Perls, Frederick S., *Gestalt Therapy Verbatim*, Bantam Books, New York, 1970.

15

The Use of Analogy in Treatment

Spiritual approaches, confrontation, and working with images allow the counselor to follow the threads of the counselee's problems and deal with them directly. The techniques sketched in this chapter and the next—analogy and tasks—make it possible for the counselor to actively lead the process of change. Through analogy and tasks, the counselor can participate with the counselee in the creation of new attitudes, new actions, and the realization of latent resources. Specifically, by using such analogous communications as anecdotes, similes, metaphors, parables, allegories, jokes, and music, the counselor can indirectly convey alternative ways of seeing or advice on how to change.

In my own life, one particular story changed my view of Christ and was instrumental in my conversion. As a boy, I took part in weekly religious observances with my parents, but I regarded religion as irrelevant. But I did have a passionate interest in naval history, and while in high school I happened to read *The Good Shepherd,* by C. S. Forester. In that story, a squadron of destroyers accompanied a convoy across the North Atlantic during World War II. A wolfpack of German U-boats attacked the convoy. The protagonist in the story was the squadron commander, who, although exhausted from lack of sleep, directed the ship's operations to beat back the attackers. During brief pauses in the action, the captain read the Scriptures and pondered John 10:11:

> "I am the good shepherd. The good shepherd lays down his life for the sheep."

The story deeply moved me on an unconscious level. Only after my conversion did I consciously realize the significance of the story. I related to the story line because it fit my interests and world view. The captain was a type of Christ with whom I could identify. The Scriptural passages interspersed with the action sequences of the battle sunk into my subconscious without resistance. The story changed the way I viewed my Christian background, thus laying the groundwork for my conversion.

The essence of counseling is advice—the offering of ideas to another in hopes of influencing the other's judgment or conduct. Solutions to the impasses of the counselee came to mind as the counselor listens to descriptions of dilemmas; the urge is to say, "I think you ought to try this." But direct advice is often discounted or resisted. Sound counsel is often met with, "Yes, but . . .". Better to translate advice into an analogy that allows the unconscious to see the wisdom of the suggestion and learn from it. Barker (1985) gives the following example:

> *The therapist's first session with the family was drawing to a close. The father, the mother, and the three children were all present.*
>
> *The therapist recommended that the family come for subsequent sessions as a family group. The father, a foreman for a construction company, was working on a project in another part of the province and got home only on weekends. He said he couldn't make it during the therapist's working hours, though he could come late in the evening or at the weekend. It seemed that therapy would have little chance of success without the father's active involvement, but the therapist wasn't available in the evenings or on weekends. An impasse seemed to have been reached.*
>
> *Then the therapist had an idea. Turning to the mother, he told her a story about how, when a hospital he had been associated with was under construction, the plumbers had gone on strike. The other trades, he explained, had tried to continue working. At first they thought they could achieve something without the presence of the plumbers. It wasn't long, though, before they found that whatever they did there was some little task that re-*

quired the services of a plumber. So they got nowhere and achieved nothing. Not until the strike ended was any real progress made.

At that, the father got out his appointment book and said, "Maybe I could get away early on a Friday every second or third week" and made an appointment suitable to the therapist.

What might a counselor hope to achieve by using analogies? Goals depend on the individual situation but will often pertain to solutions to problems discussed in earlier chapters. Analogies can be used with fixations (Chapter 2), difficulty with permissions (Chapter 5), obstacles to communion and individuation and impairments of the real self (Chapter 7), spiritual development (Chapter 8), and interpersonal struggles. In these areas, analogies might reframe a problem, provide motivation, suggest alternative attitudes, point to solutions, or enable the retrieval of resources to solve the problem. Ultimately, the counselee hopes and needs to learn something. Counseling will work best if there is rapport and a sense of cooperation and mutuality between counselor and counselee. Advice or confrontation couched in analogy protects such rapport by allowing the counselee to draw the conclusions and make responses.

How does one construct an effective analogy? How does one convert advice into parallel communication? How can such communication be part of a dialogue rather than of a lecture? This chapter addresses some general principles, examines the methods of our Lord, studies Milton Erickson's use of storytelling as a therapeutic tool, and reviews the models of two of his followers (O'Hanlon and Lankton). The literature on Erickson and his use of analogies has grown rapidly; some of these recent works are referenced under *Suggested Readings* at the end of this chapter.

General Principles of Analogy Construction

The counselor should use five principles in applying analogy:

- Praying without ceasing

- Using and including the counselee's world view and resources
- Pacing and leading
- Moving toward or away from the solution to a problem
- Gauging responses through the counselee's indirect replies, body language, and voice inflection.

Praying without ceasing creates spontaneity within the relationship and a sensitivity to unconscious processes. The counselor can experience flashes of intuition and remember applicable stories from Scripture, literature, or personal or prior counseling experiences. The counselor is free to take poetic license with such stories. For example, when relating Deuteronomy 30 to a suicidal Christian woman, I paused and slightly altered my voice when I said the punchline: *Choose life!*

Stories should include the language, interests, resources, and concerns of the counselee. The two stories related above illustrate the point. Such matching commands attention, deepens identification, and maximizes openness to new solutions.

The counselor should pace before leading. Too often we suggest solutions before walking beside the person for a time. Stories can pace by metaphorically empathizing before offering a figurative solution.

With stories, the counselor can move toward or away from solutions to problems. Jesus often told stories about people who had failed to believe, grow, learn, *etc.* Erickson told stories of people who had failed to change. Common sense leads us to say, "You should try such and such," but let the counselor instead try discouraging an obvious solution. "Such and such could be a solution, but it would be too costly, too time consuming, *etc.*" Such leading away from solutions can be couched in stories.

As a story is told, feedback in the form of a metaphoric reply, body language, or voice inflection will help the counselor reply in turn, perhaps with another story.

Jesus' Use of the Picturesque

Our Lord constantly talked with figures of speech, similes, metaphors, and parables. The few examples of picturesque language given below provide some exciting ways to communicate effectively.

- He often spoke in metaphor in the strict sense of the word.

    "You are the light of the world" (Matthew 5:14).

    "Beware of false prophets, who come to you in sheep's clothing but inwardly are ravenous wolves" (Matthew 7:15).

    "What did you go out into the wilderness to behold? A reed shaken by the wind?" (Luke 7:24).

- He frequently used similes.

    "The kingdom of heaven is like a grain of mustard seed which a man took and sowed in his field; it is the smallest of all seeds, but when it has grown it is the greatest of shrubs and becomes a tree, so that the birds of the air come and make nests in its branches" (Matthew 13:31-32).

    Such a figure creates wonder and a passion for the kingdom.
    It taps into the common experience of its listeners. It motivates.

- He often taught with parables. Parables are short, simple stories from which a person can learn. For example, in Luke 15 and 16, Jesus attempted to communicate the value of the breakdown stage of spiritual development to the self-righteous Pharisees through the parables of the lost sheep, the lost drachma, and the lost (prodigal) son. Knowing that the hearts of the Pharisees centered on money, which was the obstacle to their spiritual development, he told the parable of the crafty steward and the rich man and Lazarus. This sequence reveals the tension in our Lord's confrontations with the obdurate, murderous Pharisees. Of course, the parables help us confront and overcome our own self-righteousness and greed.

Jesus' Construction of Parables

The more resistance Jesus anticipated or encountered, the more he resorted to parables (Mark 4:33-34). To receptive disciples, he was much more direct. He repeatedly converted into parables such wisdom as,

> "If you want to know God and find the kingdom, believe in and follow me, set aside pride and the pursuit of riches, embrace your brokenness, and aid others with theirs."

In doing so, he often used two specific constructions:

- The interaction of opposites

- A focus on failure and its consequences.

Stories of either type can be extraordinarily powerful and compelling, so much so that wisdom and practice are required for their use.

In an *interaction of opposites*, two poles of an attitude, posture, objective, or action are portrayed side by side and in tension with one another in the same illustration. In Jesus' parables, the attitudes and actions pertain to spiritual development. For example, belief is the objective in the parable of the sower (Luke 8). The lifestyle of one who believes is set alongside those of several who do not. To a man stuck in the fear stage of spiritual development, Jesus tells the story of the good samaritan (Luke 10:25), juxtaposing a man who loves with those who do not. To the boastfully self-righteous, he pairs a proud Pharisee and a cheating tax collector (Luke 18:10). The very word *parable* derives from the Greek *para,* meaning beside, plus *ballein,* meaning to throw. Today's counselor can convert suggestions for solutions to fixations and other difficulties into parables.

In *focusing on failure*, Jesus paradoxically fostered spiritual development by telling stories about people who failed to believe or who failed to choose spirituality over money. Failure to transcend the love of money is the theme in the story of the rich man and the barn (Luke 12:16-21) and in the story of the dishonest manager (Luke 16:1-13). The story of the landlord and the tenants (Luke 20:9-18) is about those who fail to respect the landlord's representatives and attempt to usurp property. Each story depicts the consequences of such actions. A misuse of this method is the hell fire and brimstone sermon, which attempts to coerce people into belief through threat. This was not Jesus' intent. Rather, by telling a story that focused on failure, he hoped to set before the listener the critical choices in life. It is the fixation of people on the Talion principle that leads them to conclude that Jesus was threatening punishment. Thus, if a counselor wishes to lead a person to a particular solution or lesson, try telling the story of someone who fails. But be careful—this is an explosive method that requires practice to master.

Erickson and the Use of Analogy

Erickson pioneered the use of analogous communication in modern psychotherapy. He saw at the heart of people's difficulty a resistance to any change that would bring into question their existing notions of how things should be. He used innumerable indirect methods to confront cultural, personal, or religious rigidities; self-will; fear; rebelliousness; and other qualities that would interfere with learning. Through anecdotes, he often held up the small child's openness to new ideas as the value needed for recovery or growth. Many stories pertained to the exercise of God-given abilities to observe and think freely. He embedded his points in anecdotes of life in nature, his own experiences, and those of his patients. He often used the negative. He would motivate a person toward openness by telling a series of stories about people who resisted change. An example is the following story which he used in the process of teaching people to break out of old, restrictive patterns (Zeig, 1980).

> *When I joined the staff at Worcester, Tom and Martha, a young couple there, junior psychiatrists, were very friendly toward me. They invited me to go swimming at the lake which was adjacent to the hospital farm. I got into my bathing suit, put on a bathrobe, and got into their car. Martha was sullen and unresponsive in the car during the half-mile drive to the lake. Tom was charming, sociable, and talkative. I wondered.*

*When we reached the beach, Martha leapt out of the car, and
threw her bathrobe into the back of the car. She strolled down
to the lakeshore and plunged into the water and started swimming away. Never a worry to us.*

*Tom got out of the car cheerfully, casually. He put his
bathrobe in the back seat. So did I. He walked down to the
water, and when Tom's big toe touched the wet sand, he said,
"I think I will go swimming tomorrow."*

*So, I plunged into the lake and had my swim with Martha. On
the way back to the hospital, I asked Martha, "How much
water does Tom put into the bathtub?" She said, "A lousy one
inch."*

*Tom was offered a promotion to senior psychiatrist that week.
He told the superintendent, "I don't think I'm ready." The superintendent said, "I wouldn't have offered it to you if I didn't
think you were ready. Now you are either going to take the
promotion or you leave and find a job elsewhere."*

*Tom and Martha left. By that time, I knew Martha well
enough to know that she was very much in love with Tom and
he with her. Martha was looking forward to a nice home and
children.*

*Twenty-five years later, I was lecturing in Pennsylvania when
an old gray-haired man and a haggard old woman approached
me. He said, "Do you recognize us? I'm Tom." And she said,
"I'm Martha." I said, "When are you going swimming,
Tom?" He said, "Tomorrow." I turned to Martha and said,
"How much water does Tom put in the bathtub?" She said,
"The same lousy, stinking one inch." I said, "What are you
doing now, Tom?" He said, "I'm retired." "At what rank?"
"Junior psychiatrist." If I had had time, I would have some-
how or other managed to shove Tom into the lake.*

Erickson went on to add, "Because once you break that restrictive,
phobic pattern, the person will venture into other things."

Various researchers, including O'Hanlon (1987) and Lankton and Lankton (1986), have proposed models of Erickson's methods of analogy construction. These models are variations on themes discussed above.

O'Hanlon felt that Erickson thought in terms of classes of problems and classes of solutions. Figure 16-1 illustrates how he felt the two were related. For example, O'Hanlon examines Erickson's diagnosis and treatment of a boy with enuresis and of a man suffering from phantom-limb pain. The boy's class of problem is that of fine or automatic muscle control. The man's class of problem is that he has too much negative sensory awareness. Thus, the category *class of problem* is a generalization of which the cases are specifics. Once a class of problem has been delineated, solutions suggest themselves.

		Intervention
Negotiated		Anecdote
Presenting		Analogy
Problem		Task
		Trance phenomena

Class of Problem　　　Class of Solution
(Pattern of Experience)

Class of Problem/Class of Solution Model
(Source: O'Hanlon 1987)

The best way to suggest these solutions to a counselee is through analogous communication. Analogies can help the sufferer change the way the problem is seen, how the counselee acts in relation to the problem, and what resources he uses to solve the problem. Erickson learned that the enuretic boy played baseball, so he discussed with the lad how, in throwing a baseball, the boy could *let go* at just the right moment and how, in catching it, he could *squeeze down* at just the right time. He helped the man with phantom-limb pain change how he saw the problem by saying:

"You've got phantom-limb pain, why not also have phantom-limb pleasure?"

He illustrated this with a story of his friend John, who had a wooden leg that he enjoyed scratching at the ankle. He followed this with a story of spending the night in a foundry, learning overnight how to screen out the noise. This last story was meant to access the common ability to become accustomed to and hence ignore unpleasant stimuli.

During a class with second-year seminarians at St John's seminary, we discussed O'Hanlon's diagram. "Celibacy is hard; what kind of story could you tell that could help deal with that?" asked one student. I asked, "What is the class of problem?" After a discussion, we decided that one problem was managing sexual desire. But what was the solution? A thought flashed through my mind. "Short-term pain, long-term gain. The solution is one of motivation. Can you think of a story that would illustrate the point?" One participant raised his hand excitedly and offered this:

I'm a karate enthusiast. I recently went on a week-long workshop to further my skill. The instructor had us assume a semi-squat position and hold it motionless for several hours. It was agony. But afterward I felt a sense of zest, of strength and endurance. Short-term pain, long-term gain.

To solve a problem or resolve an impasse, a person must call on some forgotten or latent resource from within or without himself. Chapter 11 covers some available resources. Lankton and Lankton stressed Erickson's use of anecdotes to remind a person of these resources. In their model, metaphoric references to resources are embedded in a particular story line.

This is precisely the method used in Forester's *The Good Shepherd*. Forester creates a story line that has conscious hold, all the while tapping into forgotten or latent faith in the interludes during which the captain searches the Scriptures.

• *Change does not result from the story line or story outcome.*

• *Change results from the retrieving and linking of experience. Experience is retrieved by detailing, imagery, or symbols. Experience is linked by proximity, suggestions or binds.*

Story Line

= CONSCIOUS LEVEL

= UNCONSCIOUS LEVEL

(Detailing done with indirect suggestions and binds)

Change in Metaphor
(Source: Lankton and Lankton 1986)

But how does one create a story line? Forester uses the *plot skeleton,* as do many writers of television detective stories and situation comedies. According to Knight (1981), the plot skeleton has five bones:

- A believable, sympathetic central character

- An urgent and difficult problem

- Attempts by the character to resolve the problem, which fail and make the situation more desperate

- The crisis: a last chance to win

- The successful resolution, brought about by means of the central character's courage, ingenuity, faith, *etc.*

The plot skeleton forms a story of resolution. It makes use of the conscious mind's demand that tension or conflict be resolved. How often do we watch a mediocre television drama just to see how it ends even though we know from the outset that the good guy will win. Of course, there are several other kinds of plot. As the figure above indicates, change occurs, as it did with me as I read Forester's novel, with the experiences elicited by embedded messages.

A Menu of Analogies

The counselor can empathize, confront, or teach with analogy. With analogy, he or she can hope to help the counselee find the resources to change crucial attitudes or actions, whether in the spiritual, personal, or interpersonal sense. In summary, the counselor can construct analogies using the following guidelines:

- General principles, such as praying without ceasing, using the counselee's world view, pacing before leading, moving toward or away from solutions, observing feedback.

- Metaphors

- Similes

- Stories in which there is an interaction of opposites

- Stories that depict failure to learn, change, or pursue an obvious course of action

- The class of problem, class of solution model

- A story line with embedded ideas to promote the retrieval or realization of resources.

In practice, the counselor will experience flashes of insight or memories of stories from Scripture or past experiences that may apply to the counselee. Such flashes are the raw material from which, refined by the above guidelines, creative change can be fashioned.

Exercises

1. Pair up with your partners from exercise 4, Chapter 7. Studying carefully the above guidelines, write your partner a letter containing a story, personal experience, or Scriptural passage that could help further personal or spiritual development. After exchanging letters, meet to discuss and critique the letters.

2. Divide into groups of three. Using a vignette generated by exercise 3, Chapter 3, create a story, using ideas presented above, that might make a difference to its recipients. Discuss in class.

Suggested Reading

1. Barker, P., *Using Metaphors in Psychotherapy*, Brunner/Mazel Publishers, New York, 1985.

2. O'Hanlon, W.H., *Taproots: Underlying Principles of Milton Erickson's Therapy and Hypnosis,* W.W. Norton and Co., Inc., New York, 1987.

3. Rosen, S., *My Voice Will Go With You—The Teaching Tales of Milton H. Erickson*, W.W. Norton and Co., Inc., New York, 1982.

16

Tasks

Fixation => Negative Feelings => Intended Solutions =>
Patterns => Impasse

The above scheme constitutes an overarching, enduring, circular mosaic in the sufferer. Change any element of this mosaic and the whole mosaic begins to change. Spiritual approaches and working with images have the most impact on fixations, feelings, and intended solution. Confrontation works best on intended solutions, analogy on the whole gamut. Task assignments are a means of approaching patterns and intended solutions: if people hope to change, they must ultimately do something they have not done before.

Patterns are recurrent sequences of thought, behavior, and interaction, mosaics of the conscious: observable and quickly accessed. They should not be dismissed as unimportant because they are superficial. Rather, a change in a pattern can start the ball rolling and can often lead to profound change through a domino effect. Tasks can start such alterations in pattern.

> *Jill and Peter complained of terrible fights that often cul-
> minated in threats of divorce. These fights took place in their
> apartment. I assigned them the task of fighting on the beach at
> sunset. Their fighting subsided and they addressed those fixa-
> tions needing attention.*

The important change here was probably not the shift in location, but rather that there were now, by virtue of my having assigned a fight, three people involved in the fighting.

In their simplest form, task assignments, like metaphors, are advice given in the concrete. For example, how often do clergy urge their congregation as a whole to invite outsiders to church. Instead, each member might be asked to make a single phone call or other invitation on a specific occasion. In the field of marriage counseling, Stuart (1980) assigns spouses the task of demonstrating care for the other by carrying out specific actions, such as looking the other in the eye upon arriving home and saying, "I'm glad to see you, honey." Such assignments are superior to advising warring partners to love one another.

Task assignments are commonly used in spiritual direction. To aid progress along the spiritual life cycle, specific assignments can be made. Our Lord frequently ended interactions with a particular directive. In another example, a priest assigned a judgmental, self-righteous man the task of helping out for a day at an AIDS hospice—thus leading him to the breakdown phase of spiritual development. I was once told that if I really wanted to know Jesus, I should read John's gospel three times. I did so, and it worked! The reader will recognize the extent to which the church already uses task assignments.

Rituals are a form of task assignment. In the Eucharist, the church acts out communion with God. The rites of baptism, confirmation, marriage, and burial all dramatize our interaction with God. Such rituals are also profoundly useful in counseling. A priest was working with girls who had had abortions. To those who could not accept forgiveness for aborting their babies, he assigned the task of choosing names for their children. Then a funeral ritual was performed, with a ceremonial burial. After a period of mourning, the girls felt restored in their relationship with God and ready to resume living.

Given the premise that performing assigned tasks can lead to therapeutic change, how does one go about formulating tasks that will be effective? This chapter provides some general principles of task construction and a menu of particular kinds of tasks.

General Principles of Task Construction

- For change to occur, the counselee must ultimately take specific action. The counselor can prescribe a task that will get the counselee acting or thinking. For example, I persuaded a withdrawn cancer sufferer to attend a local high school basketball game. He subsequently began to gather momentum and became quite active.

- Tasks should be assigned at the end of a counseling session. In preparing such assignments, the counselor should pray without ceasing.

- Discern what previous intended solutions have been employed, including those deliberately tried and those that may actually be maintaining the problem. Then create a task that goes in the *opposite* direction from an ineffective one.

  DeShazer (1985) described the case of a woman who had to place her 72-year-old husband in a nursing home. He became combative, and more so when she visited. DeShazer, noting how hard the woman vainly tried to cheer her husband up, asked her to feign helplessness and depression on her next visit. She returned to report that she had stood up to her husband, and he had improved. Apparently, her solicitous attitude had made him feel inferior, leading him to act hostile.

- Know the prevailing patterns surrounding a particular impasse. Let your tasks add something to the pattern or transform something metaphoric in the pattern to something concrete, or *vice versa.*

  A Christian man in my counsel was an exhibitionist. Although he asked for help to stop exhibiting himself, he took no action to stop. I assigned him the task of purchasing a polish sausage; outside the grocery store, he was to unwrap it and try to give it to women passing by. He was furious, refused to do the task, but stopped exhibiting himself.

- Look for the *reductio ad absurdum* in patterns. Make concrete that absurd extreme, then design a task that accepts it.

  A diabetic boy in a group home refused to take his insulin. After several visits to the emergency room for diabetic coma, he was brought to a meeting of his house parents and peers. The counselor then announced, "Since you have a death wish and will soon die,

I want to divide up your property now. OK, who wants his stereo, his favorite belt, his pet cat?" His roommates joyfully raised their hands. From then on, the boy took his insulin religiously.

- Decide whether you want your task to go toward or away from a solution to the problem. For the "yes, but . . ." type person, restraining from change is more effective in bringing about desired results.

A 22-year-old man lived with his parents. He complained about his possessive mother and domineering father, but he met suggestions about finding work, going out with friends, and getting a girlfriend with "yes, but . . ." Finally I told him, "You've got it made, your mother cooks for you and does your laundry, and your dad gives you money—why change?" He became agitated, laughed and cried, and finally asked me in a genuine tone of voice to help him find a job.

Such *restraint from change* is also useful with phobic persons.

- How the task assignment is delivered to the counselee is important. Do it with the expectation that the counselee will take the task seriously and carry it out. Assess the counselee's reaction to the assignment. The assignment should be liberating; if the counselee appears greatly burdened or distressed by the task, re-evaluate it.

- Remember to request a follow-up at the next visit. Did the counselee do the task? If not, why not? What was learned? How did it make the counselee think?

- When learning this skill or any of the others put forth in this book, set aside time to study your cases and prepare your interventions. Talk over cases with your colleagues, also.

A Menu of Task Assignments

Categorizing kinds of tasks can aid the counselor in designing effective directives. In practice, the categories overlap and share common characteristics. The menu includes cognitive, straightforward, pattern-interruption, symptom-contingent, symbolic, ritualistic, paradoxical, and ambiguous tasks.

Cognitive Tasks

Cognitive tasks build on the cognitive bases of intended solutions and interactional patterns; certain patterns of thought contribute to all impasses. The patterns of guilt and resentment are quite familiar. Confession and apology are tasks that allay the former.

> *Al, 50, had, on a single occasion some 20 years past touched his daughter on her private parts while she slept. She had awakened, but nothing was said until 20 years later, when the now grown woman accused him ferociously. I urged him to write to her, confessing his action and apologizing. He wrote the letter, his daughter accepted the apology, and a reconciliation took place.*

Regarding resentment, Leviticus 19:17 says, "You shall not hate your brother in your heart, but you shall reason with your neighbor . . ." The counselor can invite a resentful counselee to so reach out. In the example above, perhaps a counselor had encouraged Al's daughter to confront him. If the tormentor is no longer present to confront, the empty chair technique can be used.

> *At a weekend marathon, an angry looking man named Keith announced he'd dreamt of Indians pursuing him to scalp him. Dr. Jerry Greenwald, sponsor of the marathon, asked him to put the Indians on the empty chair and talk with them. After a few minutes of dialogue, playing one part, then the other, Keith stated, "I know what this is about." He went on to describe how Tommy, an older boy and a bully, had subjugated him in the orphanage both were raised in. "And Tommy, I'm looking for you, and some day I'll find you, and then . . ." Jerry, pointing to the empty chair, said "Keith, can you forgive him?" Keith stared at the empty chair for several minutes, then said, "Tommy, I hate what you did to me, but I'm going to let you*

go." Keith no longer looked angry, and everybody in the room breathed sighs of relief.

Several psychiatric disorders have important cognitive aspects. For example, depressed or phobic persons often complain of guilt, although usually an independent observer would not perceive any transgression. I ask such persons to change the word *guilt* into the cognitive statement, "I accuse myself," which gives a more accurate picture. A task such as "Pick out five things you've accomplished recently and then deliberately accuse yourself," might be assigned the counselee.

Straightforward Tasks

Assign straightforward tasks to elicit action where before there was none. Such tasks move toward solutions to problems and are useful when a person is learning, had not thought of taking action, or has withdrawn. They may be of help to:

- A grieving person

- A student of spiritual direction

- An ill person recuperating or someone recovering from a breakdown

- A phobic person who is avoiding feared objects or situations

- A person who has metaphorically fallen from the horse and needs to get back on.

Thus, the grieving person might be asked to confess that grief to a friend. A student might be given homework, or a reading assignment, or be asked to visit a convalescent home. A cancer patient might be urged to attend a hospice meeting. A phobic person could profit from driving a street usually avoided.

Stuart's task assignments to act in a caring manner toward one's spouse are examples of straightforward tasks. For such couples and for people in general, straightforward tasks test motivation, responsibility, and readiness for change. The counselor should gently confront any failures to perform the assigned tasks.

Pattern Interruption Tasks

Such tasks introduce new elements into the patterns of thought or behavior. They utilize the idea that if a component of a pattern changes, the whole pattern may follow suit. By adding to a pattern or changing only a part of it, the counselor avoids the resistance incurred when attempting to take something away. Thus, it is better to ask a warring couple to continue to fight but to do so at a different locale or time than to ask them to stop fighting altogether. As another example, consider a case of Bergman, (1985) a husband with heart disease who persisted in smoking and overeating despite his wife's futile objections. Bergman suggested she begin buying term life insurance and looking at other men. At first the wife laughed, but she began to see his point and no longer felt helpless.

Symptom-Contingent Tasks

Tasks assigned on the contingency that some specified symptom occurs can aid highly motivated persons who are struggling to control such habits as overeating, bulimia, smoking, masturbation, and temper outbursts. For example, the counselor can assign a task to be performed when the counselee indulges. The task should be something the counselee needs to do but finds burdensome or aversive. Possibilities include writing letters, studying the student's least favorite course, exercising, or scrubbing floors or toilets. To be successful, the counselee must make an ironclad promise to carry out the task after a transgression. I finally quit smoking by writing a letter to a priest, promising him $20 (a lot of money to me at the time) if I smoked even one cigarette. Later, when I struggled with overeating, I resolved not to try to stop overeating, but rather to run a mile whenever I did. That self-imposed task has led to an ongoing fitness program with the result that I can eat pretty much what I want without gaining weight.

Symbolic Tasks

The heart's propensity to think in symbols can be put to advantage in assigning tasks. Such tasks, essentially a form of waking dream, can powerfully stimulate the heart to think deeply.

> *Zelda complained of attacks of rage that seemed to follow the slightest intimation of criticism from others. I concluded that chronic, unresolved guilt feelings were at the heart of the matter. This guilt was really an habitual self-criticism dating back to childhood events for which she felt responsible. "I've been carrying guilt around and can't seem to let go of it." Borrowing an idea from Zeig (1980), I assigned her the task of finding a heavy, ugly rock; she was to paint it black, and then carry it about in her purse. I suggested that she might find the rock comforting or burdensome or both and I speculated that she might just lose, misplace, or forget to carry it about. She returned to tell me that she had realized how reflexively she had been taking the blame for events, events that in reality angered her. Now, she found herself expressing irritation at the time of its inception, rather than storing it and exploding later. She told me that she had thrown the rock in the trash can. We both laughed heartily.*

Although symbolic tasks can be devised to call attention to fixations, masks, resources, and stages of spiritual development, they seem to work best for the counselee who is trying to resolve some negative thought, feeling, impulse, or relationship. Symbols are by nature ambiguous. This ambiguity is very useful in promoting change, as the section below on ambiguous tasks demonstrates.

Rituals

In both the church and the secular world, rituals are common, often being used to mark, dramatize, celebrate, or mourn the major transitions in life. As symbolic representations of life's transitions they are important in their own right and should be created where they do not already exist.

> *When our eldest son Luke graduated from high school, our family friend, the Rev. Jack Smith, a Catholic navy chaplain, enacted a rite in which, after a particular meal, he presented Luke with several gifts: a Bible for the values his parents wanted to impart, a key for knowledge to unlock the future, and a book on home repairs "because now you will have to do them yourself." This gave everyone a hearty laugh, but it also symbolized our faith in Luke for the years ahead.*

Perhaps we also value rituals because they help us let go. I used a ritual in the counseling of Melba, a 65-year-old, bereaved woman.

> *She complained that the death of her husband brought back to her the grief of her son's death some ten years earlier. At the appropriate time and knowing of her interest in gardening, I asked her to purchase two bushes for her garden. She was to plant them in a place where she could always see them. "They'll be roses!" she exclaimed. The planting of the bushes marked the end of her period of mourning.*

Paradoxical Tasks

Such tasks prescribe the symptom: they demand that the sufferer deliberately repeat, in some manner, thoughts or actions that before were repetitive or felt to be compulsive. Of all the tasks described, paradoxical tasks most clearly move away from solving problems; indeed, they request that the counselee deliberately continue the problem or some aspect of it. Paradoxical tasks often dramatically change the counselee and provide remarkable relief from suffering. Learning how to use them properly is not easy, but your trouble in mastering them will be rewarded by the dramatic progress of certain counselees.

Although paradoxical tasks can be as creative as the imagination of the counselor permits, they can be grouped into two broad categories:

those involving individuals and those involving systems (such as families).

> *Keith suffered from agoraphobia, experiencing overwhelming attacks of panic whenever he left his house. During evaluation, he mentioned that he longed to be able to walk around a large tree in his backyard, yet he could not, instead feeling safe only in bed or on the sofa. I directed him to avoid looking at the tree, but that every time he chanced to glance at it he was immediately to run for the sofa and curl up on it. This directive deeply annoyed him, but something in him told him that if he complied, he would benefit. He returned to report that after three trips to the sofa he felt ridiculous and proceeded to march out to the tree, surprised at his strength and determination. This marked a turning point in his treatment.*

In a paradox involving a system, the counselor *reframes* undesirable behavior as being important to the well-being of the system; that behavior is then *prescribed*. In the common case of an adolescent acting symptomatically, the counselor might label the behavior as keeping balance in the family or as preventing fights between father and mother or even as a self-sacrifice to keep father and mother together. The young person is then instructed to carry out, usually in a symbolic fashion, some aspect of the behavior in question. Such interventions often mobilize the resources of both counselee and family. As mentioned, these interventions are difficult to use and cannot be applied in cookbook fashion. Paradoxical reframing and tasks are particularly tricky, in that misused they may border on sarcasm or ridicule, something the counselor definitely does not want. Consequently, as with any task, the counselor would do well to plan out their use in advance. That injunction is especially important with paradoxical tasks.

Utilization Tasks

Utilization tasks attempt to use a counselee's world view, resources, capabilities, interests, experiences, and beliefs, to promote change. You should use whatever positive aspects present to help the counselee do something he or she would not or could not otherwise do. Consider this example of O'Hanlon's (1987) as he writes about Erickson:

In a case illustrating the use of the patient's rigid beliefs and delusions to further therapy, Erickson approached a man at the state hospital who claimed to be Jesus Christ and told him that he understood the patient had experience as a carpenter. Knowing that Jesus did indeed help his father, who was a carpenter, the man could only reply that he had. Erickson said he also understood that the patient wanted to be of service to his fellow man. To this, the patient also answered in the affirmative. Erickson then informed him that the hospital needed help building some bookcases and asked for his cooperation in the matter. The patient agreed and was able to start participating in constructive behavior rather than continuing symptomatic behavior.

Ambiguous Tasks

An ambiguous task is a nebulous, deliberately vague task that acts like the Rorschach inkblot test by actively encouraging the counselee to project insights or solutions onto it. The counselor gravely and seemingly wisely assigns a task that could be interpreted a thousand different ways. When the counselee returns after completing the task, the counselor questions what the counselee learned, but is never satisfied with the answer. To every response, the counselor responds, with seeming wisdom, "Yes, that's very interesting. But you are only scratching the surface. What else?" Such a strategy pushes the counselee to *think deeply* about the situation, something that perhaps the counselee never did before. As in a Rorshach test, the counselee can come up with some remarkable ideas (Lankton and Lankton, 1986).

Hal, a 50-year-old man in therapy for several months, was effectively dealing with his difficulties; we were going over the same material repeatedly. I directed him to drive to Santa

Barbara to spend the day viewing and studying a gigantic fig tree in a downtown park:

H. I spent the day at the tree, like you said.

A. What did you observe, what did you learn?

H. It's a big tree.

A. Is that what you learned, that it is a botanical curiosity?

H. Well, no, I figured you wanted me to look at myself.

A. *(nods wisely)*

H. I looked at the strength of the limbs, and so on, but I kept being interrupted by the street people.

A. What do you mean?

H. I learned that the tree is a hang out for transients. Several tried to bum money from me; I wound up talking to some of them.

A. *(knowingly)* What did you learn from talking to them?

H. They were down and out. Maybe I don't have it so bad.

A. That's interesting. You are getting beneath the surface now.

H. *(straining, searching)* I think I've been feeling sorry for myself.

A. *(knowingly)* uh huh. What else?

H. *(pauses, reflects)* When I was in the Army, a friend of mine broke down and had to see a psychiatrist. After a time, the doctor told him that he was feeling sorry for himself, but was otherwise okay. He was sent back to the lines.

A. Uh huh. Stay with it.

H. I think it's time I went out and did it for myself.

A. I agree.

In summary, task assignments help those who are capable of looking at themselves to break out of old patterns, to put the past behind, and to discover fresh choices and new solutions for life's difficulties. Like

Solomon's directive to the two women (I Kings 3:24-25), these tasks can be vehicles used by God to help people break impasses. Ultimately, all tasks are ambiguous; the counselor assigning a task should follow up at the next visit with the kind of inquiry noted above.

Exercises

1. Discuss selected people or couples interviewed for exercise 2, Chapter 3 from the standpoint of tasks. Using the menu of tasks described above, think of some tasks that might have been appropriate or helpful.

2. Do the same for some case vignettes generated by exercise 3, Chapter 3.

Suggested Reading

1. Ascher, L. Michael, *Therapeutic Paradox.* Guilford Press, New York, 1989.

2. Bergman, Joel S., *Fishing for Barracuda: Pragmatics of Brief Systemic Therapy.* W.W. Norton & Co., Inc., New York, 1985.

3. DeShazer, Steve, *Keys to Solutions in Brief Therapy,* W.W. Norton and Co., Inc., New York, 1985.

4. Fisch, Richard, Weakland, John H., Segal, L., *The Tactics of Change,* Jossey-Bass Publishers, San Francisco, 1982.

5. Imber-Black, E., Roberts, J., Whiting, R., *Rituals in Families and Family Therapy,* W.W. Norton and Co., Inc., New York, 1988.

6. Weeks, G.R., and L'Abate, L., *Paradoxical Psychotherapy: Theory and Practice with Individuals, Couples, and Families*, Brunner/Mazel Publishers, New York, 1982.

17

Referral

Brief counseling has its limitations. A counselor may find or anticipate it to be ineffective in certain cases. The counselee may fail to respond, or the counselor may perceive a disturbance that is beyond the counselor's time or skill. Certain cases require specialized attention. For these and other reasons, a counselor may choose to refer the counselee to a specialist or an institution. Such referrals may include a medical doctor, psychiatrist, psychologist, marriage and family counselor, social worker, Alcoholics Anonymous (AA), Adult Children of Alcoholics (ACA), or Alanon.

Referral to a Medical Doctor

A counselee's complaints may point to a physical illness. Although most likely in those over fifty, it pertains to anyone who complains for the first time of one or more of the following: depression, anxiety, memory loss, decreased stamina, personality change, unstable moods, changes in personal habits such as grooming, weight, or any other physical change. In other words, be alert to recent changes in patterns. Such changes call for medical examinations.

Various diseases can produce such changes: hypothyroidism, multiple sclerosis, diabetes mellitus of adult onset, Parkinson's disease, Alzheimer's disease, brain tumors, vitamin B^{12} deficiency, AIDS, central nervous system syphilis, chronic alcoholism, abuse of illegal or prescription drugs (especially sleeping pills and pain medicines), Huntington's disease, and the delayed effects of head injury (subdural hematoma) are some of the commonly encountered conditions.

Sister Carmen, a 50-year-old nun, consulted me for depression. Most striking was the decrease in stamina in a formerly energetic person. I suspected hypothyroidism, ordered ap-

*propriate laboratory tests, and discovered a profoundly under-
active thyroid. Thyroid medications restored her to her old
self.*

It is always safe to be open to the possibility of physical illness and to
insist on a medical evaluation to ease any suspicions.

Referral to a Psychiatrist

It is equally important for the counselor to consider psychiatric diagnosis. In Chapter 3, I advocated asking specific questions to assess
psychiatric status. Diagnosis means the recognition and identification of
needs for specific help. Being acquainted with the following diagnostic
categories can help the counselor recognize those people who could
benefit from referral to a psychiatrist: depression, psychosis, personality
disorder, alcoholism or drug dependence, panic disorder, suicidal tendencies, and adult children of alcoholics and victims of physical or
sexual child abuse.

Depression

Depression is a painful mental state known since antiquity. Psalm 88
describes the cry of a depressed person and a sense of rejection by God.
But the term has become overused: it should be reserved as a medical
term to describe a syndrome that goes beyond the everyday experience
of "the blues." In depression, the brain becomes exhausted of the
neurochemicals necessary to maintain mood, resulting in a state characterized by melancholy; withdrawal from others; loss of interest and of
the capacity to enjoy; loss of appetite; early morning waking; and
somatic complaints such as headache, fatigue, and vague pains.
Thoughts of guilt, worthlessness, futility, or hopelessness may
predominate. The condition seems partly hereditary, partly existential,
and partly psychological. Although it's not easy to escape from depression by one's self, it is highly treatable by specialists. A depressed person may respond to the methods described in preceding chapters but may
require antidepressant medication as well. These medications are often
highly effective.

Marge was 65 when she and her husband Frank moved to a resort in Arizona. They greatly enjoyed their retirement until Frank had a small stroke. Marge became depressed, withdrawn, lost interest in everything, stopped eating, and would awake every morning at 3 a.m., with her mind racing. No medical help was available, so I sent her a supply of Sinequan, to be taken at bedtime. Within two weeks, the depression abruptly lifted. She had no further problems and resumed enjoying her life.

A depressed person may become psychotic, delusionally obsessed with worthlessness, sinfulness, or the unforgivableness of past transgressions. Suicide is especially possible here, as well as in all depressions. Consider psychiatric referral in all cases of depression that do not readily respond to brief counseling methods.

Psychosis

The psychotic person has lost the ability to test reality, to discern the difference between the internal reality of the world view and the objective external world. The essence of psychosis is the delusion, an unshakable belief in an idea objectively not true. The delusional sinfulness of some depressed people is one example. Paranoia is the most common delusion; it can range from mild suspicions to pathological jealousy to severe persecutory fears. Delusions can blend into hallucinations by involving the sensory systems and hence can be hypochondriacal, auditory, or visual in nature. Four conditions may be present with psychosis: manic-depressive disorder (now termed bipolar disorder), depression, schizophrenia, and organic mental disorders secondary to afflictions of the brain.

Bipolar disorder runs in families and is characterized by periods of elation with pressured speech and insomnia alternating with periods of depression. It is highly treatable with lithium carbonate, a simple salt. Schizophrenia is a severe mental disorder often starting around age fifteen or so. It can be hereditary, but is often a condition of "leaving home." The family systems of sufferers are tight, rigid, and controlling. Antipsychotic medications and family therapy can help here. Lastly, the medical disorders described in the beginning of this chapter may cause psychosis. Obviously, all of the above conditions require prompt referral.

Personality Disorders

People who cannot love or who cannot work will not respond to brief interventions. The selves of these personality disordered people are riddled with contradictions and are covered with masks. They cannot be close or alone, cannot self-activate, and cling. St. Paul (II Thessalonians 3:6-13) wrote about them. They often lie somewhere on a spectrum between two poles. At one extreme, the person with borderline disorder is needy, will do anything for approval, and has no self-esteem. At the other extreme, the narcissist is haughty, demands admiration, and pathologically inflates self-esteem. Such narcissistic personalities may make lots of money or attain a following. Cult leaders are narcissists who surround themselves with borderlines. Rather than pursue a problem-solving approach with the counselor, such people will intensely involve the counselor with such unspoken questions as: "will you like me, stroke me, make love to me, take care of me, engulf me, abandon me, admire me, do my bidding, *etc.*?" The unwitting counselor may fall into the trap of doing these things, and the counseling will be unproductive. The following vignette, written by a seminarian, makes the point:

> *Rena was one month away from her eighteenth birthday. She was incredibly attractive: shapely, with blond hair and big blue eyes. Unfortunately, she was also suicidal (two or three failed attempts), from a broken home, with a mother who was brutal and aggressive. She had been receiving counseling from another priest in the parish who eventually broke off their sessions because he was convinced that she needed psychiatric help, which he could not provide and she was unwilling to seek.*
>
> *She arrived early for her appointment. Her motions were fidgety. (She kept turning the bracelets on her arm; she would look at me, then away quickly. She sat rigidly in her chair).*

Her answers came quick, without much meditation or thought. She seemed eager to please.

The heart of her problem: she was in love with an immature young man (19 years old, unemployed, seemingly irresponsible and selfish) with whom she had lived for three months (until his mother made him come home). She was pregnant with his child. Her mother wanted her to have an abortion. Her boyfriend thought that might be a good idea, but he said he would support her either way (though he wouldn't even drive her to a doctor's office for checkups). Rena did not want the abortion—she recognized that the Church is against abortion, and she didn't want to leave the Church. She regularly went to confession, almost weekly, so that she could receive communion. She wanted to move back in with her boyfriend (who didn't want to marry her). She strongly resisted my attempts to get her to give her child up for adoption, to seek the help of a therapist, or to break up with her boyfriend. She was strengthened by my support for her against her mother and the abortion.

At times I thought that I had gotten somewhere with her, only to discover at our next meeting that I had to start all over again with my reasoning. She would initiate each session, ask for advice, and then ignore the advice. For example, at one point she was so frustrated with her boyfriend that she resolved to dump him, yet five days later I saw them together again.

She was the source of concern and frustration for me.

Rena's impulsiveness, her ambivalent attachment to an irresponsible person, her contradictory behavior regarding boyfriend and church, her suicide attempts, and her seductiveness toward the seminarian (he thought her incredibly attractive and repeatedly fell into the trap of offering advice, only to have it rejected) are all typical of a person with a borderline personality disorder. The seminarian did well to support her decision not to have an abortion, but he could have used Masterson's *why confrontation* (Chapter 13) when she sought advice about her boyfriend and adoption of her baby and refused referral to a psychiatrist. Here is how the seminarian could have implemented the *why confrontation*:

> *Why do you keep going back to your boyfriend when he repeatedly fails to support you?*
>
> *You seem determined to keep your baby—why is that? Why do you not see the responsibility that having a child entails?*
>
> *When you repeatedly ask me for advice, it is as though you don't see yourself as having any ability to make up your own mind—why is that?*
>
> *Why don't you take the other priest's and my recommendation to see a psychiatrist?*

Rena's difficulties lie in her inability to make decisions, coupled with fantasies that her boyfriend, the priest, or even her baby will take care of her. Why questions could help her face the underlying depression that saps her strength, a depression stemming from her relationship with her brutal, aggressive mother.

A variation on the theme of narcissistic personality is the child molester, who presents a facade of righteousness, concealing the crimes from self by grandiose self justifications. With this narcissistic appeal, the molester can seduce others into helping to conceal this acting out of extreme but denied hate. If the severity of a crime is measured by its effect on the victim, child molesting is as bad as murder. Upon hearing of the offense, doctors and mental health professionals in California are required to report it to the police. Clergy hearing such confessions must at least persuade the offender to move from the family or position of trust that is being violated.

Alcoholism and Drug Dependence

Alcoholism is defined as a preoccupation or obsession with alcohol that affects personal adjustment in such areas as health, work performance, marriage, family relationships, and legal status. When a decline in one or more of these areas becomes apparent, the diagnosis is easy to make. But in the gray area of heavy social drinking, it can be difficult for the counselor to determine whether or not the counselee is addicted. Answers to the following questions can help in this determination:

- Do you have a family history of alcoholism?

- Are you undecided about whether or not you are alcoholic?

- From time to time do you abstain to prove you are not alcoholic?

- Do you always finish every drop when drinking?

- Do you perceive life as no fun without drinking?

- Do you drink in the morning, or when alone?

- Do you need a drink to get started, to calm your nerves, to relate to others, to bolster self-esteem?

- Do you become belligerent when drinking?

A positive family history increases the likelihood of becoming alcoholic. A "yes" answer to any one of the remaining questions points toward the diagnosis.

Out of fear of alcoholism, spouses or people in authority may over-react and accuse someone of being an alcoholic who is not. Also, not infrequently a person consults a counselor with the statement, "I've been sent here; I'm an alcoholic, I guess." Clearly, such a person is not seeking counsel voluntarily or with conviction. Best to contact the person who referred the counselee. When a diagnosis of alcoholism is offered, referral to Alcoholics Anonymous or a counselor specializing in addictions can be made. It can help if the counselor personally knows the specialist to whom the referral is being made.

Everything said above regarding alcohol dependency applies to drug dependence as well.

Panic Disorder

A person who experiences the sudden onset of anxiety, dread, tachycardia, shortness of breath, and sweaty hands suffers from panic disorder. Panic attacks occur "out of the blue" and convince the sufferer to self-diagnose insanity, a heart attack, a seizure, or a fainting spell.

> *Jim was teeing up his ball for an uphill golf shot when a man behind him whispered to another, "That's cardiac hill." As he strode up the hill, his heart rate naturally went up, and he had a panic attack. Fearing a heart attack, he rushed to the hospital, where the diagnosis of panic disorder was made.*

If a person having a panic attack associates it with the place where the attack occurs, the anxiety can spread and lead to agoraphobia.

> *Maureen had her first panic attack in the upper deck of Dodger Stadium. First she avoided the stadium, then heights, then crowds, and then freeways. In six months she could not leave her house.*

The panic-disordered person often is suffering from an unrecognized impasse, and is cognitively plagued with "what ifs:" "What if people don't like me? What if I make a mistake? What if I lose control?" An unchallenged "what if" leads to the panic attack. The unrecognized impasse seems to increase the sufferer's vulnerability to the "what ifs." This book offers techniques to solve the underlying impasse. Referral to a specialist in the cognitive or behavioral treatment of anxiety disorder is indicated. Two medications, Xanax and Tofranil, can be very helpful.

Suicide

How does a counselor detect the suicidal person? Such counselees may volunteer suicidal ideation, or the counselor may suspect suicidal intent and then inquire. Who should the counselor be suspicious of? Those with a history of previous, dangerous suicide attempts, depressed persons, dependent and/or violent men whose wives have left them, persons who carry impotent rage toward another, older single alcoholic men, and psychotic persons should all be considered potentially suicidal. Repeated inquiry is indicated. Once it has been established that a counselee is thinking of suicide, the counselor must evaluate just how serious the danger is. This is done by asking if the person has a plan and whether the means to implement the plan have been acquired. If the person has both the plan and the means, the danger is real and severe. That person requires immediate intervention.

> *Ted, a 30-year-old single man, became depressed after the failure of a romance. As I talked with him I asked about suicidal thoughts and learned that he had bought a rope and, with it, was in a grim dance with death. I focused all my energy on persuading him to give me the rope. He finally agreed to bring it to me, so I let him go. He returned an hour later with the rope. He went on to recover completely.*

To discern the risk and demand the actual means to implement suicide can avert disaster and set the stage for future growth. Subsequent hospitalization may be required for further protection and resolution.

Adult Children of Alcoholics and Victims of Child Physical or Sexual Abuse

Many whose breakdowns are clear cut, severe, or dramatic have a past history of mistreatment or faulty parenting from dysfunctional families. Their breakdowns may have to do with substance abuse, broken relationships, or job frustrations and are often manifested by depression or life stage crisis. One or two hours of interviewing will establish multiple fixations around the family of origin. Such people have two salient characteristics: their experience of and fit with their dysfunctional families and their own make up.

Dysfunctional families have much in common. At least one parent is alcoholic or abusive. The spouse is "codependent," ineffectual, needy, overly helpful, and protective of the dysfunctional mate. Denial, secrecy, withdrawal from the outside world, multiple shifting triangles, and family myths become intended solutions. The family atmosphere is alternately explosive and tranquil. Spouses vie in overt or covert power struggles. To try to keep the family together, children take on such roles as soother, placater, caretaker, or entertainer and may develop dramatic physical or emotional maladies that unite the parents in concern. Often one child is designated the psychological parent of the younger siblings.

Adults raised in such environments have in common a variety of personality traits. They have had to sacrifice needs for individuation and communion to placate their fears of abandonment. They suffer from shame, guilt, and resentment. They are often compliant people, eager to please, helpers to an extreme. They dissociate from feelings or memories. They may have addictive problems of their own, be prone to acting out or violence, suffer sexual dysfunctions or mood swings, and have trouble with commitment.

Such persons deserve the best of spiritual direction and training and expert counseling. Mental health professionals are becoming more proficient with these conditions. A combined approach can yield rich benefits. ACA provides an effective group program that has a spiritual base. Acquaint yourself with the AA, Alanon, and ACA programs in your area.

There are several other conditions that may call for referral. Obsessive compulsive disorder, learning disorders, eating disorders (obesity, bulimia, anorexia nervosa), posttraumatic stress disorders, and severe marital problems are a few more that could benefit from specialized care along with spiritual direction. When I talk of referral, I do not mean to imply the superiority of psychiatrists. In this age of the proliferation of mental health care providers, many psychologists, marriage and family counselors, and social workers are equally qualified. More important is that the mental health worker, regardless of the specific area of training, be competent. Psychiatrists do have the advantage of being able to prescribe medications.

Making the Referral

After deciding to refer, the counselor must persuade the counselee to accept this advice. Some counselees will be ready and willing to see a specialist and will gladly accept the referral. But others may object, perhaps feeling abandoned by the counselor, or insulted, or disheartened out of fear that something is radically wrong—after all, psychiatrists are "only for crazy people." The counselor can deal with this reluctance with empathy, helping the counselee to verbalize fears or objections. Or, using analogies, tell a few stories of some who accepted referral and benefited and others who perhaps did not. The stories stimulate deep thought about the merits of further help. Ultimately, it is very important to allow the counselee to decide to seek psychotherapy or AA or whatever treatment referral that is made. Only then can the counselee truly cooperate with the help offered.

Exercises

1. On arriving at a new assignment (church, private practice, *etc.*), contact mental health professionals and get acquainted. Don't be shy. By now you have a very good knowledge base. Take the lead in the area of spiritual development.

2. In a ministry of spiritual development, make liberal use of Scripture study and prayer groups. Teach *Christianity and Change* to your lay people, inviting selected mental health professionals to attend and contribute.

3. Attend a meeting or two of Alcoholics Anonymous, Alanon, and Adult Children of Alcoholics.

Appendix: Instructions for Multigenerational Family Systems Paper

To prepare your multigenerational family systems paper, tactfully interview your family of origin and as many relatives as time and proximity allow, using the techniques and ideas put forth in this text. Try to follow the format suggested below. Then integrate your findings in a 20 to 30 page paper that traces and explores your multigenerational family system.

- Remember always to pray without ceasing throughout your interviews, both to see deeper into your family and yourself and to seek reconciliation or healing where needed.

- Chart the system, indicating all known family members and, as available, the dates of marriages, divorces, and deaths.

- Obtain descriptions of as many of these family members as possible, including important dates, education, vocation, a one-sentence description, a characteristic quote, significant achievements, crises, tragedies, patterns, polarizations, conflicts, acting out, and instances of alienation.

- Look for any severe crises or problems, particularly alcoholism or incest, that may have influenced family organization or direction. Can you see the effects of these events today?

- Ask about children and how they were regarded. Were children conforming or resistant, good or bad? Any "angels," scapegoats, or children identified by all as sick or carrying the problem? How did siblings relate? Did they exaggerate each other's behavior? Did they follow patterns of either parent's family of origin? What was the pattern of differentiating? Did they tear away or stay fused? What rites of passage marked separations, marriages, going to college, moving out, and the like?

- How were family traits transmitted down through the generations? Look for fusion (lack of differentiation), triangling (particularly including children), and projection, as well as healthy processes.

- Ask about your own development in the family. (Reviewing family albums with parents is one excellent way.)

- As you pursue the above paths of inquiry, look for patterns. Are there recognizable patterns among generations in the number of children, personality styles, and other traits? Look for significant changes in the intergenerational processes of transmission.

- Ask about dreams, looking for recurrent themes, *etc.* If you see recurrent patterns, ask yourself why.

- Assess the spiritual development of your family, as individuals and interactionally. If the church was a major part of your family's life, consider it a relative influencing you, as above. Consider how spirituality or its lack influenced your family system.

- Ask about myths. Are there family myths you can trace? Are there myths of injustice, sin, sacrificial atonement, or superiority? Are there family secrets? How are the family ledgers? Are there family members in the red emotionally (with obligation, duty, and guilt predominant) or in the black (with rights, freedom, and open emotions)?

- Do a personal inventory on yourself. Review your journal (exercise 5, Chapter 1). List some of your beliefs, opinions, and goals. Trace back to events that led you to form them. List a few emotional reactions, positive or negative, that you have or that plague or possess you (*e.g.,* fear, self pity, sexual impulses, perfectionism, immaturities, excessive self-criticism). Do not try to change or judge them, but be alert as to how they may fit into your family system.

- Summarize and integrate your data, speculating on the heart of your family, how you fit into it, how you are differentiating from it, and your plans for the future.

- Finish with a short reflection (1 to 2 pages) on your developing view of what constitutes salvation.

References

Allen, J., and Allen, P. (1972). "Permissions and Life Scripts," *Transactional Analysis J.* 2:2

Bandler, R., and Grinder, J. (1975). *The Structure of Magic.* Palo Alto, California: Science and Behavior Books.

Barker, P. (1985). *Using Metaphors in Psychotherapy.* New York: Brunner/Mazel.

Benson, M., Wells, K., and Hoff, P. (1985). *Workbook on Introduction to Human Behavior.* Los Angeles: UCLA School of Medicine Department of Psychiatry.

Bergman, Joel S. (1985). *Fishing for Barracuda: Pragmatics of Brief Systemic Therapy.* New York: W.W. Norton.

Biddle, W. Earl. (1957). *Investigation of the Oedipus Phantasy by Hypnosis.* American Journal of Psychiatry, August 1957.

Biddle, W. Earl. (1962). *Integration of Religion and Psychiatry.* New York: Collier Books.

Biddle, W. Earl. (1963). *Images, the Objects Psychiatrists Treat.* Archives of General Psychiatry, Vol 9, No. 5, November 1963.

Biddle, W. Earl. (1967). *Hypnosis in the Psychoses.* Springfield, Illinois: C.C. Thomas.

Daim, Wilfred. (1963). *Depth Psychology and Salvation.* New York: Frederick Ungar Publishing Co.

DeShazer, Steve. (1985). *Keys to Solutions in Brief Therapy.* New York: W. W. Norton.

Downing, J. (1973). *Dreams and Nightmares.* New York: Perennial Library, Harper and Row.

Edwards, D. (1979). *Drawing on the Right Side of the Brain.* Los Angeles: J.P. Tarcher. (Distributed by Houghton Mifflin, Boston).

Erickson, M.H. (1976). *Advanced Techniques of Hypnosis and Therapy.* (Selected Papers of Milton H. Erickson, M.D., J. Haley, Ed.) New York: Grune and Stratton.

Erickson, M.H., Rossi, E.L., Rossi, S.I. (1976). *Hypnotic Realities.* New York: Irvington.

Everstine, D.S., and Everstine, L. (1983). *People in Crisis: Strategic Therapeutic Interventions.* New York: Brunner/Mazel.

Farrelly, F., and Brandsma, J. (1974). *Provocative Therapy.* Cupertino, California: Meta Publications.

Haley, J. (1973). *Uncommon Therapy: The Psychiatric Techniques of Milton H. Erickson, M.D.* New York: Norton.

Haley, J. (1980). *Leaving Home: The Therapy of Disturbed Young People.* New York: McGraw-Hill.

Hall, M.C. (1983). *The Bowen Family Theory and Its Uses*. New York: Jason Aronson.

Horney, K. (1950). *Neurosis and Human Growth*. New York: Norton.

Kaufmann, W. (1973) "Do you Crave a Life without Choice." in *Psychology Today*. April 1973.

Kernberg, O. (1984). *Severe Personality Disorders*. New Haven and London: Yale University Press.

Knight, D. (1981). *Creating Short Fiction*. Cincinnati: Writers Digest Books.

Langs, Robert. (1985). *Workbooks for Psychotherapists: Understanding Unconscious Communication*. Emerson, New Jersey: New Concept Press.

Lankton, S.R., and Lankton, C.H. (1986). *Enchantment and Intervention in Family Therapy*. New York: Brunner/Mazel.

Marsh, John. (1968). "Saint John." Baltimore, Maryland: *The Pelican Gospel Commentaries*, Penguin Books.

Masterson, J. (1985). *The Real Self*. New York: Brunner/Mazel.

Masterson, James F. (1983). *Countertransference and Psychotherapeutic Technique*. New York: Brunner/Mazel.

Morgan, W., and Engel, G. (1969). *The Clinical Approach to the Patient*. Philadelphia: Saunders.

O'Hanlon, W.H. (1987). *Taproots: Underlying Principles of Milton Ericksons's Therapy and Hypnosis*. New York: W.W. Norton.

Perls, Frederick S. (1970). *Gestalt Therapy Verbatim*. New York: Bantam Books.

Rico, Gabrielle L. (1983). *Writing the Natural Way*. Los Angeles: J.P. Tarcher, Inc. (Distributed by Houghton Mifflin Co., Boston).

Strupp, H. (1972). *On the Technology of Psychotherapy*. Archives of General Psychiatry, Vol. 26, No. 3, March 1972.

Stuart, R.B. (1980). *Helping Couples Change*. New York: Guilford.

Watzlawick, Paul. (1979). *The Language of Change*. New York: Basic Books.

Watzlawick, Paul, Weakland, John H., and Fisch, Richard. (1974). *Change: Principles of Problem Formation and Problem Resolution*. New York: Norton.

Weeks, G.R., and L'Abate, L. (1982). *Paradoxical Psychotherapy: Theory and Practice with Individuals, Couples, and Families*. New York: Brunner/Mazel.

Winnicott, D.W. (1971). *Therapeutic Consultations in Child Psychiatry*. New York: Basic Books.

Zeig, J. (1980). *A Teaching Seminar with Milton H. Erickson*. New York: Brunner/Mazel.